German

GERMAN

Biography of a Language

RUTH H. SANDERS

OXFORD
UNIVERSITY PRESS

2010

OXFORD
UNIVERSITY PRESS

Oxford University Press, Inc., publishes works that further
Oxford University's objective of excellence
in research, scholarship, and education.

Oxford   New York
Auckland   Cape Town   Dar es Salaam   Hong Kong   Karachi
Kuala Lumpur   Madrid   Melbourne   Mexico City   Nairobi
New Delhi   Shanghai   Taipei   Toronto

With offices in
Argentina   Austria   Brazil   Chile   Czech Republic   France   Greece
Guatemala   Hungary   Italy   Japan   Poland   Portugal   Singapore
South Korea   Switzerland   Thailand   Turkey   Ukraine   Vietnam

Copyright © 2010 by Oxford University Press, Inc.

Published by Oxford University Press, Inc.
198 Madison Avenue, New York, NY 10016

www.oup.com

Library of Congress Cataloging-in-Publication Data
Sanders, Ruth H.
German : biography of a language / Ruth H. Sanders.
p.   cm.
Includes bibliographical references and index.
ISBN 978-0-19-538845-9
1. German language—History.
2. German language—Social aspects.
3. Sociolinguistics—Germany. I. Title.
PF3075.S26 2010
430.9—dc22
2009038656

Frontispiece: *Thusnelda im Triumphzug des Germanicus* 'Thusnelda in the triumphal procession of
Germanicus', painting by Carl Theodor von Piloty, 1873. Thusnelda, wife of the Germanic leader Arminius,
with their young son Thumelicus and her retinue, paraded in Rome as captives of the Roman general
Germanicus on May 26 of the year 17 AD. Photo: Blauel/Gnamm—Artothek. Neue Pinakothek, Munich,
Germany. By permission of Artothek.

3 5 7 9 8 6 4

Printed in the United States of America
on acid-free paper

Preface

THE German language has a long history, beginning perhaps as early as six thousand years ago. Linguists, that is, scientists of language, have been tracing its roots since the late eighteenth and nineteenth centuries, working with at times nothing more than scraps of ancient Germanic languages, often written in foreign alphabets or runes. These scientists provided the first piece of the puzzle: the stages of development of the language; pronunciation changes, grammar changes, and vocabulary additions, and how they came to be. Modern linguists have continued their work, and in fantastic detail they have reconstructed early German in its many historical stages going back thousands of years.

Recently other sciences—anthropology, archaeology, genetics—have developed exacting methods to turn their microscopes, in closer focus than ever before, on prehistoric peoples and languages. Their results enable us to see a second piece of the puzzle, that is, when and where Neolithic (Late Stone Age) peoples settled, when they began using agriculture and animal husbandry, what cultural contacts they made, and hence what languages could have influenced other languages (including Germanic). Their work has dated some linguistic events earlier than had previously been estimated, in some cases by more than a thousand years.

In the last centuries of the pre-Christian era, Greek and Roman historians and military men (for example, Julius Caesar) described their encounters with the Germanic peoples. What they wrote not only defined how the Greeks and Romans viewed these peoples, whom they called "barbarians," but also colored our own view, since until recently we had few other sources. The pre-medieval speakers of Germanic languages did not (with the exception of the Goths) have writing, so their side of the story is largely lost to history. However, anthropologists, archaeologists, and geneticists have discovered ways to reanimate the Germanic peoples of Roman times and even earlier, through their bones, their craft work, their graveyards, their trash piles, and their genetic material. These findings have begun to provide the human picture, which can tell us which peoples intermarried with which other peoples, when the Germanic peoples took up the foods and clothing styles of the Romans, and which ones gave up their native language and which ones didn't.

In tribal times the Germanic languages were divided; by medieval times they began to coalesce into what would become German and what would become its sister languages: English, Netherlandic (Dutch and Flemish), Afrikaans, Frisian, Yiddish, Danish, Norwegian, Swedish, Icelandic, and Faroese. But by then the written record could yield the story of German, sometimes even through the lives of individuals. Here the findings of historians who have performed their reanimation tasks in archives and libraries take over the narrative.

This story, then, is one told by many scholars of many disciplines. Bringing all the parts of the story into one narrative, as this book attempts to do, involves the risk that the author will misinterpret the findings of fields other than her own. It seems to me, however, that the German language is due for a wide-ranging historical assessment, using the knowledge not only of linguistics but also of other sciences, and I can only hope I have been equal to the task.

Many colleagues and friends have graciously read and commented on the manuscript, or parts of it, as it developed. For their insight and encouragement, I express here my thanks to Renee Miller, Audrone Willeke, Gerda Bikales, Winfried Thielmann, Gene Willeke, K.E. Smith, Michael Bachem, Jacqueline Vansant, Mila Ganeva, Mathias Schulze, Robert DiDonato, Karen O'Hara, Pirkko Suihkonen, and Stephen Nimis. Thanks too to Dan Meyers, who provided technical assistance. To Kevin Kirby, special thanks are due for getting me off to a good start by giving me his copy of Orrin Robinson's *Old English and Its Closest Relatives* (1992). To the anonymous reviewers of Oxford University Press, my gratitude for their generous comments as well as their exacting standards. To my editors at Oxford University Press, special thanks: to Brian Hurley, for his good judgment and encouragement at all the right moments; to Joellyn Ausanka, for her skillful editing and hard work. Of course, whatever errors remain in the book are mine alone.

One additional note: I have quoted in English from many works in German; unless otherwise noted, all translations are my own.

Miami University in Oxford, Ohio, gave me essential support in the form of a year-long leave that enabled me to do much of my research in Munich, Germany; and the Institut Deutsch als Fremdsprache of the Ludwig-Maximilians-Universität in Munich provided me with a professional home during my year in Munich. Miami University's King Library, particularly its Special Collections and Digital Initiatives departments, was extremely helpful in locating materials. My thanks to these institutions and the people who make them work.

Finally, to my husband, Alton Sanders, my deepest gratitude not only for his reading of and comments on the manuscript, but even more for his steady support and encouragement. It is to him that this book is dedicated.

Contents

Introduction

Turning Points of a Language

As they gathered thousands of years ago to talk around their fires or to take to the sea in their boats, the prehistoric coastal and island people in what is now Denmark and southern Sweden wouldn't have known much about the world beyond their clans' seafront territories and nearby fishing grounds. Still less would they have imagined that their dialect would one day grow into a world language.

Between their time and ours, though, that dialect migrated from the clans' homeland over most of the European continent, eventually developing into German, today the continent's second most commonly spoken language (after English). This book investigates the turning points of the language's path from its Germanic prehistory into the present.

German is the linguistic daughter of the Proto-Indo-European language once spoken throughout vast stretches of Eurasia. The history of German has at least two parts: it is the story of language development over thousands of years, and also of the lives and societies of its speakers throughout that time. The narrative as told in this book starts with those seafront clans and continues with the acceptance by some tribal Germanic societies, and the resistance of others, to colonization and Latinization by the Roman Empire, through the turbulent Middle Ages, the age of the European printing press, the formation of the nineteenth-century German Empire, and Germany's twentieth-century military and cultural horrors.

These were significant historical events, and this book will consider them also as linguistic events. The speakers of Germanic languages through history have their stories as well, and these continue to be revealed in sometimes startling detail by the findings of our contemporary archaeologists and geneticists.

For instance, genetic and archaeological studies are pushing back known dates for the settlement of Europe, based on early peoples' ancient grave remains and fragments of their material culture. DNA analysis has enabled the outlining of prehistoric migration of peoples at a level of detail and accuracy not previously possible. Radiocarbon dating and other technology have revealed that some samples of pottery, wheeled vehicles, and representations of gods and people, for example, are much older than was previously thought, while new techniques of locating buried remains have uncovered relics from deeper and older layers than ever before. Analysis of plant remains and pollen preserved in dwelling places, graves, and even under water allow scientists to track and date the spread of agriculture. Even the discovery of old latrines plays its role in providing the details of social history: those along the *limes*, the wall built by the Romans along the Roman-Germanic borders early in the Christian era, have provided specifics about Roman and Germanic diets of the time.

The peoples of our story, in both prehistoric and early historic times, did not understand themselves to be Germans, or even Germanic peoples. They were, however, speakers of Germanic languages. The clans and tribes we follow in this book are more accurately viewed as language groups than as ethnic groups (Lowenthal 2005 and Goffart 2006, passim). The peoples joined, separated, made war, and joined again with neighboring clans and tribes, migrating to other territories. In our times speakers of the Germanic languages inhabit the largest part of northern and central Europe. The story of German in these pages ranges over millennia, presenting an analysis of the events that determined the direction the language took at its turning points.

A spotlight on turning points, leaving the connecting events largely in the dark, inevitably leaves out a great deal. In return, however, the pruning of detail in these interim years allows the emergence of a strong narrative line, a shape of the story.

Six events are outlined below, each of them a defining moment in the development of the German language, each the topic of a chapter in this book. Emphasis throughout is on the spoken, not the written, language, though obviously, once the language gained a written form, the spoken and the written forms influenced each other. The first and the third events are nodes of linguistic-systematic change; the second, fourth, fifth, and sixth represent sociopolitical turning points. Other authors might add different signal events to their own lists, but the significance of these particular six seems beyond argument.

The six are:

- the prehistoric breakaway of a "pre-Germanic" language from its Indo-European mother language, via a systemic set of changes in pronunciation of certain consonants in the mother language at that time;
- a decisive military victory of Germanic tribes over Roman troops sent to colonize the territory east of the River Rhine, preserving into modern times a Germanic-speaking peninsula in a Western European sea of Latin and its daughters, the Romance languages;
- a second systemic shift in pronunciation which eventually demarcated two kinds of West Germanic languages, one becoming the source of Modern German, the other the source of English and Netherlandic;
- a "people's" Bible translation that gave shape to a standard German language emerging from a dozen spoken dialects to form a single language, forerunner of today's Modern German;
- the nineteenth-century political unification of German-speaking territories north of the Alps that was pivotal in making the new nation of Germany a European power, and German a world language;
- the beginning of a postwar recovery of the moral and cultural capital of the German language, which had been squandered in the brutal deeds of two world wars instigated by Germany.

These events provide a vantage point from which to look at the German language as a social product and as a linguistic system, but they of necessity leave out or touch only lightly on a great deal that German philology and German history have traditionally considered important.

The Gothic language, for example, is explored only briefly in chapter 2, even though, of all the pre-medieval Germanic tongues, Gothic was the only one to leave an extensive written record of itself. However, as a language it is now extinct, without daughter languages. Gothic texts written for the most part in the fourth century AD are preserved in manuscripts dating from the sixth century, and its people and some of their cultural habits are described in Classical Greek and Roman commentary. The Goths, who arrived about 300 BC at the mouth of the Vistula river in today's Poland, probably came over the

Baltic sea from Scandinavia, specifically Sweden (though some scholars question this notion; see Christensen 2002, passim). After several centuries of cultural and military accomplishments, the Goths were absorbed into the peoples of their eventual areas of habitat: Italy, Spain, France, Bulgaria, Romania. Their language disappeared. No path leads from the Goths or the Gothic language to Modern German.

Also lacking its own chapter here is the National Socialist, or Nazi, Party, which ruled Germany from 1933 until its 1945 defeat in World War II. Its linguistic incursions are described briefly in chapter 6. The Nazi episode had a cataclysmic effect upon its victims, upon the German nation, and upon European history. The Nazis left no positive or long-lasting effects on the German language after their twelve-year reign in the two largest German-speaking countries, Germany and Austria. What survives is only a collection of words—some of them neologisms, others ordinary words used as euphemisms—both types meant to disguise, glorify, or excuse murderous deeds. These Nazi words were isolated from the German language immediately after the military defeat of the Third Reich. They are used now only in their historical sense; an example is *Führer* ('leader'), once a neutral and useful word, now seldom used in any sense other than as a designation for Hitler, because it still forcefully reminds both German speakers and the rest of the world of its history as Hitler's preferred title.

The German people of the Nazi era were nearly ruined and certainly shamed by Nazism. The German language, on the other hand, cannot be blamed for Nazism's deeds, is not ruined, and cannot be shamed for words that Nazis coined or perverted. However, the German language did pay a price for Nazi crimes, in the coin of its moral and cultural authority, which had been at its height before World War I and reached its nadir during the Nazi rule. The cultural standing of the German language began a slow recovery only after Germany's defeat in World War II, concomitant with Germany's rejoining the company of responsible nations.

This is the story of German as it has been used by ordinary people. The spoken language is emphasized here, wherever historical evidence gives us access to it. Accordingly, historically significant written monuments such as the medieval epic poem *Das Nibelungenlied*, courtly love poetry, *Faust*, nineteenth-century realistic dramas, or twentieth-century prose will not be focal points. The accomplishments of the great writers such as Walter von der Vogelweide, Hans Jakob Grimmelshausen, Johann Wolfgang Goethe, Friedrich Schiller, Heinrich Heine, Franz Kafka, Bertolt Brecht, Anna Seghers, Thomas

Mann, Ilse Aichinger, and countless others, significant though they are, will be mentioned only in passing. Nor do we include here the logicians, mathematicians, and scientists who, starting in the sixteenth century, used German rather than Latin for their writing and lecturing and, in so doing, helped to develop German into an expressive tool for the most sophisticated thought. All have found, and will continue to find, other chroniclers.

We take up the biography of German at what linguists consider its cradle, nearly six thousand years ago at the northern edges of the European continent, on the coasts and islands of the Baltic and the North Sea. The marvels of archaeology and genetics provide occasionally detailed, though inevitably incomplete, portraits of that time and place. One such portrait of pre-Germanic society and, where possible, of its language, is sketched in chapter 1.

1

Germanic Beginnings

4330 BC: Linguistic Ancestors

On a day over six thousand years ago, about ten miles from what is today Copenhagen, the bodies of a young woman and a newborn boy were laid in a grave. The infant's body was cushioned by a large swan's wing.

This touching gesture was not repeated in any of the nearby graves in Bøgebakken, Vedbaek, on the island of Zealand, Denmark, all of them dating to around 4330 BC. An unusually large number of grave offerings were found with the woman and the baby: 190 pendants made of perforated snail shells had been buried with them, and around the woman's pelvis were fifty pendants made of the teeth of red deer, elk, boar, and seal, writes Christopher Tilley (2003, 39). The swan's wing on which the baby's body lay may have been a religious expression; according to Joseph Campbell, birds have been associated since at least the early Stone Age with the soul and the spirit world (1969, 167).

Death in childbirth? Disease? Accident? Murder or clan conflict? There is no way to know now what happened to the woman and the baby, or to the twenty-two other bodies found in eighteen graves from this time in Bøgebakken. Most of Bøgebakken's nearby graves of men also contained grave offerings; but some contained only one pendant, while most of the women's graves contained none. The bodies of both men and women were sprinkled around the heads and pelvises with red ochre, frequently found in graves of this time (Tilley 2003, 39).

At Skateholm, in today's Skåne, Sweden, on the nearby Baltic coast, twenty-two people and two dogs were found in a burial ground dating to around 4340 BC. Here a woman was buried with a dog—perhaps her pet—decapitated and laid across her shins. Some bodies had been buried sitting up, some crouched or supine, some face down (Tilley 2003, 35–38).

We know little about these individuals and others whose remains have been found at about forty prehistoric coastal and island sites in today's Denmark and Sweden. We know more, however, about their communities, dating to the millennia between 7000 and 3000 BC, before agriculture was practiced in northern Europe. The people here lived from fishing and a little hunting, pieced out by edible finds in berry bogs or by wild grasses and grains.

In the fifth millennium BC, when the woman and her baby were buried at Bøgebakken, the cultivation of grains and vegetables and the domestication and raising of animals for meat and milk still lay in their community's future, but the people were laying the groundwork for the coming shift to agriculture by learning to find, cook, and eat wild grains. Their language was one of the many languages current on the Eurasian continent, perhaps even a local dialect of Proto-Indo-European (PIE), the now extinct mother language of future Germanic languages. The prefix "proto-" indicates a historically reconstructed (and now extinct) language hypothesized from indirect evidence, rather than directly from living speech or written documents; "Indo-European" refers to the geographic origin of this family of languages: the Indian subcontinent and Europe.

Experts are not in agreement as to how early PIE was spoken in Europe, or even whether another language or languages predated PIE in North Sea/Baltic Europe. Though it was settled at least as early as 7000 BC, this part of northern Europe shows exclusively Indo-European place names, whether of land or bodies of water (Renfrew 1987, 256). If non-Indo-European languages had been spoken here, they might be expected to have left traces behind in place names, which according to the linguistic subdiscipline of *onomastics* (the study of proper names) may retain traces of their linguistic origins for millennia (Keller 1978, 43–44). The exclusively Indo-European place names suggest, but do not definitively prove, that the language of the original settlers was PIE. On the other hand, the existence of a significant body of words in the

Germanic word-stock which appear to be of non-Indo-European origin suggests that a non-Indo-European language was in some way instrumental in the formation of Germanic.

Indo-European: Protolanguage and Culture

Living languages such as German or English, or even extinct ones such as Luvian (probably the language of ancient Troy), which survive only in inscriptions, are *attested*, or available from the direct evidence of the writing or the speaking of their native speakers. The ancestor of these languages, Proto-Indo-European, which is believed to have been a living language for thousands of years from 7000 BC or earlier (Renfrew 2000), flourished too early to be attested by written or spoken evidence. Its existence, now universally accepted by scholars, was hypothesized as early as the eighteenth century, most famously in 1786 by Sir William Jones, who presented in his presidential address to the Bengal Asiatic Society the idea that Sanskrit, Greek, and Latin were "sprung from some common source, which, perhaps, no longer exists." By the early nineteenth century, linguists such as the German Franz Bopp and the Dane Rasmus Rask had begun outlining the foundations of what was to be known as Indo-European philology.

Proto-Indo-European is called by linguists a *protolanguage* because it has not survived in written or spoken form, and because of its status as an extinct ancestor of living languages. Indeed, Proto-Indo-European (often referred to by its initials, PIE) is currently embodied only as a reconstruction, the linguistic equivalent of a dinosaur whose whole skeleton is deduced from a set of surviving fragments and represented in a museum by plaster casts of the missing bones. Such language reconstruction is accomplished by the *comparative method*, in which linguists comb over languages known or believed to be more or less closely related, comparing surviving words in related daughter languages with what is known about how languages develop through time, to hypothesize the original form of words and even grammatical constructions. Although its form is only hypothesized, the language was real and was used by real speakers, Elmer Antonsen explains: "Our reconstruction of a proto-language is theoretical and partial; but the language itself was necessarily real and whole. As a real language, it shared with all real languages the characteristic of non-uniformity. Some of its speakers spoke differently from others; they spoke differently from their linguistic predecessors and successors" (2002, 139).

The peoples who spoke PIE might have had little in common other than their language, however, just as many unrelated peoples speak English today. "If there was an Indo-European language, it follows that there was a people who spoke it: not a people in the sense of a nation, for they may never have formed a political unity, and not a people in any racial sense, for they may have been as genetically mixed as any modern population defined by language.... The Indo-Europeans were a people in the sense of a linguistic community," writes M. L. West (2007, 2).

Proto-Indo-European must have been a single language before it began to split into dialects, which then developed into daughter languages, the mother language becoming extinct. No written documents in PIE survive to demonstrate this progression to later ages, almost certainly because PIE never had any form of writing. The earliest written evidence (ca. 1300 BC) of a PIE daughter language comes from the Mycenaean dialect of Greek, in the form of clay tablets inscribed with a nonalphabetic script. As one of three kinds of inscriptions found together (the other two have not yet been decoded) and named "Linear B," it was discovered in 1900 on Knossos, Crete, by Sir Arthur Evans. Two other Indo-European languages attested from ca. 600–700 BC are Italic, an ancestor of Latin, and Continental Celtic, a now-extinct branch of Celtic once spoken throughout central Europe (Watkins 2000, x *ff*).

In a massive language shift that took place over thousands of years in a territory spreading from the Indian subcontinent and the Mediterranean in the south, northward to the North Sea, and westward from the Black Sea and the steppes of what is now Russia to the Atlantic Ocean, Proto-Indo-European (or its dialects) replaced whatever languages were previously spoken in these areas.

But, although the language shifted, the population in Europe remained substantially unchanged. The populations of this huge area simply stopped speaking their previous languages over time and began speaking a new language. Why would they do this?

Countless times throughout recorded history, and almost certainly countless times in prehistoric ages too, peoples on a large scale have changed languages. Sometimes this change occurs when newcomers in an area numerically overtake the indigenous population and replace their language by breeding both people and language into extinction. Genetic studies show that this was not the case with Indo-European.

Another possibility is warfare: the new population may conquer the old population and force them to take up the conquerors' language, or may crowd out the old language by insisting on the use of the new language in public venues. Alternatively, an entering population's superior technology may cause the indigenous population to adopt both the technology and the language, considering them to be of a higher status than its own. These latter scenarios are now the accepted alternatives for the coming of the Indo-European language to Europe, including the northern European homeland of the Germanic-speaking peoples.

Over generations, the peoples who gained knowledge of new technology—whether it was knowledge of breeding horses, agricultural techniques, or new ways of making pottery or of burying the dead—from neighboring peoples, invaders, or immigrants might improve their social status, and with it their chances of finding a desirable mate, by speaking the language associated with the new ways.

When a new language comes to dominate an already populated territory in the absence of genocide or other removal of the original population, a lengthy period of bilingualism among the indigenous peoples is to be assumed. But where people stop believing that competence in both languages is advantageous, they fail to pass on the second language to their children, and it dies out. This seems to have been the fate of most of the pre-Indo-European languages of Europe. A few non-Indo-European languages, however, flourish in Europe. Basque, which may once have reigned linguistically over a large territory in Europe, is still spoken in a small area at the heart of Indo-European language territory, perhaps thanks to its speakers' remote and inaccessible home in the Pyrenees. A second example is Hungarian, a survivor perhaps of a time when the Finno-Ugric language family was widespread on the European continent. Its sister languages Finnish and Estonian are thriving on the Baltic edges of the continent—having likely come there from the steppes of Russia in prehistoric times.

Currently, over half the world's population speaks an Indo-European language. These include the Germanic languages (German, Yiddish, English, Netherlandic, Afrikaans, Frisian, Swedish, Danish, Norwegian, Icelandic, Faroese), the Romance languages (French, Spanish, Portuguese, Italian, Romanian, and Catalan), the Baltic languages (Latvian, Lithuanian), the Slavic languages (Bulgarian, Serbian, Croatian, Czech, Slovak, Polish, Russian, Ukrainian, and Kashubian), the Indo-Iranian languages (Hindi/Urdu, Bengali, Farsi, Pashto, Kurdish, Sindhi, and Romani), and Greek, Albanian, and Armenian (Crystal 1997, 302–303).

Reconstructing Ancient Languages: The Comparative Method

Proto-Indo-European has been reconstructed from scraps of related extinct languages and through comparisons with both living and extinct daughter languages. Since PIE was not written, this reconstruction entails representing what linguists believe to be the sounds of the language using modern writing systems. Not only individual words are reconstructed, but also grammar (including morphological endings such as cases, conjugations, and plurals) and syntax (sentence structure), as well as the phonology (sound structure).

Table 1.1 lists some word roots of the Indo-European protolanguage as reconstructed by linguists using the comparative method. The left-hand column gives the postulated root and its postulated meaning; in the columns at the right are the cognates, or historically related words, from modern German and English. Note that the modern words may not express exactly the same meaning as the PIE original, but it is usually easy to see that the meanings are closely related.

Table 1.1. Proto-Indo-European to Germanic

Indo-European root and meaning[a]	Modern English	Modern German
*drem *sleep*	dream	Traum
*dwo *two*	two	zwei
*er *earth, ground*	earth	Erde
*gheldh *pay*	yield	Geld
*lik *body, form, same*	like, -ly	Leiche, gleich
*medhyo *middle*	middle, midst, medium	Mitte, mit
*per *for, through*	for	für
*reidh *ride*	ride	reiten
*sengh *sing*	sing	singen
*ters *dry*	thirst, toast	Durst
*ud *out*	out	aus
*we *blow*	weather	Wetter
*upo *under, over, up*	up, upon	auf
*wed *water, wet*	water, wet	Wasser
*yu *you*	you	euch

Table after Watkins 2000, xxi–xxxxv.

[a] *The single asterisk is used to indicate that a language form has not been attested in written text but has been reconstructed.*

A Reconstructed Specimen of PIE

Professor Geoffrey Sampson of the University of Sussex, England, has collected examples of reconstructed texts in PIE, built by scholars from known vocabulary to provide a fanciful but not entirely baseless sample of the language. The following story, based on an extract from Old Indic literature, was translated into (hypothetical) PIE by S. K. Sen. As Sampson writes (2006; also at Mallory and Adams 1997), "material that was transmitted from generation to generation by word of mouth . . . may represent the earliest genre of literary composition recorded in any IE language . . . S. K. Sen picked a simple passage in which the Old Indic vocabulary is believed to correspond to PIE roots, and took a consensus view from the experts on what the passage would look like if the Old Indic structures and sounds were rolled back two or three further millennia to their PIE antecedents" (Sampson 2006). Here is an excerpt, translated into English from the original Sanskrit:

> Once there was a king. He was childless. The king wanted a son.
> He asked his priest: "May a son be born to me!"
> The priest said to the king: "Pray to the god Varuna."

Sampson describes the following PIE version "as it might have been uttered by a PIE speaker—by one of our linguistic ancestors, some six millennia ago." Because the passage is reconstructed rather than attested, every word in it could be marked with an asterisk, but for ease of reading, this has not been done here:

> To réecs éhest. So nputlos éhest. So réecs súhnum éwelt.
> Só tóso cceutérm prcscet: "Súhnus moi jnhyotaam!"
> So cceutéer tom réejm éweuqet: "Ihgeswo deiwóm Wérunom."

While the above passage looks at first glance completely unfamiliar to speakers of English, it does contain some words that we can recognize with a little help. Some of the examples provided by Sampson include *réecs*, 'king' (cf. Latin *rex*, English derivatives 'regal', 'regicide', 'reign'); *súhnum*, 'son'; and *deiwóm*, 'god' (cf. Latin *deus*, English derivative 'deity'). The passage, though not genuinely PIE, suggests how linguistic information may provide clues to the society of its speakers. In fact, much about very early Proto-Indo-European society, including its religious beliefs, has been surmised from its words, filtered through several millennia and several daughter languages.

Indo-European Homeland and Society:
The Linguistic Evidence

Language reconstructions can be used by linguists as evidence of the society the speakers of that language might have had, a method called *linguistic paleontology*. This procedure has been questioned by many scholars who doubted that it was possible to adduce facts about a people and a society spread over such a large geographical area, and for thousands of years, simply through language (Schmidt 1993, 38–39). However, the results have gained credibility in recent years, particularly where archaeological remains have produced supporting physical evidence.

Though PIE was eventually spoken by many different peoples of presumably many ethnicities and in many locations, there must have been one place where it all started. In the quest to determine the PIE homeland (linguists often call this by its German equivalent, the *Urheimat* "primeval homeland"), much has been made of PIE's vocabulary concerning plant and animal life. Calvin Watkins has summarized and updated the scholarly coordinations between Indo-European vocabulary and society (Watkins 2000, vii–xxxv). For example, the PIE word for "beech" has survived in related form in many Indo-European languages; does this mean that the homeland is located in an area in which the beech tree is native? Similarly, the word for "salmon" has survived; must the Indo-European homeland be a place where salmon are also at home? The controversy remains unsettled, however, in part because the related words of the daughter languages don't always have the same meaning. For example the word in Greek which is cognate to "beech" means "oak" of a kind native to the Mediterranean (Renfrew 1987, 82); "salmon" in some Indo-European languages refers to a saltwater fish, in others a river or a lake fish, and so on. Other plant clues are apple and cherry trees (the only fruit trees documented in PIE), as well as a lack of words for "palm tree" or "vine," which argue against, though are not proof against, a Mediterranean homeland. A surprising fact: "mouse" and "louse" have rhymed since PIE times: *mus / *lus. None of this is conclusive in choosing between the two major hypotheses about the origins of Indo-European: a Middle Eastern or Mediterranean homeland, or a homeland in the steppes of Russia or farther east into Asia.

Religion

There were many gods in PIE; the general word for god was related to the verb *dyen, to shine, linking deity to a bright sky. The phrase "overcome death" was in existence, as was the concept of "grace" and the idea of oral prayers, including the formula: *pa-wiro peku, 'protect, keep safe, man and cattle!' which has been attested in four now-extinct daughter languages, Latin, Umbrian, Avestan, and Sanskrit. The chief god was *dyeu-pater (which lived on in Latin as one word, *Jupiter*). The second element of that name, *pater, named the head of the household (and also designated 'father'); his mate was *mater (also meaning 'mother'), indicating a patriarchal household organization. That Indo-European society appears to have been patrilineal and patriarchal is not controversial, but the additional argument of anthropologist Maria Gimbutas that pre-Indo-European Europe (which she called "Old Europe") was "matrifocal . . . and matrilinear" (1991, 89) has not found general scientific acceptance, since it has been neither documented on linguistic evidence nor confirmed by anthropological findings (Eller 2000, 38–39).

Economic and Domestic Life, Technology, and Nature

The principle of exchange and reciprocal gift-giving appears to have been central to social organization; there were words for ransom and enslavement of captives in war. Metallurgy of copper and perhaps bronze, gold, and silver was practiced. Farming and stockbreeding, however, seem to have been the main economic support.

The word for 'house' (*dem-) indicated a social or family unit as well as a structure, as it does in modern English. Words for household activities included cooking and ripening fruit and vegetables (the verb in both cases *pekw-), kneading dough and shaping mud and clay into vessels (a single verb, *dheigh-), spinning (*[s]ne-), weaving (*webh-), and sewing (*syu-). Several houses made a village, frequently located on a hilltop fortified for defense.

Domesticated animals included cows, sheep, goats, swine, horses, and dogs. Stock was the measure of wealth, and the metaphor of a god or a priest as a shepherd of his "flock" of people, which survives to the present, dates back at least to PIE times. That large animals were used for transportation and for heavy work is documented not only by lexicon but by prehistoric artwork. The wheel was known, writes Watkins, citing "archaeological findings that date the distribution of the wheel in Europe to the latter part of the fifth millennium BC, the latest possible date for the community of Proto-Indo-European proper" (2000, xxi).

Numbers from one to one hundred are recorded. The number system was decimal (based on ten); 'ten' was *dekm, 'hundred' was *(d)kmtom, 'ten tens'. The time was measured by the *yer 'year' and by lunar months. Celestial bodies known included the sun, the moon, and the stars; and the dawn was lucky (or even worshipped); 'right' also was lucky, but 'left' was unlucky or taboo. Snow was known, but there are no words for 'sea', only for inland waters.

Rituals and Society

PIE contained a rich vocabulary of abstractions, including words for mental activity, a sacral kingship, religious law, pledge, payment of compensation for an injury, punish, justice, and believe (expressed in a metaphor, "put to heart," which is preserved in the Latin *credo*). A duty of children to cherish their aged parents was recognized, and the phrase "imperishable fame" was known. Even poetic stylistics have been combed for evidence of their origin in Indo-European culture. Beginning in the German philological tradition of the nineteenth century, scholars began comparing elements of elevated discourse in different branches of Indo-European, particularly in Greek and Indic, with an eye to demonstrating that relics of prehistoric poetic language were still visible in modern literary forms (West 2007, 3).

Conclusions about the society of PIE speakers, while the subject of constant adjustment based on new findings of archaeology and genetic studies, for the most part support earlier linguistic findings. However, current anthropological findings have suggested that the entry of PIE into Europe, and the breakup of PIE into dialects and daughter languages, may have occurred thousands of years earlier than had been hypothesized from linguistic evidence alone.

These earlier dates have consequences for dating the development of Proto-Germanic from Indo-European. For example, PIE might have come to Northern Europe as early as the fifth millennium BC. Subsequent immigration or invasion could not have brought unified PIE, only dialects (Watkins 2000, xxxiv–xxxv). Renfrew (2000) dates the breakup of PIE into dialects as early as 7000 BC. If this is true, it implies that when speakers of PIE joined the indigenous peoples in the Germanic homeland, either PIE was already present there, or the immigrants brought a new dialect with them, from which a new, pre-Germanic language was to develop. Not all linguists have accepted these earlier dates and the hypotheses that depend on them, which so far rest on incomplete archaeological evidence. For now, this scholarly disagreement remains unresolved.

The Germanic Homeland

Many newcomers migrated in these early times to this Scandinavian landscape and the neighboring North Sea coasts of what is now the European mainland, apparently desirable for its forests, its wildlife, and its mild climate. The combined indigenous bands and immigrants are the ancestors of future *Germanen*, the name I will give to the early Germanic peoples in this book. Because the people here are the foremothers and forefathers of the Germanen, and because changes in the language of this region were to lead to the development of the Germanic languages, we will regard this landscape for our purposes as the Germanic homeland. It has long been so regarded by historians of German (Keller 1978, 46).

Prehistoric people cannot accurately be referred to as *Germans*, as no *Germany* existed at that time; at the beginning of our story they lived not yet in tribes, but rather in very small bands or clans, surely without awareness of themselves as members of a "Germanic" ethnicity. However, they are the linguistic forebears as well as, to a large extent, the genetic ancestors of many of today's Germanic language speakers across northern and central Europe. "Germanen" is an anachronistic as well as a foreign name, its base being of unknown origin (even recent hypotheses as to its source have proven unlikely), but taken into Latin as a name for the tribes; I have added a modern German plural ending. "Germanen" is thus meant to suggest a reality historically distant from our own. These ancient people were in several senses the forerunners of today's Germanic peoples, but they were not modern Europeans, and their Stone Age culture and characteristics cannot reasonably be attributed to Germany or Germans of today.

The people of these coasts, populating territories in and around the area that will much later be called *Deutschland*, or Germany, will migrate, millennia into the future, and at times will rule over vast realms throughout western and central Europe. At this time in our story, though, they appear more self-contained than dominating, thriving in their own environment.

Their way of life seems to have been dominated by fishing, no surprise in this seafront land and its nearby islands. At Gønghusvej, one of the fifth-millennium BC settlements in Denmark, an oval hut with a central fireplace and a floor of branches contained the bones of land animals and fish. At Tybrind Vig, another settlement, a cobblestone surface leading from the settlement into the water may have served as a dock for the two boats found there.

The middens, or garbage dumps, of these ancient settlements are valued by archaeologists as evidence of what the people ate. At Ertebølle in North Jutland the midden yielded the remains of meals of shellfish including oysters, cockles, and mussels; game including deer, wild boar, elk, and aurochsen, one of several wild ancestors to today's domesticated European cattle (Beja-Pereira 2006, 8113); water animals such as seals, swans, and ducks; and marine and freshwater fish.

At Kongemose, 25 kilometers from the coastline, buried remains of two dogs who had eaten mostly fish suggest that the dogs (and undoubtedly their human hosts as well) had commuted between the seacoast and inland. It seems the people were partially settled, partially still nomadic. Dogs must have been then, as now, the people's working partners, probably also pets, in any case buried rather than being left in place where they died, as wild animals are. In fact, at Skateholm, in the cemetery previously mentioned, a dog was buried with three flint blades by its hip, a red deer antler laid along its spine, and a decorated antler axe on its chest, making it "one of the most richly furnished graves in the entire cemetery" (Tilley 2003, 35). Dogs were valued members of a hunting society, "the only domesticated animal in the Mesolithic. . . . clearly accorded a human or semi-human status . . . buried in exactly the same manner of people and with a rich range of gravegoods associated with the hunt" (Tilley 2003, 35).

The settlers cooked their meals: large pointed-base pottery jars as well as flat elongated bowls found there retained traces of seal, probably blubber. Some cooking pots contained scraps of hazelnuts, fermented porridge, and fish, perhaps caught with the wicker cage trap also found. Fish soup with vegetables seems to have been a frequent menu item; cereals were also an important part of the diet, as investigation of the human remains reveals. Fish tapeworms, which can be acquired through the consumption of undercooked or raw fish, left their traces in the human skulls. Elk and aurochs were hunted, but perhaps not often with success, judging from the minimal traces they left in the corpses or on the cookware. Or did these early northern peoples simply prefer fish, as many in coastal areas do today?

Remains of mammals that were not eaten—pine marten, wild cat, fox, otter, badger, polecat—had been held in traps, cutmarks on their bones. This and other evidence, especially plentiful after about 4500 BC, suggest that these animals were trapped and killed for their fur and that there may have been a fur trade among the peoples of what is today coastal Germany, Denmark, and southern Sweden (Karsten 2004, 68). These areas were at that time connected by a land bridge over the shallow waters of the Baltic, then still a large freshwater lake and not the slightly salty sea it has since become.

Agriculture Comes to the Germanic Homeland

Life in the Germanic homeland had probably been relatively prosperous for a long time. Complex burial practices, ritual activity, and trade suggest that these were not subsistence cultures but complex and successful ones: societies perhaps not of plenty, but at least of sufficiency, resistant to change.

But before the end of the sixth millennium, something disturbed the cultural equilibrium among the bands of hunter-fishers in their forests of oak, elm, and lime, in the mild and humid Atlantic climate: the elk and aurochs nearly disappeared, possibly because of a warming climate. Fishing and gathering alone failed to provide sufficient nourishment for an increasing population, and the people turned on each other. The results were not pretty: in east Jutland, human bones had been split for marrow, the bodies decapitated, the heads scalped. At one site in Dyrholmen on Jutland, "cut marks on human skulls are identical to the butchery marks which occur on animal bones," writes Tilley (2003, 43).

Around 3300 BC, peoples from the Pontic steppes (dry grasslands stretching from today's eastern Romania across today's southern Ukraine) established long-term relationships with peoples to the west, perhaps as immigrants, perhaps as explorers, in any case as culturally and most likely linguistically influential actors, according to David Anthony (2007, 344). Colin Renfrew dates arrival of such peoples on the Scandinavian coasts to around 2500 BC (1991, 50). About this time, new cultural habits also came to these coasts: burial of a stone battle-axe with each male corpse; burial mounds called *kurgans*; and pottery decorated with cordlike ridges. The new peoples were technologically advanced, becoming culturally and perhaps militarily imposing. The remains of their horse-drawn wagons, their pottery, and their tools provide evidence of dominance, though not of any modern-style large-scale invasion (Anthony 2007, 214). It seems possible that they, or perhaps only their culture and their language, a dialect of PIE, reached the coasts of Denmark and Sweden and replaced the local language (which may itself have also been PIE, but a different dialect).

What was the specific source of this cultural and linguistic dominance? Anthony suggests several:

- the Pontic steppe peoples' expertise in horse breeding and horse trading, a technology new to this geographical area, provided a means to shorten travel times;
- the steppe peoples' concept of the sanctity of oaths became advantageous in the development of trade and political institutions;
- their traditions of hospitality and, developing from that, the possibility to incorporate peoples they dominated into clients who would get favorable treatment in return for cooperation (as opposed, for example, to an ethos of conquering and making slaves of dominated peoples); and
- the celebratory functions of the steppe peoples such as funerals, weddings, and feasts, which were accompanied by ritual speech and songs (Anthony 2007, 343).

The last two in particular would have provided a positive motivation for the client peoples to learn the language of the newcomers; often these factors provide an impetus for the new language to replace, over generations, the old language:

> The pre-Indo-European languages of Europe were abandoned because they were linked to membership in social groups that became stigmatized. . . . The general situation in Europe after 3300 BC was one of increased mobility, new pastoral economies, explicitly status-ranked political systems, and inter-regional connectivity—exactly the kind of context that might have led to the stigmatization of the tightly closed identities associated with languages spoken by localized groups of village farmers. (Anthony 2007, 340–341)

Current archaeological evidence in general supports, though suggesting an earlier date for, several hypotheses previously outlined by scholars. For example, linguist John Waterman (1966, 42) accepted an estimate that around 2000 BC a northern PIE dialect began splitting into two further dialects: the ancestors of Germanic and Slavic. The date comes from the application of a method called lexicostatistical dating. The method was outlined in detail by Morris Swadesh (1952, 452–457), who proposed a list of 207 basic words on which to measure languages' degree of relatedness, and a "retention rate" of 76 to 85 percent of these words per thousand years. The method has been used to estimate the length of time since two languages split off from their common ancestor. Since Swadesh's original proposal, changes have been proposed to make the method more reliable; nonetheless many scholars continue to be skeptical of lexicostatistical dating. Subsequent archaeological and genetic research, meanwhile, has suggested an even earlier dating for a pre-Germanic dialect, as was noted above.

At this time, PIE was a continuum of closely related dialects spoken by many peoples, geographically and genetically distant from one another, whose migrations spread their language over much of Eurasia. Genetic studies make it clear, though, that Proto-Indo-European peoples, whoever they may have been and wherever they may have come from, did not spread their language by wiping out the native populations of Europe.

> There was no Indo-European invasion of Europe. . . . Instead a succession of Pontic steppe tribal segments fissioned from their home clans and moved toward what they perceived as places with good pastures and opportunities for acquiring clients. [They] then used their ritual and political institutions to establish control over the lands they appropriated for their herds. (Anthony 2007, 369–370)

Far from genetically replacing the populations they dominated, these newcomers more likely melted into them. In fact, a study of worldwide human DNA shows that 87 percent of the DNA of today's Europeans can be traced to peoples who came to Europe before the end of the Ice Age that preceded the Neolithic (Late Stone Age) (Wade 2006, 108). In other words, the bringers of the Proto-Indo-European languages did not replace the hunters and gatherers; at most, small numbers of the newcomers joined the earlier inhabitants, contributing in the process only 13 percent of the current European DNA.

The appearance of the Neolithic pre-Germanen, as far as we know, hardly differed from the appearance of Scandinavians, northern Germans, and northern Slavs today: on average, they were relatively tall and relatively fair-haired. Grave finds in Scandinavia from the Stone Ages and the Bronze Age have documented a predominance of tall bodies and long skulls; the peat bogs of Denmark have yielded whole corpses with facial features and hairstyles intact. Height and skull-length measurements of these millennia-old human remains are similar to those made of Swedish Army recruits in the nineteenth century. In a 2006 genetic study, Peter Frost argued that the fair hair and light-colored eyes common in northern Europe today are a consequence of high male–female ratios in post Ice-Age northern Europe (2006, 98). Frost hypothesizes that in the pre-agricultural hunting conditions of northern Europe (not only in pre-Germanic, but also, for example, in Celtic and Uralic-speaking populations), a high death rate for (exclusively male) hunters as they plied their dangerous trade hunting large game tipped the male–female sex ratio, giving the surviving males many females from which to choose. According to Frost, the men's preference for the fair led to a "population bottleneck" in which blond and light-eyed women were more likely to find mates and to reproduce. By contrast, in societies with a more evenly matched male–female ratio, virtually every adult would have mated and reproduced. Their offspring of both sexes would have been at least somewhat likely also to be fair, and over many generations the trait of fairness could have become dominant in both women and men. The results may be seen throughout Europe today, from Italy and Spain in the south to Finland and Russia in the north: dark hair and brown eyes predominant in the south, fair hair and blue or gray eyes predominant in the north. Frost provides some eye-color and hair-color maps of Europe as documentation of these trends (2006, 87–88).

Agriculture may have been brought by newcomers to the North Sea and Baltic landscapes; or perhaps it was developed independently here. Colin Renfrew hypothesizes that agriculture had arrived with Indo-European-speaking farmers who came in a gradual migration from the Mediterranean and the Middle East, starting in the seventh millennium BC and arriving in coastal northern Europe around three thousand years later (Renfrew 1991, 52–56). Other scholars do not agree with Renfrew's hypothesis. T. Douglas Price writes that around 4000 BC, agriculture appeared "almost simultaneously across a large area from northern Germany to western Norway and middle Sweden," though he finds no convincing evidence that it was introduced to the area by new peoples (Price 2000, 18).

In any case, pastoralism and agriculture replaced hunting, fishing, and gathering as the economic basis of the society of Northern Europe and Scandinavia. The people in the Germanic homeland learned to breed and herd domestic animals for meat and milk, using slash-and-burn methods to clear the forest in order to pen animals and grow grain. These technologies—agriculture, and domestication of animals to provide food—can support a much larger population per acre than hunting and fishing, and the settled lifestyle favors caring for dependent infants and children. By contrast, peoples on the move must either carry or leave behind anyone who cannot walk, including children under five or six years old.

Barley and the primitive wheats known as einkorn and emmer were planted with hoes and ground with querns—flat stones on which grains were laid, to be crushed into meal or flour by hand with a flat-topped stone. The earliest known evidence of a domestic animal other than the dog was found in Øgårde on the island of Zealand, Denmark, in the form of a cow bone dated to around 3850 BC (Price 2000, 277). Livestock, including cows as well as pigs and sheep, was not only domesticated from the forest but also imported. Analysis of remains of pigs and cattle at some sites revealed that they were not of local origin, though they had been fed with local acorns. Instead of the large hunting dogs of earlier times, smaller watchdogs, or companion dogs, became common. The people buried their dead in graves known as *dysser*, round or oval mounds surrounded by stones. Settled villages replaced the temporary shelters suitable to a people who followed game migrations or changes of season. Regional architectural fashions even arose. Dwellings in the Scandinavian villages were free-standing houses, according to the style already established in other European locations, whereas in the Near East rows of connected habitations, or buildings grouped around courtyards, were more typical (Milisauskas 1978, 45).

Some social patterns found here at this time were to be long-lasting. For example, sex roles were differentiated: the men were buried with weapons, the women with jewelry. And it will sound familiar to today's readers that graves of men showed on average more riches than those of women. But the status of women was on the rise; toward the end of the period of these Danish settlements, increasing weights of gold, bronze, and jewelry are found in women's graves. The graves of both men and women in fertile farmlands contained more of these riches than those in less fertile areas, demonstrating the connection between agriculture and prosperity (Phillips 1980, 210–211).

A Proto-Germanic Language Emerges

By about 1500 BC new styles of weapons, pottery, and burial customs, along with the knowledge of smelting of copper and tin to make bronze, had completely replaced earlier implements and practices of the Stone Age Germanic homeland, beginning the Nordic Bronze Age. The people in this Germanic homeland had long been localizing their PIE language into a pre-Germanic dialect. The first phase of the pronunciation changes that were to result in what linguists term Proto-Germanic was still occurring at this time; the entire sound shift may have been in process for as long as two millennia.

Germanic linguist Winfried Lehmann, writing in 1967, pointed out the long gap between the probable breakup of PIE into dialects and daughter languages and the documented existence of Germanic: "Proto-Germanic is scarcely to be dated before 500 BC, yet a very conservative estimate of Proto-Indo-European would set for it a final date of at least 2500 BC. The intervening period of two thousand years during which some species of Germanic was spoken is generally shrugged off with the label pre-Germanic" (1967, 73). David Anthony estimates an even earlier date—around 3300 BC—for the pre-Germanic split from another PIE dialect (Anthony 2007, 82). The splitting is defined by the transition to at least some of the consonant changes of the Germanic Sound Shift (see below). Scholars do not generally refer to the language as Proto-Germanic until it has completed the entire sound shift, including all the consonant changes as well as the shift to a first-syllable accent pattern.

Harigastiteiva, a third-century BC inscription of one or perhaps two words on a bronze helmet cast sometime in the fifth century BC, is the earliest *written* evidence of Germanic. The fragment appears on one of twenty-eight brimmed helmets dug up by Jurij Slazek in 1811 as he was planting an apple orchard in what is today Zenjak, Slovenia. All the experts agree that at least parts of the inscription represent a Germanic language, though they are scratched in the right-to-left alphabet of the Etruscans, non-Roman inhabitants of the western Italian peninsula. Almost everything else about the find, as well as quite a bit about the Germanic language it intriguingly samples, is still under debate.

The meaning of the helmet's inscription is not settled: "for Harigast of God," "to Harigast the god," and "Harigast made this," among others, have been proposed. The date of manufacture of the helmets, as well as of the inscription, can only be estimated; the Etruscan writing was once believed to be runes; the words themselves may be all Germanic or partly Germanic, partly Italic (i.e., pre-Latin). Linguists agree that *Harigast* (its *–i* ending possibly indicating the dative case) is Germanic, but is it the name of the helmet maker, the warrior for whom it was made, or an alternative name for Odin or Wotan, the chief Germanic god? The interpretation of the Etruscan representations of Germanic (or Italic) is disputed: the following word, *Teiva* (the inscription, like others of its time, does not show spaces between words), may be the name of the chief Germanic god, or an Italic verb, providing the interpretation "made for Harigast," "Harigast made this," or perhaps something else altogether (Keller 1978, 66–68).

Named the "Negau helmet" because it was found in the Negau district, part of the Austro-Hungarian Empire, in 1811, it is today on display in a glass case at the Kunsthistorisches Museum in Vienna. The inscription may have been scratched onto the helmet by a later owner two hundred years or more after the helmet was cast in bronze. Still later, around 50 BC, all twenty-eight of the helmets were buried in what eighteen hundred years later was to become Mr. Slazek's apple orchard, possibly placed there to keep them from being taken as booty by invading Romans.

The helmet's inscription suggests that, in approximately the third century BC, a specifically Germanic language existed. It also provides evidence for the existence at some earlier time of Proto-Germanic ("proto" because scholars believe it must have existed, but there is no written or spoken evidence of it other than its daughter languages). Proto-Germanic is the ancestor of today's Germanic languages (German, Yiddish, English, Netherlandic, Frisian, Afrikaans, Norwegian, Danish, Swedish, Icelandic, and Faroese) and is itself a daughter language of Proto-Indo-European (PIE). But the Negau Helmet cannot tell us when the language of the Germanic homeland ceased being PIE and started being pre-Germanic or Proto-Germanic.

The Negau inscription is the earliest physical evidence we have of any Germanic language, although most historians of language believe that Proto-Germanic must have been either a separate language or a distinct dialect of PIE long before. Narrowing down when and how a PIE dialect's Germanic *tendencies* became a Germanic *language* is a problem with which comparative linguistics has concerned itself for over a century. It seems fair to say that progress on the *how* has been markedly better than progress on the *when*.

The Germanic Sound Shift

The linguistic marker between PIE and Proto-Germanic is the *Germanic Sound Shift*, or *First Sound Shift*, known in German as *die erste Lautverschiebung*. This sound shift was not a random or scattered change, but a change from one system to another. It has two parts: first, a shift of consonant sounds, and second, a shift in syllable stress, affecting every single word.

The consonant shift, in which certain consonants became other consonants as PIE changed into Germanic, may appear to the modern observer as a single event because all the changes are usually analyzed together and the phenomenon has a single name. Nonetheless it took place over possibly thousands of years and was apparently complete by the time of the Negau inscription in the third century BC.

The second part of the Germanic Sound Shift was not as complex as the consonant shift, but it affected every word of more than one syllable. This was a change in the stress patterns. PIE had shown a wide variety of accent, or "free" spoken stress, in different words; that is, some words were accented on the first syllable, others on the second, and so on, with no systemic rule or predictability.

As a result of the First Sound Shift, though, every word that came into Proto-Germanic from PIE was stressed on the first syllable, no matter what syllable its stress fell on in the mother language. This pattern remains dominant, though not exclusive, in Germanic languages to the present.

In addition, the eight noun cases of PIE were reduced in Proto-Germanic to four, and many verb forms disappeared as well. In most of the modern Germanic languages, this tendency toward reduction in grammatical endings continued in subsequent eras, and it appears to be still at work today, though at different rates in different Germanic languages: Modern German is less inflected than Old High German, while Modern Swedish, Norwegian, Danish, Dutch, and English are less inflected than their medieval forms. For example, English, probably the least inflected of the Germanic languages, has lost genders of inanimate nouns as well as most case indicators. It retains traces of a case system only in the possessive of nouns and pronouns ("school's" or "his"); subject and object forms of first and third person personal pronouns ("I/me," "she/her," "he/him," "we/us," "they/them," while "you" has flattened out to a single form); and the relative/interrogative "who/whom"—though "whom" appears well on the way to obsolescence as fewer and fewer native speakers know how to use it. Interestingly, Icelandic and Faroese, the "Insular" (because their home is on islands) Scandinavian languages, seem to have been much less affected by the Germanic trend toward loss of inflection. Today they retain case indicators in both nouns and adjectives and in general have a richer inflectional system than any of the other Germanic languages, including their "Mainland" Scandinavian sister languages Swedish, Norwegian, and Danish.

The First Sound Shift

In 1818 Danish philologist and founder of comparative linguistics Rasmus Rask published his analysis of the regularly occurring consonant difference between Germanic and non-Germanic languages of the Indo-European language family. His work was elaborated and formulated as a law in 1822 by German philologist Jacob Grimm. Grimm's Law claimed that Proto-Germanic had been derived from Proto-Indo-European (PIE) through a sound shift among three kinds of consonants. This sound shift affected virtually every single word that came from PIE into Germanic.

The systematic nature of language ensures that such wide-ranging sound shifts, once they begin, will continue to affect other sounds until the system stabilizes. The phonology, or sound structure, of a language rests upon maintenance of as much "distance" between its sounds as possible, so that when one sound or group of sounds shifts, other sounds shift also to maintain this equilibrium, as Astrid Stedje explains (2001, xx).

In Table 1.2 a simplified accounting of the consonant shifts (in part from Ernst 2005), the earliest available attested examples are used. Hence, PIE or Latin (or, in one case, Tocharian, a very early and extinct Indo-European language) is used to represent Indo-European; Gothic, Old Saxon, or Old Norse are used for Germanic. Modern English equivalents are provided for clarification of meaning, but not for the sound shifts per se; these sound shifts are often shown in English, but in the intervening centuries other changes have occurred that may confuse the picture, so that it is considered best practice in linguistics to use the older examples for illustration.

There are a few additions to Grimm's Law. It does not apply in clusters beginning with *s*: *sp*, *st*, *sk*, *sk*^{w}. Further, Grimm's Law does not always apply when the consonant does not occur at the beginning of the word. Danish philologist Karl Verner resolved this apparent exception in 1875 with Verner's Law, which stated that *$^*f$, *$^*þ$, *$^*s$, and *$^*x$ became voiced as *$^*b$, *$^*đ$, *$^*z$, and *$^*g$ when they immediately follow an unstressed syllable in the word and between voiced consonants or vowels. For example (from Bury 2005, 18), *$^*p$→*$^*b$ (not *$^*f$) in Latin *septem*, Old High German *sibun* ('seven'), *$^*k$→*$^*g$ (not *h) in Latin *oculus*, Old High German *ouga* ('eye').

With the addition of Verner's Law, Grimm's Law could now be applied without exception, in every single one of the specified consonants in PIE words that survived into Proto-Germanic.

However, modern Germanic languages borrowed many words from other languages after the Germanic Sound Shift was complete; these words are not affected by the consonant shift even if they are ultimately of Indo-European origin. Further, later sound shifts may also have affected the consonants, such as when *s* or *z* in English and the Scandinavian languages mutated to *r*. In this way, the presence or lack

Table 1.2. Some Examples of the Results of the First (Germanic) Sound Shift: The Consonants (Grimm's Law)

Consonant Shift[a]	From (non-Germanic) Indo-European	To Germanic[b]
*p→*f	Latin: *pater*	Gothic: *fadar* 'father'
*t→*þ (*th* as in English 'thorn')	Greek: *treīs* Latin: *tres*	Gothic: *þreis* 'three'
*k→*x (as in Scots *loch*; probably by Gothic times sounded like English *h*)	Latin: *canis*	Gothic: *hunds* 'dog'
*kʷ→*hw	Latin: *quis*	Gothic: *hwer* 'who'
*b→*p	PIE: *slab*	Old Saxon: *slapan* 'sleep'
*d→*t	Latin: *quod*	Old Saxon: *hwat* 'what'
*g→*k	Latin: *iugum*	Gothic: *juk* 'yoke'
*gʷ→*kw	PIE: *gwewo*	Old Norse: *kvikr* 'quick'
*gʷʰ→*gw→*w	PIE: *gʷʰíbʰ*	Proto-Germanic: *wiban*, earlier *gwiban* 'woman'
*bh→*b	PIE: *bhrater*	Gothic: *broþar* 'brother'
*dh→*d	PIE: *bhendhon*	Gothic: *bindan* 'bind'
*gh→*g	PIE: *ghostis*	Gothic: *gasts* 'ghost'

[a] *The single asterisk is used to indicate that a language form has not been attested in written text but has been reconstructed. The sound changes in the far left column are starred because they show changes from one reconstructed language into another (PIE to Proto-Germanic), even though the examples are sometimes taken from attested (nonstarred) languages.*

[b] *Some Germanic examples show more than one sound shift; the one being illustrated is underlined. Note that because the sound shift was in spoken language, not written language, the sound changes notated in the leftmost column are not necessarily identical to the spelling in attested languages (for example, Latin) in the columns on the right.*

of a sound shift in borrowed words can be used to date the borrowing into a Germanic language.

The second part of the Germanic Sound Shift, the moving of the accent to the beginning of the word, was a seemingly small alteration that had large ripple effects. Over time, accenting the first syllable of each word "caused a progressive sloughing off of the phonetic elements in final position" (Waterman 1966, 23). This alteration affected many Germanic words. Waterman illustrates by comparing one word of Latin, an Indo-European but non-Germanic language, *hostis* 'stranger', with Germanic equivalents in Gothic *gasts*, showing weakening of the Latin *-is* to *-s*, and Old High German *gast*, where the ending has disappeared.

In time, the first-syllable stress fired the imagination of Germanic speakers and led to countless alliterating word-pair idioms, beginning at least in Old High German times and probably earlier. Germanic poets working in this tradition combined alliteration with poetic rhythm (German *Stabreim*), by making the "beats" of their lines fall on words beginning with the same or a similar sound. Though this pattern was gradually replaced as a standard poetic device by the end rhyme that became common in European verse in Christian times, alliteration has remained into modern times a frequent feature in folk proverbs, prose, and poetry in Germanic languages. German furnishes many examples of its idiomatic presence: *Wind und Wetter, Nacht und Nebel, Haus und Hof* (a list is in Jeep 1995, 1–46); similarly, English "hearth and home," "bag and baggage," "black and blue." Shakespeare is still paying tribute to the old Germanic technique in *The Tempest*: "Full fathom five thy father lies. . . ."

As a daughter language of PIE, Proto-Germanic retains much of the structure of its mother language. The three grammatical genders— masculine, feminine, and neuter—continued into Proto-Germanic, though in some of the modern Germanic languages, such as English, these have fallen away. Also retained in Modern German and, to a limited extent, Modern English, are conjugations incorporating person, number, tense, and mood (German *ich werfe/ er wirft*; English 'I throw/ he throws'). Comparison of adjectives is similar to that of PIE: there are three grades (positive, comparative, superlative), indicated by similar suffixes on the comparative and the superlative: *-r, -st* (Modern German *klein, kleiner, kleinst-*; Modern English 'small', 'smaller', 'smallest').

Though Proto-Germanic retained much from the mother language, considerable changes occurred as well. Some characteristics of verbs disappeared; where PIE verb forms expressed tense and aspect (beginning, duration, completion of actions), Proto-Germanic retained only the present and preterite (simple past) as one-word tenses, expressing other tenses and aspects with additional words, as in Modern German *hat gemacht, wird machen* and Modern English has done', 'will do'. Additionally, Germanic distinguished "strong" verbs, those with consonant and vowel alternations in the past tense and past participle. Examples are Modern German *sehen, sah, [hat] gesehen*, Modern English 'see, 'saw, [has] seen'. "Weak" verbs are those whose past tense shows a dental (d or t) suffix, as in Modern German *arbeiten, arbeitete, [hat] gearbeitet*, Modern English 'work, worked, [has] worked'.

PIE's eight noun cases (nominative, genitive, dative, accusative, ablative, locative, instrumental, vocative) became in Proto-Germanic just four. Modern German retains indicators for nominative (for sentence subjects), genitive (possessive), dative (for indirect objects), and accusative (for direct objects). Older Germanic languages indicated these cases by endings on every noun, as in Latin. In Modern German the noun case system survives in attenuated form: an *(e)n* in all cases except nominative singular for masculine "weak" nouns, an *(e)ns* in the genitive, an *(e)n* in the dative for neuter "weak" nouns; an *(e)s* in the genitive singular of most masculine and neuter nouns; an *n* in the dative plural of most nouns in all genders. The articles (such as words for "the" and "a") and adjectives retain case endings; and personal pronouns, as in English, show distinctive forms for the cases.

In some Germanic languages, adjectives gained "weak" and "strong" endings depending upon the articles preceding them. Examples are Modern German *das alte Haus* 'the old house' (weak) versus *ein altes Haus* 'an old house' (strong; both nominative case), Modern Swedish *det gamla huset* 'the old house' (weak) versus *ett gammalt hus* 'an old house' (strong). Old English still retained the strong/weak distinctions: *ān alte hūs* 'an old house', *đa alte hūs* 'the old house' (weak); but *alt hūs* 'old house' (strong; all three nominative case). The strong/weak distinction is lost in Modern English, though it was still present in Chaucer's time (Middle English).

Substrate Hypotheses

The changes grouped under the First Sound Shift can be explained with reference to Proto-Germanic's mother language, PIE. But did other languages play a role as well? About one-third of the vocabulary words of modern Germanic languages, including English, are not traceable to PIE; their source has not yet been found. Examples from English and German include: ship/*Schiff*; boat/*Boot*; keel/*Kiel*; sail/*Segel*; rudder/*Ruder*; mast/*Mast*; swim/*schwimmen*; weapon/*Waffe*; sword/*Schwert*; eel/*Aal*; carp/*Karpfen*; hand/*Hand*; bone/*Bein* (Eggers 1963, 26). It should be noted, however, that this list is constantly being pared down as more roots are identified in mostly extinct Indo-European languages (such as Tocharian; Watkins 2000, xxvii). Because quite a few of these apparently non-Indo-European words are from the realm of seafaring, linguists have speculated that the Indo-European homeland was not on the sea. Dwellers in the seafront Germanic homeland could have borrowed maritime vocabulary from an unidentified neighboring language or kept it from their previous language, also not yet identified.

The search for this other language has suggested a related line of inquiry: whether an earlier language in the Germanic homeland, or spoken at an earlier time by its people (in linguistic terms a *substrate*, sometimes called *substratum*), influenced the type of PIE spoken there and caused the changes that led ultimately to Proto-Germanic.

"There is for Northern Europe an extensive, bitter and thoroughly inconclusive controversy on whether the systematic change of all PIE consonants in Germanic should be attributed to non-Indo-European natives who spoke 'broken Indo-European,'" writes J. P. Mallory (1989, 175), summarizing the debate on the substrate hypothesis. If PIE served as a lingua franca for several local non-Indo-European languages, the non-native speakers might have brought their errors in and made them part of the new language, writes Hans Henrich Hock (1991, 479).

Germanic linguists do not reject the substrate hypothesis in principle, though there is considerable controversy as to its relevance in the Germanic Sound Shift. According to Mallory, for example, there is "fairly clear evidence for substrate languages affecting some of the Indo-European languages" (1989, 156). So while the substrate hypothesis for Proto-Germanic is not generally accepted by linguists, neither has it been completely ruled out. Many scholars continue to pursue the question; several lines of inquiry are summarized in the following sections.

Uralic Influence?

If a substrate was responsible for the main events of the Germanic Sound Shift, what language might it be, and what is the evidence? Proto-Uralic, mother language of Finno-Ugric and hence grandmother to Modern Finnish, is the usual suspect for proponents of the substrate hypothesis. The Uralic family, the exact composition of which is a matter of linguistic controversy, consists of two subgroups, Finno-Ugric and Samoyedic. Currently the only nonendangered Finno-Ugric languages are Finnish, Hungarian, and Estonian. All of the Samoyedic languages, spoken on the Arctic shores of Russia by a total of no more than 30,000 speakers, are considered endangered.

If a Uralic language is suspected as the linguistic forerunner of PIE in the Germanic homeland, what would be its means, motive, and opportunity? The *means* could be some sound patterns of Proto-Uralic, not characteristic of PIE but among the changes made by the Germanic Sound Shift. Finnish linguist Kalevi Wiik, among others, argues that Proto-Germanic's shift to the first-syllable stress pattern and some of its other phonetic characteristics could be explained by influence from Proto-Uralic, which also had these patterns (Wiik 2003).

Wiik also argues that the people of the North Sea/Baltic area were Proto-Uralic speakers when PIE speakers migrated into the region (Wiik 1999). His assertion is unproven, but there is evidence of long contact between Proto-Uralic and PIE in the Baltic or, before that, in the Russian steppes, which might provide *opportunity* for Proto-Uralic influence. The evidence includes both objects found in these regions, but far from their place of origin, and some very early borrowings from PIE into both Sámi (Lappish) and Finnic languages (Koivulehto 1988). Borrowing in the opposite direction, that is, Uralic loanwords in Germanic, though, is rare; even the Germanic languages' non-Indo-European seafaring words mentioned earlier are not of Uralic origin. Perhaps it may be said, then, that *motive* is lacking: there is no evidence of substantial Proto-Uralic language spread into southwestern coastal Scandinavia, where the Germanic Sound Shift took place.

Currently most scholars of Germanic or Uralic linguistics consider Uralic influence on the Germanic Sound Shift either unproven or unfounded, and in particular they do not accept Wiik's hypothesis (Aikio and Aikio 2002; Kallio, Koivolehtu, Parpola 1997). However, the issue of Uralic-Indo-European influence continues to exert fascination, especially in Finland, the Germanic speakers' Baltic neighbor. Finland's Scandinavian-style culture, its geographical location in Scandinavia, and its non-Scandinavian, in fact non-Indo-European, language make for an unusual combination. Finns curious about their own national and linguistic origins have made historical linguistics a lively academic specialty, as well as a popular hobby, in their northern land.

Vasconic or Semitic Influence?

German scholar Theo Vennemann hypothesizes still other sources for otherwise unexplained anomalies or shifts in vocabulary, sound, and grammar of PIE and Proto-Germanic. Vennemann names as a source Vasconic, the mother language of today's Basque. He argues that Vasconic people resettled the European continent after the last Ice Age and before the arrival of the Indo-European speakers, an argument for which he claims support in the form of DNA evidence (Vennemann 2003, 139).

Up to now we have discussed a substrate, an "underlying" native language of an area invaded or settled by foreign-language speakers. When two languages collide in a disputed or conquered territory, one may be a substrate, in which case the other is a *superstrate* or *superstratum*. Operationally, the substrate is a language of lower prestige, the superstrate a language of higher prestige (such as the language of military invaders). If neither of two languages in a single geographic area has a prestige advantage, each is considered an *adstrate* or *adstratum*. With the passage of a long time, it may be difficult even for experts to determine precisely what the relationship of two languages was.

As for Proto-Germanic, Vennemann explains its non-Indo-European words as evidence of both a substrate and a superstrate. He believes that Germanic was fundamentally influenced by a substrate, Vasconic (the mother language of modern Basque), and a superstrate, ancient Semitidic (Semitic, Egyptian, and Berber [introduction by Patrizia Noel Aziz Hanna to Vennemann 2003, xx]). Vennemann speculates that the superstrate was the language of Semitidic-speaking seafarers who settled the European Atlantic coast in 5000–4000 BC and left behind traces of their language along with megalithic (giant stone monument) culture, characterized by the monuments at Stonehenge and similar Neolithic Age sites in the British Isles, France, and Italy.

Vennemann considers superstrate influence proved by the estimated one-third of the original Germanic vocabulary that is non-Indo-European, especially words in three categories: war, law, and public life. Examples from Modern German of these non-Indo-European words include *Schwert* 'sword', *Waffe* 'weapon', *stehlen* 'steal', *Dieb* 'thief', *Volk* 'people" and *Adel* 'nobility' (Vennemann 2003, 1–20).

These, according to Vennemann, are precisely the categories of words that are typically borrowed from a prestigious society's language into the language of a less advanced or less prestigious one. "Even if the rulers—perhaps under conditions of large numerical and possibly also cultural superiority of the conquered people—give up their own language and take on that of the conquered people, they at least keep their legal vocabulary" (Vennemann 2003, 9). Even the other types of non-Indo-European borrowings (for example, in navigation, construction, animal and plant names, and everyday words) could have come from either a superstrate or a substrate, Vennemann writes:

> If the ruling people come by sea, their nautical terminology will prevail. If they bring superior construction techniques, the conquered people will take on the vocabulary as well as the techniques. In every area of daily life the ruled listen to the expressions of the rulers, even if they have fully adequate expressions in their own language. If the rulers' language dies out in conditions of bilinguality, the surviving language . . . will retain expressions from the earlier ruling language. (Vennemann 2003, 9–10)

Thus, Vennemann considers it possible that all of the non-Indo-European vocabulary of the Germanic languages might be attributable to a superstrate. Vennemann's hypotheses, though published in respected journals of historical linguistics, remain controversial and are not universally accepted by his fellow linguists, such as Edgar C. Polomé (1992, 47).

The case is not closed. A substrate "can often neither be proved nor disproved, because it is no longer available for comparison," cautions linguist Terry Crowley (1992, 194). It is likely that, as more evidence is gathered through the increasingly sophisticated methods of DNA research, archaeology, and anthropology, questions of language origins will be revisited.

Language Prestige

Prestige would have played a role in language change in prehistoric times just as it does today. If newcomers in a territory are conquering invaders or have high status (perhaps through wealth, superior technology, or know-how), their language may exert a powerful, even stifling influence on the indigenous language. Meanwhile, the indigenous population, even while using the new language, may as a defensive tactic devise its own in-group phrases or other alterations of the new language as a mark of identity (Crowley 1992, 258). Such a use of language could have been at work in the prehistoric Germanic homeland. In this case, the native pre-Germanen might have stubbornly retained some language features in their use of the new language as a covert resistance to, for example, the migrants and their superior technology (weaponry, agricultural knowledge, wheeled vehicles) and economic means (metals, jewelry, horses and other domesticated animals).

When the nonnative speakers use the new language, they sometimes make changes in the grammar, and these changes may persist into subsequent generations. Joe Salmons comments that "rule loss is often found in second and third generation speakers, as is consistent with generative theory. That is, rule addition should be more common among adults and rule loss more common among childhood learners" (1992, 39). Under this hypothesis, the children learning a new language would have simplified or reduced its sounds and rules for their own use, passing their form of the language down to their children.

German linguist Hans Eggers pictures the prehistoric Germanen as grasping the rules, but not the exceptions, of PIE, transforming it to "schematic regularity" (1963, 26). The historical accuracy of this statement cannot be known, but if true it would provide an explanation for why Proto-Germanic ended up with a heavily pruned version of the PIE noun case and verb tense systems.

Was it the second-language learners' use of PIE as a lingua franca, their inexpert mimickry of the new language, their transference from their native language, or their reduction of language rules that caused a regularization in the sound system and grammar of the PIE in the Germanic homeland? Or perhaps none of the above? When the historic dust settled, a streamlined (or impoverished, depending on one's view of language) Proto-Germanic could be seen to have arisen from the exquisitely detailed morphology and grammar of its mother language, PIE.

Why Did a New Language Replace the Old One?

Language replacement typically does not happen quickly:

> When two languages come into contact, people speaking one of them do not immediately abandon their own and adopt the language of the other. A prerequisite to language shift is societal bilingualism. This may remain quite stable over a long period but in the case of Indo-European expansions it was obviously a prelude to the adoption of Indo-European. (Mallory 1989, 258)

The technological accomplishments of the newcomers would have had a halo effect on PIE, making the language attractive to peoples who had contact with the newcomers. In time the old language would die out, as there was less reason for parents to pass it on to their children.

"Generally even the most ferocious teachers in schools with the most fearsome whips cannot turn time back, as far as language is concerned," writes Crowley (1992, 31). In other words, in spite of other factors, the language in a bilingual society seen by that society's speakers as advantageous will dominate and eventually become exclusive, the old language passing out of use.

What are the factors affecting language dominance in a bilingual society? As a general principle, adstratal languages, of equal prestige, borrow and loan basic vocabulary. Illustrations from many languages and time periods tell the story. For example, with the ninth- and tenth-century Norse (sometimes called Viking) incursions into English-speaking northern Britain came Norse words, including 'egg,' 'get,' 'give,' 'guest,' 'hit,' 'husband,' 'sky,' 'skirt,' 'take.' These words borrowed into everyday English seem to indicate that Norse remained an adstrate, living side by side with Anglo-Saxon, in a position of more or less social equality. In fact Anglo-Saxon and Norse were so similar at that time that speakers of the two languages probably understood each other with little difficulty and, as subsequent genetic studies indicate, intermarried freely.

> If the donor language is a superstratum, loans are from prestigious parts of the lexicon and are themselves prestigious; if the donor language is a substratum, loans are 'need' borrowings, such as place names, or have derogatory connotations. But the relative prestige of a given language does not affect . . . whether it will replace the other language or be replaced by it. (Hock 1991, 411)

Hock notes that English ousted an adstrate (Norse), a superstrate (French), and a substrate (Celtic). For example, the (French-speaking) Norman conquest of England in 1066 established French as the prestige language of England for three hundred years and left behind many French words in English yet French failed to replace English over the long term. Explaining this turn of events, David W. Anthony comments:

> The Normans conquered England . . . but . . . failed to establish their language among the local populations. . . . Immigrant elite languages are adopted only where an elite status system . . . is also open to recruitment and alliance. For people to change to a new language, the shift must provide a key to integration . . . and those who join the system must see an opportunity to rise within it. (2007, 118)

Apparently the Normans had opened no routes for the English to succeed to the French-speaking ruling class; there was no social or economic payoff for the population in learning French.

Borrowing of foreign words does not in itself lead a language to extinction, as modern language examples demonstrate—English vocabulary is 65 percent foreign, Swedish 65–75 percent and Albanian, 90 percent, yet all three languages currently retain their distinctiveness. Syntactic and morphological structure, more than vocabulary, sustain the identity of languages; these are not as easily borrowed from foreign sources as are individual words.

Governments often try, though usually without success, to stop the population from borrowing foreign words: "the general population (as opposed perhaps to officialdom) is not concerned with linguistic nationalism, rather more with prestige" (Hock 1991, 415)—meaning that the people will continue to borrow foreign words if they perceive them as of high status.

The Sound Shift accomplished, the Germanic world had acquired a language, and though the people little knew it at the time, that language would sketch an identity for its speakers. Both language and people continued on their way for a long time unnoticed by the world beyond them. Not until the final years of the second century BC, when the Germanic tribes began to migrate into Roman territories, would the Germanic world attract the wider world's attention (Lockwood 1972). That is the subject of the next chapter.

Timeline: From the Earliest Settlements in Northern Europe to the Beginning of the Christian Era

Year (all BC)	In the Germanic Homeland	In the Rest of the World
35,000		All human population in Europe is entirely modern (*Homo sapiens sapiens*)
10,000	First documented human habitation in Bromme, Denmark	End of Paleolithic (Old Stone Age) and beginning of Mesolithic (Middle Stone Age) in Continental Europe
7000–5000	Hunter-gatherer communities, North Jutland, Denmark	

continued

Year (all BC)	In the Germanic Homeland	In the Rest of the World
4999–4000	Settlements in Vedbaek Bøgebakken, Denmark	Proto-Indo-European (PIE) one of many languages spoken across Eurasia. Earliest settlements exist in Mesopotamia; Egyptian calendar with 360 days, 12 months
3999–3500	Earliest agriculture in Denmark; domesticated oxen; Neolithic Era begins in Scandinavia	First year of Jewish calendar, 3760 BC. Disastrous floods in Mesopotamian region; copper, gold, and silver smelted by Egyptians and Sumerians; multicolored ceramic ware from Russia reaches China
3499–3000		First phase of Stonehenge; earliest known numerals in Egypt; wheeled vehicles in Sumeria
2999–2500	Mainland Scandinavia populated by food gatherers, megalith (giant stone monuments) builders	Gaulish dialect of Indo-European spoken in northern and central Europe; Proto-Finno-Ugric (ancester of Finnish and Hungarian) borrows words from PIE; European Bronze Age; Baltic amber traded to Italy, France, Greece; epic tales of Gilgamesh; mother and son deities worshipped by Hittites, Egyptians, Phoenicians, Scandinavians

Year (all BC)	In the Germanic Homeland	In the Rest of the World
2499–2000	Oldest pictorial representation of skiing, on rock carving in Rodoy, Norway; Dolmen (stone funerary chamber) period in Scandinavia	Earliest Egyptian mummies; first domesticated chickens, Babylon
1999–1500	Harvesting of grains (wild einkorn, emmer); reports of first trumpets in Denmark	Nomad pastoralism in Eurasian steppes; Code of Hammurabi in Middle East
1499–1000	Bronze Age in Southern Denmark	Germanic influences on Finnic language and culture; Moses of Bible tradition returns from Mt. Sinai with the Ten Commandments
999–900		Gold vessels and jewelry in Europe; classic paganism in Greece; King Solomon builds Yahweh Temple in Jerusalem
899–800		*Iliad* and *Odyssey* (ascribed to Homer)
799–700	Beginning of Iron Age in Denmark	City of Rome founded (traditional date 753 BC); first recorded Olympic Games in Greece
699–600		Marduk Temple in Babylon (Tower of Babel) begun; first written laws in Athens
599–500		Oldest surviving Latin inscriptions; Rome declared a republic and its last king, Tarquin the Proud, expelled

continued

Year (all BC)	In the Germanic Homeland	In the Rest of the World
499–400		Wine cultured in wooden barrels in Italy and Gaul; age of Euripides, Sophocles, Aeschylus in Greece
399–300	Greek explorer Pytheas of Massalia (Marseilles) sails to Britain and "Thule," probably Iceland or the Shetlands	Euclid's work on geometry appears
299–200		Great Wall of China built; Greek New Testament, *Septuagint*, written
199–100	Germanic tribes, Cimbri and Teutones, leave Denmark and enter the Roman Empire	Rosetta Stone is engraved; war between Sparta and Rome; Erastosthenes of Cyrene computes the circumference of the earth at 40,000 kilometers (currently figured at 40,075.16 km)
99–1	The Germanic Suevi invade Roman Gaul; Caesar conquers Gaul, declares the Rhine the border between Roman Germanic and the Germanic tribal territories; massive Roman incursions into Germanic territories between Rhine and Elbe Rivers	Cleopatra, last queen of Egypt; birth of Jesus at Bethlehem

Table is after Grun 2005. With a few exceptions, dates are not firmly attested, though all are part of current and generally accepted scientific discourse.

2

The Germanic Languages
Survive the Romans

The Battle of Kalkriese, 9 AD

By 12 BC the largely Celtic territory west of the Rhine called by the
Romans "Gaul" was a Roman colony, but the lands of the Germanen
immediately eastward had not been conquered by the Romans. In that
year, Roman Emperor Augustus set out to correct this situation. He
intended to conquer, once and for all, the territories located between
the rivers Rhine (at that time the eastern border of Gaul) and the River
Elbe. The Romans knew these territories as *Germania*, home of the
Germani. Both names are now categorized by scholars as of non-Latin,
non-Germanic, but otherwise undetermined origin, abandoning
previous hypotheses as linguistically unlikely, according to Herwig
Wolfram (2005, 20).

Following Augustus's orders, the Roman Consul Publius Quintilius
Varus, "a man of evilly acquired but princely wealth" (Detwiler 1999, 6),
had begun a harsh and corrupt occupation in Germania. The Romans
believed the area to be pacified by 6 AD, as Varus, now General of the
Roman Army of the Rhine, subdued the *Germanen* with tactics such as
confiscating their winter food supplies and killing entire villages if they
resisted Roman rule. The tribes themselves were hardly a unified force,
and the Romans found it easy to use divide and conquer techniques against

them. Neither General Varus nor Emperor Augustus in Rome considered the barbarian tribes capable of a victory over the Roman Army.

In the late summer of 9 AD a horrific three-day battle near Kalkriese, a hill near Osnabrück in Lower Saxony, proved them wrong and resulted in the slaughter of 23,000 Romans, destroying Roman complacency about the Germanic tribes and making not only military but also linguistic history.

The Germanic tribes that allied at the Battle of Kalkriese under their leader Arminius, a Germanic-born Roman officer, meant to defeat the Romans and rid themselves of a hated and brutal Roman administrator. In this goal they succeeded, but the battle had other consequences as well. After the shocking loss of three legions of the Roman Army in a defeat carried out by one of its own officers, the Empire withdrew from territories east of the Rhine by order of Emperor Augustus. Several years later, after his death, there was a Roman campaign in the area, but it was relatively small scale and in any case not successful; the Empire eventually withdrew altogether and, in its remaining five hundred years of existence, did not again attempt to colonize in Germanic territory, as Erik Durschmied writes (2000, 17).

Withdrawing along with the Romans was the Latin language, leaving a body of Germanic language territory sitting on an arc of Roman—and Latin-speaking—Europe.

Tradition long called this battle the Battle of the Teutoburg Forest (in German, *Teutoburger Wald*), the name deriving from the Roman historian Tacitus's name for its location, the *saltus teutoburgiensis*. Twentieth-century archaeological research located the battle about 70 kilometers away from the Teutoburg Forest, in the swampy woods near Kalkriese. Amateur archaeologist Tony Clunn, who is credited with the discovery (working with archaeologists at the nearby university), has described his successful location of the battlefield, right down to the findings of human and animal bones, the metal face guards, and the battle pay in Roman coin (Clunn 2005, 325–335).

The architect of the battle that defeated the Roman legions was Arminius, a Germanic tribesman but also a Romanized, Latin-speaking Equestrian of the Roman Army, who turned against Rome to lead the Germanic warriors against the Empire. Son of a Cheruscan tribal chieftain, he received his Roman name during the military training in Rome that was customary at the time for ambitious young Germanic noblemen. His Germanic birth name is undiscovered by history, though later centuries named him the nearest German equivalent, "Hermann," and generations of irreverent American graduate students in modern times have dubbed him "Hermann the German." After several years of distinguished military service to Rome, Arminius became a trusted colleague of General Varus. But, perhaps because he was repelled by Varus's brutal methods, Arminius turned against both Varus and Rome. Arminius noticed that Varus was a careless military man who underestimated the Germanen, and he used his knowledge to design the battle that was to change both Germanic and Roman history, uniting tribal elders of his own and neighboring tribes in a plot against Varus. Arminius's pro-Roman father-in-law, Segestes, discovered the plan and warned Varus. Varus, however, discounted the warning as motivated merely by a family feud, since Segestes was known to be angered by his daughter Thusnelda's marriage to Arminius after having broken off her betrothal to another tribal member (Durschmied 2000, 23).

On that late summer day in 9 AD, General Varus was en route from the legions' summer camp at Aliso on the River Lippe to winter quarters near the Rhine; he had rerouted his three legions into unfamiliar territory at the advice of Arminius. It seemed that there was a Germanic uprising that needed quelling. So Varus's troops proceeded, single file in a muddy and slippery ditch, the Germanic forest deep and dark on both sides. Roman Legions XVII, XVIII, and XIX picked their way through the tree roots and stones, led by Varus and followed by three squadrons of cavalry and a large contingent of servants, extra horses, wagons of provisions, and pack animals. Also along for the trip were the soldiers' "field wives," local women who were not necessarily prostitutes, as might be suspected, but rather temporary partners taken by military men who were often stationed in faraway outposts like Germania for years at a time. The women (along with the children who inevitably resulted) followed the Roman soldiers on their travels and provided them with domestic services such as cooking and other homely maintenance, as well as affectionate company.

The uprising that Varus and his troops thought they were going to put down was fictitious, a ruse to lure the Roman legions onto this dangerous route; Arminius had prepared an ambush in his tribal homeland. Waiting in the forest to attack them were his fellow Cherusci, collected under Arminius's direction with tribesmen of the Marsi, the Chatti, and the Bructeri—about 18,000 men, the normally infighting tribes finally comprising a unified force unexpected by the Romans.

When the Germanen attacked, the Romans were virtually helpless, according to the Roman historian Cassius Deo and other contemporary sources (Krause 2005, 99–103; Durschmied 2000, 29–30). In a ditch and surrounded by forest, they could not get into their accustomed battle formations. A powerful thunderstorm came up over the battle, with heavy rain, bolts of lightning that split trees, and hail the size of robins' eggs. The Roman historian Tacitus, writing in his *Annals* nearly a century later, described the Roman troops as terrified, convinced that the storm was an omen warning that Jupiter was against them. The Germanen, however, had the home advantage. The gloomy forest that seemed threatening to the Romans was familiar to them, and they considered the storm a favorable sign from Thor, the Germanic god of thunder.

About 23,000 Romans—soldiers, camp followers and servants, women and children among them, along with their animals—died in the three-day battle, most of them slaughtered with axes. The camp followers who survived were taken captive as slaves. The Germanen poked out the eyes of the Roman soldiers, cut off their hands and their tongues, and sewed up their mouths. They nailed Roman skulls to trees, they strung up horses and pack animals from high branches, offerings to the Germanic gods. About a thousand Roman soldiers survived to escape by night, eventually taking the news of the terrible battle back to Rome. Many others were trapped, and, knowing that defeat and slaughter awaited them, committed suicide rather than be taken. Varus himself, having first fallen on his sword as Roman tradition prescribed to losing generals, was afterward beheaded by the Germanen, and his head was sent to Emperor Augustus in Rome. The ragtag barbarians had conquered the Imperial Roman Army, and in a most spectacular way.

The horrific slaughter so appalled the Roman Emperor Augustus that during his lifetime he permitted no attempt to reinvade the territories east of the Rhine, considering that "to pacify, assimilate, and govern Germania against the will of its intractably unpredictable inhabitants would overextend the resources of Rome," writes Donald S. Detwiler (1999, 7). Elderly and ill, Augustus was reported to have wandered through his apartments in Rome crying out: "Varus, Varus, give me back my legions."

The defeat at Kalkriese had significant consequences in Rome, where it had not been imagined that the primitive barbarians could orchestrate a battle so catastrophic to the disciplined and well-equipped Roman army. The three lost legions, XVII, XVIII, and XIX, were never reconstituted. The Romans feared that the Germanen would march against Italy and Rome itself. In response, Augustus instituted a draft of all military-age men under a threat of financial penalty and loss of citizenship, ordered all Germanen living in Rome to be immediately deported, and cancelled all pending Roman festival celebrations (Krause 2005, 106).

After Augustus's death, his stepson and successor Emperor Tiberius sponsored several campaigns between the years 14 and 16 AD to regain the territories east of the Rhine. However, these campaigns were costly and inconclusive, and Tiberius eventually settled for a Rhine–Danube border with the eastern Germanen (Detwiler 1999, 4). In 15 AD a Roman delegation returned to the battle scene at Kalkriese and conducted funeral rites for the dead (Detwiler 1999, 8), recording for Roman history the extent of the slaughter.

The Germanic leader, Arminius, lived to fight the Romans again, escaping with his army after losing the Battle of the Weser River in 14 AD. His pregnant wife, Thusnelda, however, was betrayed to Roman General Germanicus by her father, Segestes. Segestes evidently expected his daughter to denounce Arminius, the son-in-law he hated, and join her father in Roman triumph. But after the Romans took her captive, Thusnelda refused to denounce Arminius. While in captivity she gave birth to their son Thumelicus. In 17 AD both were displayed in a triumphal parade in Rome (see frontispiece). Her father, who had betrayed her to the Romans, is shown on the steps above her, slumped over, presumably in shame (Lankheit 1984, 20). The story was reported by the Greek historian Strabo (Strabo 1917, VII, Ch.1/4, 292), who appears in the right-hand lower corner of the painting (Neue Pinakothek 2003, 283). Thusnelda's ultimate fate is not known. Her son, according to Tacitus, was trained as a gladiator in Ravenna and died young. Arminius did not marry again; in 19 AD he was killed in a dispute with his own tribesmen.

This dramatic family story, overlaid by an anachronistic narrative of Arminius as an early hero of the future German nation, was told many times in the German art and literature of later centuries. Thusnelda's noble acceptance of her fate as reported by the Roman historian Tacitus (109, I) became, centuries later, an icon of German national pride: she and her husband were celebrated in Klopstock's 1753 ode "Hermann und Thusnelda," as well as in a 1786 painting (now lost) by Angelika Kaufmann and an 1822 painting by William Tischbein. The battle at Kalkriese was the subject of Heinrich von Kleist's 1818 drama *Die Hermannsschlacht* 'The Hermann slaughter', while Arminius's and Thusnelda's son Thumelicus was the subject of Friedrich Halm's tragedy *Der Fechter von Ravenna* 'The gladiator of Ravenna', which premiered in Munich in 1856. Finally, in 1875, during the height of nineteenth-century German nationalism, the government of Kaiser Wilhelm I glorified Arminius yet again by erecting a huge bronze statue near the German city of Detmold portraying him in a (historically inaccurate) winged helmet.

The Roman fear that the Germanen would invade Rome proved prophetic, although that would not happen for many years. The Romans never colonized east of the Rhine and in time stopped going to Germania, though the Germanen were to go to Rome.

Whether the eventual domination of Rome by the Germanic peoples owes much to Arminius at Kalkriese remains an open question. Possibly the Romans were already overextended and could not in the long run have conquered the Germanen east of the Rhine even if the Battle of Kalkriese had never happened, suggests Detwiler (1999, 10). However that may be, the Battle of Kalkriese was a signal event in the history of Rome, the Germanic peoples, and the Germanic languages in Europe.

Why Did Arminius Ambush the Roman Legions?

To the Romans in the first century, the ambush at Kalkriese was an act of treachery (Strabo 1917, VII, 1/4, 292), for Arminius, the Germanic nobles, and the Cherusker had all sworn loyalty to Varus and to Rome. To Germans in later centuries, it seemed a heroic act of national liberation, though this is strictly speaking impossible, since Germany did not exist as a nation until nearly nineteen hundred years later.

Arminius has been described as a dominant personality type who wanted to be "a Germanic king according to the Roman example" (Krause 2005, 163), bringing his people the advantages of Rome, and enjoying the privileges of a Roman king, without himself being subject to Roman rule. Arminius may have lost his taste for cooperating with the Roman Empire after having witnessed Varus ordering pitiless and massive slaughter of his fellow Germanic tribesmen. Perhaps, then, his treachery can be understood as both an emotional display of revenge and a calculated act of ambition, for which he, his wife, and his son were to pay a bitter price. The eventual effect on the Germanic languages is, however, another story entirely.

The Linguistic Consequences

The Battle of Kalkriese set the stage for the survival of the Germanic languages in this part of Europe, through the centuries of the Roman Empire, the Middle Ages, and into modern times. Had the Romans been able to carry out their planned conversion of these territories into a Roman colony, on the pattern of the Latin-speaking *Gallia Romana* 'Roman Gaul' to the west, the almost certain result would have been a replacement of the Germanic tongues of the region by Latin, just as Celtic in Gaul had been replaced by Latin. The next step would have been its development in time into a daughter language of the Romance family (as with French in Gaul). Germanic languages would likely have survived only in Scandinavia, where there was little Roman influence, and possibly in present-day Holland. There would have been no Germanic-speaking Angles and Saxons on the German North Sea coast to invade and settle the British Isles four centuries later, so that no Germanic language would have arrived on that island to become the ancestor of English.

In the rest of Europe, hundreds of years of Roman domination effectively erased the local, often Celtic and Germanic, languages and replaced them with Latin. During the Middle Ages and the rise of European principalities and kingdoms, Latin evolved into what we now know as the modern Romance languages: Spanish, French, Portuguese, Italian, Romanian. To the west, Gaul, roughly where modern France is now located, had already been colonized by the Romans, and its Celtic language had already been replaced by Latin when the Germanic Franks came to rule there. While the Frankish ruling elites continued for a time to speak their own language, it was Latin that had staying power; it would later give birth to the language now known as French. The Franks' native language, Franconian, survived, but in the Low Countries, where it eventually became Modern Netherlandic, that is, Dutch and Flemish. A few holdout areas such as Bretagne in France and the Basque territories in Spain retained their own non-Latin, non-Germanic languages. "When about 1200 AD, the [German-French] linguistic frontier becomes clear from contemporary records, it is seen to be virtually as it is today, apart from some losses to French in French Flanders," writes Lockwood (1972, 104). Throughout Germany, Holland, Denmark, and part of Belgium, then, the dominant language family was and remained Germanic, albeit enriched by thousands of words borrowed from Latin.

The Germanic tribes spoke not *Deutsch* but rather various dialects, their geographical distribution reflecting the tribal settlements after the migrations in the fourth to sixth centuries. A single standard German language would not begin to emerge until the 1500s.

The Germanic Tribes: From Clans and Warbands to Tribes

By the early years of the Roman Empire, far distant from the Empire's territory, Germanic clan groups in their homelands came together for trade and self-defense, or to commit mayhem on their neighbors, and they began to coalesce into tribes. Tribes were larger and more cohesive than clans; each had a name for itself and an awareness of itself as a people. The tribes very likely had, however, no ethnic or national awareness in the modern sense, even when they were made up mostly of related clans. Further, it sometimes happened that one dominant tribe absorbed another, smaller or weaker tribe; these mergers could easily cross ethnic lines.

About 98 AD the Roman historian Tacitus (1999, passim) enumerated in his *Germania* the Germanic tribes known to him, all of them at that time living in the far north of Europe. Tacitus was no ethnographer and his comments should not be taken at face value, particularly as he lacked any personal experience with the Germanen; his writings are of interest more as an expression of the Roman view of the tribes than as a reliable account of them.

Tacitus both admired and felt superior to the barbarians, as the Romans called them, expressing the ambivalence that the Romans were to experience concerning the Germanen for the next four centuries. On the one hand, he described the tribes as wild, uncivilized, and dangerously hostile, interested in little except fighting, disinclined to work, and content to be slothful between battles. On the other hand, Tacitus admired their bravery in battle; he describes them as hardened to hunger and cold by their unfavorable climate and unyielding soil. Well impressed by these Germanic customs, Tacitus recounts that Germanic men and women were faithful to their spouses and, further, that they believed their gods had given women the power of prophesy. As a wedding gift, Germanic women received a horse equipped for battle, a javelin, and a sword, and they accompanied their men into battle to feed, encourage, and perhaps fight alongside them, unlike Roman women, whose place of honor was solely within the household.

Tacitus named three Germanic groups, each according to tradition descended from one of the three sons of their god Mannus. They were the *Ingvaeones*, living next to the ocean; the *Irminones* (also called *Herminones*), living in the middle country; and the *Istvaeones*, all the rest. Each of the three groups contained many tribes. Some of those named by Tacitus may in actuality have been Celts, and many of them did not figure prominently in later history. Tacitus believed that the Germanic peoples must have originated in their homeland, which he described as "gloomy forests or nasty marshes," not the sort of place that anyone would have moved to from somewhere else, such as warm, sunny, and civilized Rome.

The Romans named the northern seas after the Germanic tribes that lived on their coasts: the Baltic, the *Mare Suebicum* after the Suebi tribe; the North Atlantic, the *Mare Frisia*, after the Frisians. Tacitus could not know that within two hundred years the number of Germanic tribes would explode and the territory they ruled would expand to cover much of the European continent, while the Germanen would become an almost constant threat to the Roman Empire, eventually overwhelming it.

Of the fifty or so tribes mentioned by Tacitus in 98 AD, only one, the Frisians, stayed at home (except for a few incursions into nearby areas), remaining a seafaring folk that even, while modernizing, kept many of its ways, its English-like language, and even its name into the twentieth-first century (see Table 2.1). Most of the tribes undertook migration that observers at the time considered significant. Tribal migrations, even before the *Völkerwanderung* beginning in 376 AD (see section later in this chapter) brought Germanen to regions from Poland to Italy, from Romania to Spain, and even to North Africa. In the process they merged with one another and then split again into new formations and acquired new names, attacked and then made treaties with Rome, and even joined their realms to the Roman Empire. The resulting peoples eventually became major players in the European nation-building of the Middle Ages.

The names of most of the Germanic tribes listed in Table 2.1 are preserved in place names in German-speaking countries or elsewhere on the European continent, where the eventually Romanized tribes established their realms during the pre-medieval centuries of the Roman Empire. The barbarians feared by the Romans did indeed conquer Rome, but instead of destroying it, they ushered in the Middle Ages as its new rulers. Table 2.1 represents a partial listing of the 100 Germanic tribes mentioned by Krause (2005, 269–276); additional information is taken from other sources as noted. It omits non-Germanic tribes even if they were prominent in Europe (for example, the Celts).

Table 2.1. Some Germanic Tribes and What They Did

Tribal Name	Probable Origin	Facts About	Name Lives On As
Alamanni	Elbe River region, Germany	Possibly a coalition rather than a single tribe; their name means 'all men'. Under Frankish influence from about 500 AD, the tribe became part of the Frankish kingdom in 746.	"Germany" in several languages (e.g., French *Allemagne*); today *Alemannic* refers to the dialects of southwestern Germanic speech area in modern times; *Alamannic* refers to the tribes and their language.
Angles	Jutland, Denmark, and Schleswig, North Germany	With the Saxons and the Jutes, invaded England perhaps in 5th century AD, becoming the Anglo-Saxons, their language the forerunner of Modern English.	*Angeln*, place name in Schleswig, Germany; *Engla-lond* ('England' in Anglo-Saxon English).
Burgundians (Burgundi- ones)	Sweden	Migrated to Germany, founded a king- dom west of the Rhine in 411 AD, their story told in the 12th-century *Nibelungenlied*	Their home, *Bornholm* Island in Sweden (*Burgundarholmr* in Old Norse); the *Burgogne* region in France (and its wine, called in English *Burgundy*).
Chatti (Catti)	Hessen, N. Germany	Part of Arminius's coalition in 9 AD at Kalkriese; mentioned by Tacitus in 98 AD. Much later merged with the Franks. Mentioned in the English epic *Beowulf* (ca. 1000 BC) as the Hetwaras.	*Chatti→Hessen* "Hessia" (through a series of sound shifts), region in northern Germany.

Tribe	Location	Description	Notes
Cheruscans (Cherusci)	Rhine valley between modern Osnabrück and Hanover	Tribe of Arminius, leader of the Battle of Kalkriese, flourished between 1st century BC and 1st century AD.	Tribal name may mean "the deer people" (modern German *Hirsch* = 'deer' through sound shift ch→h).
Cimbri (Kimbri)	Jutland, Denmark	Migrated to the Danube valley in 2nd cent. BC; joined with Teutones, battled the Romans, who defeated the tribes in 101 BC; the women of the two tribes committed mass suicide rather than be taken captive, deeply impressing the Romans.	*Himmerland* (formerly *Himberland*), their home in the Jutish region of Denmark (through sound shift k→h); however, this tribe is not related to the modern-day *Cimbri*, a Germanic-speaking ethnic group in northern Italy.
Franks	Possibly Denmark, later the Rhine area	Took their name in 11 BC; later became a confederation of tribes, including the Chatti, Salians, and many others. Established a realm in Gaul around 340 AD.	The first Germanen to settle permanently in (Latin-speaking) Roman territory, Gaul, which became a nation, *France*. They spoke at first Germanic *Franconian* (ancestor of Netherlandic) and then Latin, which evolved into *French*.

continued

Table 2.1. (continued)

Tribal Name	Probable Origin	Facts About	Name Lives On As
Frisians (Frisii)	North Sea coast	Coalesced along the North Sea coast around 700 BC; the waters there were called by the Romans *Mare Frisia*; avoided destruction by the Romans with a treaty in 28 AD. Frisians may have been among the invaders of Britain (with the Angles and the Saxons) around 450 AD. (Robinson 1992, 137)	Of the tribes mentioned by Tacitus, only the Frisians have maintained their name until the present. *Fries*, a minority language in Holland, Denmark, and Germany, is the language closest to English, as this proverb shows: "Good butter and good cheese are good English and good Fries."
Goths (Goti)	Sweden	Migrated to Poland in 1st century BC Split in 3rd century AD into eastern Ostrogoths and western Visigoths. Conquered eastern, southern Europe.	The Swedish island *Gotland* (possibly their home), Swedish city *Göteborg* and Spanish *Catalonia* are variations of *Goth/Gothic*.
Jutes	Possibly Jutland or middle Rhine (Germany); they have been identified with the Ripuarian Franks (Robinson 1992, 137)	With the Angles and the Saxons, invaded Britain around 450 AD, forming the Anglo-Saxons.	*Jutland*, in Denmark; *Jutta* (German woman's name).

Tribe	Origin	History	Legacy
Lombards (Langobardi)	Scandinavia	Migrated to the River Elbe area in northwest Germany in 1st century AD; in the 5th century to Pannonia (western Hungary), and in the 6th century conquered northern Italy, to rule for another two centuries.	*Lombardy* region of northern Italy.
Marsi	Area between Rhine, Ruhr, and Lippe rivers in northwest Germany	Part of the coalition of Arminius. In 14 AD, while drunk at a celebration for their goddess Tanfana (according to Tacitus), the tribe was massacred by the Romans in revenge for the Kalkriese slaughter.	German cities: *Marsberg, Obermarsberg* in eastern North-Rhine-Westphalia; *Volkmarsen* in northern Hesse; however, this tribe is not related to the *Marsi* of Italy.
Rugians (Rugii)	Rogaland, Norway	Migrations to Hungary and Italy; founded a realm in Austria; later allied with Ostrogoths.	Lived for a time in Pomerania (northeast Germany) and gave their name to the Baltic *Isle of Rügen* there.
Saxons (Saxones)	Jutland, parts of today's eastern Netherlands	Their name may be derived from *seax*, a kind of knife. In approx. 450 AD they invaded Britain with the Angles and the Jutes, forming the Anglo-Saxons.	The names of three modern German Federal States include *Saxony* (Ger. *Sachsen*); Saxe-Coburg and Gotha, home of Prince Albert, husband of English Queen Victoria; Celtic names for 'English' (Scottish *Sassenach*, Breton *Saouzon*, Welsh *Sais*); Finnish and Estonian name for Germany (*Saksa*).

continued

Table 2.1. (continued)

Tribal Name	Probable Origin	Facts About	Name Lives On As
Suebi	Baltic Sea coast	Intruded into Roman Gaul in 70 BC. Later merged with the Alamanni. In 410 AD established the kingdom of Gallaecia in northwest Spain, near the city of Braga.	*Swabia* (German *Schwaben*), in current German Federal States of Baden-Württemberg and Bavaria.
Suiones, Svíar, or Svear	Sweden	Their kings claimed descent from the Norse god Freyr. Migrated eastward; in the 9th century established a kingdom in Novgorod, Russia.	Their home region, *Sweden*; their descendants the *Rus* gave their name to *Russia*.
Teutones	Scandinavia, possibly Jutland	In 2nd century AD, with the Cimbri, fought the Romans. After the Battle of Aquae Sextiae the defeated Teuton and Cimbrian women killed their infants and then committed suicide rather than submit to capture, thus passing into Roman legend for their bravery.	*Teuton, Teutonic* currently mean 'German', 'Germanic' (German *teutonisch*), but the Teutones were not recognized by historians as Germanic ancestors until the 13th century.

Thuringii	Harz Mountains, Central Germany	May have been part of the Alamanni; first mentioned in 400 AD.	Their home region *Thuringia* (German *Thüringen*), eastern Germany
Vandals	Scandinavia	Migrated to Silesia (now Poland) in 2nd century AD; entered the Roman Empire in 5th century; settled in the south of Spain before leaving to create a state (429–534 AD) at Carthage in North Africa.	The Spanish state of *Andalusia* (orig. *Vandalusia*; later, Arabic conquerers called it *Al-Andalus*). Similarity of names suggests tribal origin in *Vendel*, Sweden, or *Vendsyssel*, Denmark. English 'vandal', meaning 'pointless destroyer', derives from their invasion and two-week sack of Rome in 455 AD.

Table after Krause 2005, 269–275.

The Celts

In their long heyday, the Celts, who like the Germanen were a loose collection of tribes united by little more than their related languages and their common deities, were very nearly masters of all of Europe. During the first millennium BC, Celtic was spoken from the North Sea to the Black Sea and the Balkans, into Asia Minor, from France to Turkey and from Belgium to Spain and Portugal. The Celts of Asia Minor, called Galatians, are even mentioned in the New Testament of the Bible; it was they to whom Paul's *Epistle to the Galatians* is addressed.

From the first millennium BC or earlier, the Celts were neighbors of the early Germanen, and the comparatively more advanced Celtic culture had a strong influence on the Germanic. Celtic skills in working bronze, silver, and gold into both decorative and practical objects were admired and imitated throughout Northern Europe. Germanic metalworkers were often apprenticed to Celtic masters, spreading the intricate and sinuous styles to the Germanic peoples too. The curved beauty of the metal objects made by the Celts, as well as the harsh and primitive ways of the people themselves, were perceived by the Greek and Roman elites as a thrilling as well as threatening contrast to the measured formality, comfortable lives, regulated civilizations, and modern armies of their classical world.

By about 600 BC, Proto-Celtic, an Indo-European language, had split into different language groups and the Celts had settled widely distant areas in Europe. Celts had probably settled both Britain and the Iberian Peninsula by 500 BC; chariot burials, the earliest archaeological finds in Celtic Britain, date to around that time. It was Celtic Britain that Julius Caesar invaded in 55 and 54 BC; Roman occupation in Britain (central and northern Scotland were never occupied by the Romans) lasted until 383 AD, not, however, replacing the Celtic majority population with Romans, nor the Celtic language with Latin.

Celts were the majority population in Roman-era France and were known by the Romans as Gauls, described by Julius Caesar in his *Gallic Wars*. Celts were also for a time the rulers of northern Italy, where they founded a city they called Mediolanum (modern Milan); and Celts sacked Rome itself in 390 BC.

In 192 BC the Roman Army defeated the last Celtic kingdom in Italy, and the Celtic language thereafter gradually retreated northward, even as the Celtic population for the most part stayed and switched to Latin, blending with the locals. As the Roman Empire declined, the

Celts of Gaul and Iberia were overwhelmed and dominated by Germanic invaders. In Britain the Celtic language retreated before the Anglo-Saxon language of the conquerors to coastal areas, and Anglo-Saxon's daughter language, English, eventually predominated.

Today two branches of Celtic languages survive: the *Brythonic* languages Breton (in Bretagne, on the northwest coast of France) and Welsh, and the *Goidelic* languages Irish and Scots Gaelic in the British Isles. While the Celtic languages have retreated to the edges of the British Isles and France, the modern descendants of the Celts remain in the local populations not only throughout Britain (where they predominate in most areas of the country), but throughout all of Europe.

Tall, powerful, pale-skinned, and bearded, the Celtic warriors made a strong impression on the Romans. They were said to behead their foes and decorate their homes and temples with the skulls. Yet the Celts and the Romans traded peacefully with each other, and Celtic metal weapons and gold jewelry were sought after in Rome.

The Celtic priestly caste, the Druids, had sacral knowledge not to be shared with laymen and were the custodians not only of religious ritual but also of the law. As the Roman Empire encroached upon Celtic territory and vice versa, the Druids opposed Rome and Roman influence. So seriously did Roman authorities take this opposition that Caesar Claudius in 54 AD banned Druids from Roman territory.

Recent work in population genetics has shown that large-scale population replacement of indigenous peoples by invaders is unlikely ever to have been the engine for language and cultural change in Europe: not in the spread of Proto-Indo-European through the Middle East and into Europe, not in the spread of Celtic throughout Europe, not in the spread of Germanic through the formerly Celtic areas, and not in the spread of Latin through the Roman Empire. Rather, the indigenous peoples remained in place and the language and culture of the minority invaders spread into their territories by force, by cultural influence, or by diffusion. The invaders themselves were as often as not eventually absorbed by the native populations.

For example, DNA studies on the English population suggest that Celtic bloodlines predominate today in most of Britain. Only in northern England (Yorkshire, East Anglia) and the Orkney and Shetland Islands is the picture different. Here the Danish invasions from about 800 AD were followed by long-standing settlements and Danish rule (the Danelaw), and Scandinavian genetic influence is strong (Royal Society of Edinburgh 2007). The Anglo-Saxon invaders of the fifth century, on the other hand, left in the British Isles a powerful heritage in their language, ancestor to modern English, though their genetic influence in the modern British population is minimal (Elliott and Robbins 2001). These Germanic invasions, then, the Scandinavian and the Anglo-Saxon, did not wipe out the preexisting peoples of the British Isles, and the Germanic language that prevailed and became English did so through social rather than genetic means.

The old Celtic tribal names, like the names of vanished Germanic tribes, have survived in the place names of their former territories, even those far from Britain. Examples include *Bohemia* (now part of the Czech Republic; named for the Celtic *Boii*), and *Belgium* (named for the Celtic *Belgae*).

The Germanen Go to Britain: The Anglo-Saxons and the English Language

According to archaeological evidence, it was the Romans who brought the first Germanen to Britain, as mercenaries to help subdue the Celtic chieftains (Blair 2000, 3). Even after Britain became a Roman province in the second century AD, it remained an attraction to Germanen on the North Sea coast, possibly because both the Roman and the Celtic cultures in Britain were more advanced and more prosperous than their own. The Saxons and the Jutes in particular (from the neighboring coasts of today's Germany and Denmark, respectively) continued to raid Britain, seeking not only booty but also land for settlement. In 383 the overextended Roman Empire began recalling its troops, and in 436 the last Roman soldiers left Britain.

The Age of Anglo-Saxon

The beginning of the Anglo-Saxon Age in Britain is usually dated to 450. In that year the brothers Hengist and Horsa ("stallion" and "horse," their names possibly honoring a horse cult; Wolfram 2005, 116) came to Britain. "The historical sources refer to a British (i.e., Celtic) 'proud tyrant' . . . who invited . . . Saxons . . . into the country to help his people resist attacks from the Picts and Scots of the north," writes Robinson (1992, 136). The Celtic tyrant was identified as Vortigern by the Venerable Bede, eighth-century Anglo-Saxon historian. "If this story is true, the invitation was a gross miscalculation," adds Robinson, as the Saxon tribesmen soon became "more of a threat than the peoples they had been brought in to fight" (136). Settlements in most of southeastern England by the Saxons, the Angles, and the Jutes followed, leaving place names that still live in today's England: Sussex (South Saxon), Essex (East Saxon), Wessex (West Saxon), East Anglia. By the year 600 most of southern Britain was controlled by the Germanen, soon referred to as Anglo-Saxons. Celtic rule and the Celtic language remained only in western areas such as Wales and Cornwall, though, as modern genetic studies have shown, the Celtic population itself remained largely in place, easily absorbing the Germanic invaders.

Both population and culture (artifacts such as metalwork and other treasures, as well as poems and legends) in Anglo-Saxon England were mixed, including elements of Celtic, Scandinavian, Germanic, and northern French. The Germanic language here was called first Anglo-Saxon, then (and after some radical changes), English. "Here then was a new sort of 'international' community, poised between the Roman and non-Roman worlds. . . . The values and social customs which they brought with them would prove astonishingly tough, even through centuries of assimilation to Christian culture," writes Blair (2000, 5).

Fifth-century life in Celtic Britain probably differed little from that in Saxon-dominated Britain, except for religion: the Celts were Christian, the Saxons still pagan. The legendary or historical (it is not certain which) stories of King Arthur reflect the struggle of Christian Celts against the pagan Saxons. However, by the sixth century the proselytizing by missionaries, for the most part Irish monks, was succeeding (Wolfram 2005, 116).

The Scandinavian invasions that began in the eighth century resulted in Scandinavian control of large parts of northern England (the Danelaw) until 1066. During this time Anglo-Saxon borrowed many words from Norse which became a permanent part of the English language (examples are "sky," "leg," and "they").

Anglo-Saxon (Old English)

Most of the surviving texts in the Anglo-Saxon language (also called Old English) date to about 1000 (Robinson 1992, 143). Foremost among them are the epic poem *Beowulf*, originally written in 750 AD, which recorded in highly formalized and beautiful language (making liberal use of that old Germanic poetic device, alliteration) the heroic deeds of the Anglo-Saxon forebears in a Scandinavia of many centuries earlier; and *The Anglo-Saxon Chronicle*, a diary-like history of the Anglo-Saxons, commissioned by Alfred the Great, king from 871 to 899.

Anglo-Saxon shows a close relationship to Old Saxon, the language of the Saxon territory in north-central Germany. Old English and Old Saxon, however, diverged in the fifth century and had been developing separately for centuries before the great flowering of Anglo-Saxon writing.

As might be expected, Anglo-Saxon shows some features lost in modern English, such as five noun cases, gender for all nouns, and verb-final word order. It also shows some features that are characteristic of English today (and not typical, for example, of Modern German), such as possessives before the noun (*thaes cyninges thegnas* 'the king's thanes').

A bit of Old English: "Parable of the sower and the seed," the Bible, Mark 4:1–9)

> *And eft he ongan hi aet thaere sae laeran.*
> And again he began them at the sea to teach.
> *And him waes mycel menegu to gegaderod,*
> And him was great multitude to gathered,
> *swa thaet he on scip eode, and on thaere sae waes;*
> so that he on ship went, and on the sea was;
> *and eall seo menegu ymbe tha sae waes on lande.*
> and all that multitude around the sea was on land.
> (after Robinson 1992, 148; translation mine)

The Battle of Hastings and the Norman Conquest

In the fifth century, Britain absorbed the Angles, the Jutes, and the Saxons to become Anglo-Saxon England, but another Scandinavian conquest, this time via France, was to give their adopted land, and their language, a new turn. This took place in the year 1066, when the Normans, French-speaking Viking descendants who had been living in France since 911, sailed across the English Channel with their king, William the Conquerer, to claim the English throne and rule England. The Battle of Hastings in that same year made Britain a Norman conquest.

Norman French (later called Anglo-Norman) was spoken at court and by the new Norman nobility of England. Surprisingly, the Norman

French of the conquerors did not replace Anglo-Saxon. Within a few generations, the descendants of the Normans were speaking Anglo-Saxon and had even issued manuals to help their children learn their ancestral language, Norman French (suggesting that the children did not learn it at home as their mother tongue, but had to learn it from books).

Anglo-Saxon continued to be spoken by the common people, but it borrowed thousands of words from Norman French. Many of these words survived into Modern English alongside native English words of similar meaning. In many cases the Modern English word derived from Norman French indicates a higher social class usage than the word derived from Anglo-Saxon. Examples are: the Anglo-Saxon farm animals *pig*, *cow*, and *sheep*, when turned into cuisine, took new names from Norman French, becoming *pork*, *beef*, and *mutton*; the prosaic Anglo-Saxon *wood* became the poetic Norman French *forest*; the people's Anglo-Saxon *house* became the prosperous Norman French *mansion*.

The Norman rule of England dissipated when the Black Death of the fourteenth century killed a large portion of the population, throwing society into chaos for a time and erasing the distinction between Norman and English people. The language, enriched with many borrowings from Norman French, began to call itself English. Later scholars have given the name "Middle English" to the language of about 1100 to 1500. It was a time of creativity and accomplishment in the world of literature, producing among many other great works Geoffrey Chaucer's epic poem *The Canterbury Tales*.

The Germanic *Völkerwanderung*, 375–568 AD

News that Germanen were massing at the borders of the Roman Empire from the Danube to the Black Sea reached Rome around 375 AD. The traditional view is that tens or hundreds of thousands of tribesmen were on the move; Peter Wells cautions that modern-day anthropologists believe that the migrations were considerably less massive than Roman reports indicate (2008, 30). The tribesmen were Goths fleeing an invasion of their empire by Huns, an Asiatic people from the east. The Goths were followed by other tribes such as the Vandals, the Burgundians, and the Gepids, who had resided on the eastern fringe of the empire (Krause 2005, 47). More were to come; for the next two centuries, Germanen came to the Roman Empire, sometimes politely requesting entry, sometimes invading, sometimes attacking and even plundering Rome.

This migration of the Germanic tribes is called in German the *Völkerwanderung*; in English, the Migration Period. It is made up of two phases: the Germanic phase of 376–568, and the second, partly non-Germanic phase, lasting until 900, of Slavic, Turkish, Magyar, and Scandinavian peoples (the latter were later called "Vikings").

The *Völkerwanderung* does not reflect the first contact of the Germanen with Rome, nor even the first military confrontations. The Germanic tribes, as we have seen, had been migrating since pre-Christian times, as the tribes moved out of southern Scandinavia and the Baltic coast of Germany deeper into the mainland. Dealing with Germanen on the move was to become a major challenge for the Roman Empire.

The reports concerning the tribal movements starting in 375, as written by Ammianus Marcellinus, the most prominent Roman historian of the time, certainly got the attention of the political and cultural elites in Rome, where there was great fear about the possible consequences. Not only the Germanen were involved. The attacks of non-Germanic, eastern nomadic peoples such as the Scythians, the Alans, and the Mongolians were a constant danger to the settled realms of Europe. Perhaps the most relevant of these to the history of the Germanen were the Huns, nomads from the Eurasian and Central Asian steppes. As it turned out, when the Huns moved, the Germanen moved too.

The Huns' ways were frighteningly alien to both the Romans and the Germanen. Ammianus gave incredible reports concerning the Huns: he wrote that they cut deep wounds into the cheeks of their young boys to prevent the growth of beards; instead of cooking meat, they tenderized it in leather bags by pounding it under their legs as they rode their horses. They were said never to dismount, even relieving themselves while astride—this last report was probably connected with the Huns' use of stirrups (unknown both to the Romans and to the Germanen), which enabled them to stand up while on horseback.

As the Huns moved westward, they collided with Europe first in the Ostrogothic (eastern Gothic), then in the Visigothic (western Gothic) kingdom (Krause 2005, 149–150), subjugating the Ostrogoths and causing the Visigoths to flee. The Huns were to press westward as far as Gaul, eventually finding allies and even admiration among some who initially fled from them. The Goths, for example, took up some of the Huns' more attractive habits, such as the culture of riding horses and the Hunnish style of gold jewelry; they even adopted the Hunnic custom of binding the soft skulls of infants, especially girls, so that they grew up with noticeably elongated heads. This custom was also adopted by relatives of the Goths, the Burgundians, in their kingdom in what is today France, as remains of Burgundian skulls have shown.

Meantime, nature also provided reasons for peoples to be on the move. Rising levels of rivers and lakes flooded some tribal settlements and caused the peoples to seek new lands. The more tribal migrations there were, the more the migrations themselves caused other tribes to migrate, all seeking refuge in the apparently safe and prosperous Roman Empire. Throughout the two centuries of the *Völkerwanderung*, Germanen did what the Celts before them had done—they went to the Balkans, the Black Sea, Asia Minor, Italy, Spain, Gaul, and Africa. Often they managed to have their own kingdoms and also to shelter in the Roman Empire: Roman *confoederatio* 'confederation' status, won by several of the tribal realms, made them independent of but protected by and allied with the Empire.

The Goths and the Gothic Language

Of the pre-medieval Germanic tongues, only Gothic, the language of the Goths, became a written literary language (Musset 1975, 12). That it did so was thanks to Ulfilas (also called *Wulfila*, 'little wolf'), a Greek missionary who converted the Goths to Christianity and became their Bishop in 340 AD. Between 348 and his death in 383, he invented an alphabet based on Greek and translated almost all of the Bible, as well as other religious texts, into the Gothic language. This is the earliest extensive body of written text in any Germanic language. Fragments of his translations survive, in several different handwritings.

The best known is the *Codex Argenteus* (Silver Bible), named for its silver letters. Of its 336 original pages, 187 are preserved as a purple-dyed parchment manuscript. Copied around 500 AD at the Ostrogothic court of Theoderic in Ravenna, it turned up a thousand years later in the German Cloister of Werden on the Ruhr River, was taken as war booty in 1648 by Swedish troops in the Thirty Years' War, and in 1669 came to the Uppsala University Library in Uppsala, Sweden, where it remains today (Krause 2005, 156).

Also surviving in Gothic are other fragmentary manuscripts, including deeds, runic inscriptions, and a commentary on the Gospel of John called *Skeireins* (Gothic "explanation"). Together these provide

| | Codex Argenteus | | Codex Carolinus | Cod. Ambros. S. 45 super. | Cod. Ambros. S. 36 super. | |
	Manus I	Manus II			Manus I	Manus II
a	Λ	Λ	Λ	λ Λ	Λ Λ	Λ Λ
b	ʙ	ʙ	ʙ	ʙ ʙ	ʙ ʙ	ʙ ʙ
g	Γ	Γ	Γ	Γ	Γ	Γ
d	ẟ	ẟ	ẟ	d	ẟ	d d
e	Є	Є	Є	F	Є	Є Є
q	U	U	U	U	U	U U
z	Z	Z	z	z	z	Z
h	h	h	h	h	h	
þ	ψ	ψ	ψ	ψ ψ	ψ	ψ ψ
i	I ï	I ï	I ï	ı ï	I ï	ı ı
k	κ	κ	κ	κ	κ	κ
l	λ	λ	λ	λ	λ	λ
m	м	м	м мᷓ	ɴ м	м	м
n	N	N	N ᵭ	N	h	N
j	Ç	Ç	Ç	Ç	Ç Ç	Ç
u	ῆ	ῆ	ῆ	ῆ	ῆ	ῆ
p	Π	Π	Π	Π	Π	Π Π
ч	Ч	Ч				
r	ᴋ	ᴋ	ᴋ	ᴋ ᴋ	ᴋ ᴋ	ᴋ
s	s	s	s	ꞇ ꞇ	s	s s
t	т	т	т	т	т	т
v	Y	Y	Y	Y	Y	Y
f	Ⅎ	Ⅎ	Ⅎ	Ⅎ	Ⅎ	Ⅎ
χ	x	x	x	x	x	x
ƕ	Θ	Θ	Θ	⟨·⟩ ⟨·⟩ Θ	⟨·⟩	⟨·⟩
o	Χ	Χ	Χ	Χ	℧ ℧	℧

The Gothic alphabet invented by Bishop Ulfilas in order to translate the Bible into Gothic. By permission of Carolina Rediviva Library at Uppsala University, Uppsala, Sweden. Facsimile edition (Codex Argenteus Upsaliensis Jussu Senatus Universitatis Phototypice Editus. Uppsala, [1927], Tab. IX).

us with almost all we know of Gothic, the major representative of the now-extinct East Germanic language group. In addition, these texts are the only written documentation of any Germanic language of this time. "Comparable records of other Germanic speeches do not appear until almost three centuries later," writes Patricia Mason (1979, 258).

During the Goths' seven-century history, they developed from a rough and pagan tribe known to their fellow Germanen for fierce warring and physical prowess, to the highly cultured rulers of realms spanning most of southern Europe and Asia Minor. The Goths, Christianized in the fourth century, were adherents of Arianism, a branch of Christianity named for its founder, Arius of Alexandria (no connection to *Aryan*). They believed that Jesus was a separate creation of God rather than being of the substance of God, a doctrine rejected as heresy by the Roman Church in the fourth century. The Goths remained Arian Christians for several centuries, even attempting at times, though without much success, to force peoples in their kingdom to accept the Gothic religion.

By the sixth century AD, however, the Goths had ceased to be a religious, political, or military power, and by the eighth century they had all but disappeared, their population and their culture absorbed into other peoples and cultures, their language dead and without descendants.

A history of the Goths, *Getica, sive de origine actibusque Gothorum* 'Gothica, or on the origin and deeds of the Goths', was written in 551 by Roman Christian Bishop Jordanes, who claimed Gothic ancestry. Jordanes, describing himself as drawing on Gothic tradition, wrote that the Goths, leaving their homeland on the island *Scandza* (not precisely identified), arrived in three ships on the coast across the sea in a place that would correspond to today's Poland, at the mouth of the Vistula River. In Jordanes's account they pushed out the resident Germanic tribes, the Rugii and the Vandals, settled in, and named the place *Gothiscandza*. There is some evidence supporting this narrative. Near the modern Polish city of Gdansk archaeologists have discovered evidence of first-century BC. Scandinavian immigration and settlement. The names of both the Baltic island of *Gotland*, off the eastern coast of Sweden, and *Götaland*, in central Sweden, suggest the possibility of a Gothic homeland in either place, and of Sweden as *Scandza*.

However, Gothic origins in Sweden, generally accepted by Swedish archaeologists, are currently questioned by American scholars, writes linguist Dennis Green (1999, 32); though "their settlement for some time on the Polish coastland between the Oder and the Vistula commands general assent nowadays" (1999, 11). The Polish city of Gdansk was long thought to owe its name to *Gothiscandza*, the Gothic settlement; but Green doubts this theory on phonological grounds (1999, 17). "Jordanes' dependence on Gothic oral tradition may tell us how the Goths later imagined their trek," concludes Green, "but not how it actually took place" (Green 1999, 17).

Another scholar's doubts about the reliability of Jordanes's Gothic origins narrative have arisen from text analysis. Arne Søby Christensen believes Jordanes's history of the Goths is not a Gothic tradition but no more than "an abbreviated version of the Roman historian Cassiodorus's *History of the Goths*" (2002, 89). Christensen concludes:

> nothing in the first third of Jordanes's *Getica* has anything whatever to do with a history of the Goths. This was the part in which Jordanes described the emigration of the Goths from *Scandza* in the year 1490 BC, outlining their history until they became divided into two groups after the Hunnic assaults in the mid-370s—the part of his narrative that was allegedly based on Gothic tradition, a Gothic *Stammessage* or *Wandersage*. . . . On the other hand, there is no doubt that the last two-thirds of the *Getica* occasionally provide truthful accounts relating to the history of the Goths. The "Visigoths" did in fact migrate to Gaul and Spain in the early fifth century, and we are equally sure that at the end of the same century the "Ostrogoths" actually travelled into Italy, where they were subsequently vanquished by the Eastern Romans in the middle of the sixth century. (2003, 319)

However the Goths got to the mouth of the Vistula, it is agreed that they settled in for another two hundred years before moving southeast toward the Black Sea. For the next 600 years the Goths continued to grow in numbers and conquered huge territories throughout Europe, establishing their kingdoms spanning an area from today's Ukraine and Turkey to Italy, the Iberian Peninsula, and the south of France.

By the year 551, when Jordanes wrote their story, the great Gothic kingdoms of Europe and Asia Minor were gone. The Western Roman Empire had fallen in 476. Jordanes's manuscript described a people and a culture that had passed their historical moment. Like other peoples in our story, they first spread and conquered, then they fell from power, and finally their language and their identity faded as they blended in with the local populations in areas where formerly they had ruled: "The Goths of both branches ceased to be a distinct ethnic and linguistic group in Europe in the eighth century. In Spain and Italy they were assimilated into the native populations to become Spaniards and, along with the later Langobards, Italians" (Wolfram 2001, 13). Even today, Wolfram continues, it is possible to see on the Spanish Canary Islands the unfriendly graffito *fuera godos* 'out Goths', *godos* 'Goths' being a pejorative slang term for mainland Spaniards.

Musset writes: "the brief appearances of the Goths and the Vandals on these islands [Sicily, Corsica, Sardinia] do not seem to have left anything behind" (1975, 142). But, as Robinson adds, "Only in the east are there some late echoes of their existence" (1992, 47). The subdued Crimean Goths—vassals to the Byzantines, the Khazars, and other powers—retained their identity and their language for perhaps another thousand years in the long-ago conquered former Gothic kingdom on the northern shores of the Black Sea. A Gothic language may have been spoken in the area as late as the sixteenth century.

Though the Gothic population eventually grew very large, the original settlers at the mouth of the Vistula may have been a small group. There could have been subsequent Gothic migrations from the homelands, and it is also likely that local tribes threw in their lot with the Goths, who were reputed to be particularly effective warriors (Krause 2005, 150–151). Such joining of tribes was common, as small groups sought to maximize their chances of survival and prosperity.

In the third century AD, having migrated to the Black Sea near the Roman province of Dacia (Romania), the Goths divided into two groups, which were later named Ostrogoths (those to the east of the Dniestr River) and Visigoths (to the west of the river). Though the Ostrogoths and the Visigoths differentiated themselves as peoples, they shared a language (Mason 1979, 264), which is usually referred to simply as Gothic.

It was here, among the western Goths, that the Arian Christian bishop Ulfilas translated the Bible into Gothic. Then in 375 the western Goths fled from invasions by the Huns and gained admittance to the Empire, becoming in 376 the first Germanic tribe to be settled in the Empire, granted status as Roman *foederati* "federates," and allowed to live under its own leaders. Meanwhile the eastern Goths were conquered by the Huns. Following the death of the Hunnic leader Attila in 453, they won independence from the Huns and entered the Roman Empire. There they founded a kingdom in Italy and the Balkans, which lasted until 535 (Robinson 1992, 45–47). The Goths who arrived in Spain by 414 undertook to conquer those they considered barbarians—the Germanic Swabians and Vandals and the Asiatic Alans. Successfully routing these groups, the Western Goths, or Visigoths, as they were called in Spain, were rewarded with a permanent home in Aquitaine, in southwest Gaul, in 419. They established an independent kingdom with a population of about 90,000 and a capital at Toulouse (Mason 1979, 263). However, under pressure from the Franks, the Visigoths retreated from Gaul and shifted their center of power to Barcelona and Toledo. Their kingdom there was overthrown in 711 by Arab invaders, who succeeded in conquering what is today Spain. The Christian reconquest, led by Visigoths, began in 718, and although the Visigothic kingdom was never reconstituted, descendants of the Visigoths were to play a prominent role in the Frankish empire of Charlemagne several generations later.

The Gothic Element in Spanish

The Germanic tribes left traces in the Latinate languages wherever they settled in the Roman Empire. However, as Patricia Mason writes, it is specifically the Goths who are credited for this influence in Spanish: "When a word of Germanic origin is found in Spanish and in no other major Romance language, it is generally attributed to the Visigothic super-stratum" (1979, 264). The Iberian Peninsula was the only Romance language area occupied by the Visigoths long enough to influence the local language, and they were the last Germanic invaders there, so that the traces they left behind are not likely to be conflated with later Germanic influences.

The surviving book of Visigothic laws, the *Lex Visigothorum* (which replaced in the year 654 the earlier doubled codes of Roman and Visigothic laws), provides written documentation for some lexical borrowing from Gothic into Spanish; linguists have worked out the etymology of other borrowings. Lexical items contributed by Gothic to the Spanish language include terms related to warfare (Sp. *guardia*←Got. *wardja*); the law (Sp. *sacar* ←Got. *sakan* 'to plead'); clothing (Sp. *escotar* 'to cut a dress to fit'←Got. **skauts* 'edge, trimming'); and many others, including personal names (Sp. *Rodrigo* ←Got. *hroths* 'reputation'+ *reiks* 'powerful', Sp. *Fernando* ←Got. *frithu* 'peace'+ *nanth* 'daring'). Other names of Visigothic origin include *Elvira, Alfonso, Ramiro*, and *Adolfo*. Additionally, the Gothic patronymic ('son of') suffix–*ez/iz* survives in Spanish surnames such as *Velazquez, Sanchez, Muniz*, and others (for more examples see Mason 1979, 267).

The Death of Gothic

A few hundred years after the Goths' triumphant arrival in the Iberian Peninsula, the Gothic language was all but dead. What could have caused this apparently dominant language to die out so quickly? Mason identifies several factors (1979, 268–272), namely the following:

- Numbers: The Gothic population in the Peninsula at the time of first settlement is estimated at 100,000 at most, as against the Hispano-Romance population of eight million. The Visigoths were definitely a small minority;
- Gothic habitation in a geographically small area: The Visigoths settled in a small area of their kingdom, apparently in order to create a concentrated Visigothic community with the aim of preserving their culture. However, this step served to limit their cultural influence over the rest of their kingdom;
- Linguistic influence of Latin on Gothic even among the Goths themselves, resulting from the two previous centuries of residence within the Roman Empire;
- Religion: The Goths were Arians, whereas their subjects the Hispano-Romans were Roman Christians. In 589 the Visigothic king Reccared converted to Roman Christianity and declared the Peninsula also Roman Christian. Since the relationship between Arianism and the Roman Church had been characterized by enmity on both sides, the conversion was either an indication or a cause of the declining social prestige of the Visigoths, which would be expected to lead to a decline in the influence of the Gothic language.

Add to these factors the one mentioned by Anthony, that "immigrant elite languages are adopted only where an elite status system is not only dominant but is also open to recruitment and alliance" (2007, 188). The Goths, it seems, considered themselves superior and preferred to keep their culture and their language to themselves rather than to encourage their subjects to aspire to their elite ranks. Their elitism may have been the last straw for the survival of the Gothic language.

By the seventh century the distinctive Gothic styles of dress had disappeared, the old Gothic art was replaced by East Roman art, and the Gothic custom of burying goods with the dead was abandoned. The Visigoths, in spite of having retained their sense of separateness from the Hispano-Roman population for a long time, had for all practical purposes merged with that population, and their language was no longer spoken.

Nine Centuries Later: A Small-Scale Gothic Survival?

In the sixteenth century, evidence emerged pointing to surviving Gothic speakers, the so-called "Crimean Goths" (German *Krimgothen*). These were assumed to be the descendants of the Ostrogoths, conquered by the Huns, and those Visigoths who stayed behind while their countrymen fled the Huns in 376. Ogier Ghislain de Busbecq, Austrian ambassador to Istanbul from 1555 to 1562, fascinated by stories that Gothic was still spoken in the Crimea (a spit of land, located in Ukraine, jutting into the Black Sea), invited two Crimean visitors to dinner and asked them about their language. The guests spoke in Greek, which was translated into Italian for Busbecq, and his notes in Latin of 101 words of what Busbecq believed to be Crimean Gothic were published by a French printer (Busbecq 1595). Later analysis of this list, which is fascinating to linguists but unreliable because of the many languages through which it was filtered that night, documents that the language was Germanic, possibly Gothic in origin. However its vocabulary was much changed from the Gothic known from Ulfilas's documents. Robinson says "perhaps the most reasonable classification of this language is as a late Ostrogothic dialect" (1992, 51). The complete story of the Crimean Goths and their language is still unknown to us.

A Sample of the Gothic Language, ca. 350 AD

Below is a four-line excerpt from the Lord's Prayer in Gothic (with interlinear English equivalent), from the *Codex Argenteus*, the Gospel of Matthew (transliterated from the Greek-based Gothic alphabet of Ulfilas into the Latin alphabet in Stedje 2001; interlinear translation mine):

> *atta unsar thu in himinam weihnai namo thein*
> father our thou in heaven blessed name thy
> *quimai thiudinassis theins wairthai wilja theins*
> come kingdom thy become will thy
> *swe in himina jah ana airthai hlaif unsarana*
> as in heaven so on earth loaf our
> *thana sinteinan gif uns himma daga jah aflet uns*
> this daily give us this day and forgive us

The Vikings: Raiders, Traders, Neighbors

While the other Germanen were migrating out of and into various regions of Europe and Asia Minor during the *Völkerwanderung*, their Scandinavian cousins were on the move as well, though before the eighth century their migrations were mostly confined within Scandinavia. But then, seamen from what is today Denmark, Norway, and Sweden began to attack and raid in Ireland, England, the Shetlands, and the Orkneys (Robinson 1992, 69–73), initiating what was later called the Viking Age, 793–1066 AD.

By the ninth century, the marauding Scandinavian seamen had established a Norse kingdom in Ireland which served as a base for many later attacks, such as on Muslim Spain in the ninth century and on England in the tenth century (Robinson 1992, 71).

Scandinavians were not then called Vikings, but variously *gaill* (Irish = foreigners), *Northmanni*/Northmen, *Dani*/Danes, Swedes, and Norse or Norsemen. The term "Viking" was introduced to modern usage in English-speaking countries by Sir Walter Scott's 1828 novel *The Pirate* (Richards 2005, 4). And it was as pirates in longships, raiding and pillaging on the coasts of Britain, France, and Spain, that the Scandinavians of the Viking Age were remembered first and foremost by later ages. These raids "represent the great epilogue of the history of the Germanen, which began a thousand years previously in south Scandinavia. . . . Its end would take place here in northern Europe as well" (Krause 2005, 233).

The word "Viking" may be of Norse origin, derived from *vik* 'bay', or from the area called *Vik*, around Oslo Fjord, or perhaps *vika* 'duty turn', from oarsmen's work; or perhaps it is derived from Old English *wic* 'armed camp' (Richards 2005, 4). In any case, it originally denoted not a people but an activity. To "go a-viking" meant raiding and stealing, whether abroad or at home. The peoples of Denmark, Norway, and Sweden considered themselves farmers and traders and did not for the most part go a-viking, even if they saw nothing wrong in it. In fact, in some places going a-viking was considered a seasonal occupation, pursued by the young and the vigorous who might be mostly farmers or traders but would take up marauding in season, if opportunity presented itself (Krause 2005, 238, 241). Their pagan tribal ethos approved the age-old method of taking goods from weaker tribes. Christianization with its concept of theft as a sin was still in the future for Scandinavia.

Raiders

In the year 793 Northmen sailed in their long warships to Lindisfarne on the northern coast of England and came ashore to destroy and plunder, burning down the monastery there and killing many of the monks. That year has entered history as the beginning of the Viking Age. Fear of the Northmen was thereafter great throughout Britain. The raid in 793 was not the first sign of Viking activity in Europe; earlier raids had been reported in both England and France (Richards 2005, 13). Nonetheless, the attack on the monastery in Lindisfarne "represented a new, terrifying level of violence. Heathens had attacked a holy place!" writes Krause (2005, 233). Robinson calls the English reaction "nothing short of hysterical" (1992, 71). In any case, thereafter hardly a kingdom in Europe was spared from the Viking attacks, and many kings found no defense successful except paying tribute to the raiders, a practice which in England was financed by a tax known as the *Danegeld* 'Dane money'.

What caused the Norse farmers and traders to turn to large-scale piracy and pillage? Population increase in response to the bumper crops of a milder Scandinavian climate may have caused shortages of the goods needed in an economy still based on gift exchange, chieftains rewarding underlings for loyal service ("ring-giving"). "[I]t was the shortage of portable wealth in Scandinavia that was the driving force for overseas expeditions," writes Richards (2005, 53). The Northmen's raiding and settlements abroad are documented by the Icelandic sagas, partly historical, partly fictional epics written centuries after the fact.

Traders

In the midst of the eighth-century raiding, some of the Northmen stayed at home and engaged in international trade. Norwegian grave finds of the era included goods from Ireland and England, and Scandinavian towns had gold and silver coins from as far away as Arabia. Glass beads made from Italian materials were found at Ribe in south Jutland, dating to around 704 (Richards 2005, 40).

Scandinavian merchants, however, not only focused on luxury goods but also trafficked in Germanic slaves, for whom there was high demand in the Middle East. Swedish Vikings flourished as traders, both of slaves and of goods, in the Middle Volga, where they were called *Rus*. In 921 they were described in the chronicle of Ibn Fadlan, an emissary of the Caliph of Baghdad (Smyser 1965, 92–119). There has been some dispute, mostly among Russian scholars, about the Scandinavian identity of the Rus described by Ibn Fadlan, though this is accepted by most German and Scandinavian scholars; James E. Montgomery provides an account of the dispute, as well as the complete text of Ibn Fadlan's manuscript (2000, 1–25). Ibn Fadlan describes the Rus as "tall as date palms, blonde and ruddy," and tattooed from fingernails to neck with dark green trees (¶ 80), but "the filthiest of God's creatures," having intercourse with slave girls while others watched, not washing their hands afterwards, and in fact washing only in basins of water shared with many others, for washing and spitting (¶ 85). Ibn Fadlan's habits of Muslim ritual cleanliness no doubt exceeded the hygienic standards of the Scandinavians. His implications that the Rus cared little for bathing and personal grooming are, however, contradicted by archaeological finds of large sauna-like bath houses with facilities for heating air and water, elaborately carved combs with fine teeth for removing lice as well as for styling hair, and comb-cases, brushes, and mirrors.

The Rus established a number of settlements in Russia, eventually founding the city of Kiev. They began speaking Slavic, intermarried with the locals, and were finally absorbed into the population, leaving behind signs of a mixed Scandinavian-Slavic culture as well as their name (which lives on as "Russia" and as *Ruotsi*, the Finnish word for Sweden).

Neighbors

The Icelandic sagas called settlement *landnáma* (land-taking), and it was an ongoing activity for the growing population of Northmen, since much of the land in Scandinavia was unsuited for agriculture. Norwegians sailed westward, exploring and establishing colonies in nearby unoccupied islands such as Iceland, the Faroes, and Greenland, as well as a place they called "Vinland" (which was not unoccupied). Iceland and the Faroes are still populated by their descendants; the Greenland colonies, settled in 985 AD, were abandoned by the Norse in the fourteenth century. Inuit people migrated to Greenland from northern Arctic islands in about 1200 and lived more or less in harmony with the Norse settlers; in 1261 Greenland was incorporated into Norway, then in the nineteenth century into Denmark. Today it is a self-governing Danish territory with Danish and Greenlandic (Kalaallisut) as official languages.

The Norse Vinland was identified in 1960 as L'Anse aux Meadows, Newfoundland, Canada, by archeologists who found there traces of an eleventh-century Scandinavian settlement of eight buildings, which had been occupied for about three years and abandoned for unknown reasons.

In England the arrival of the Scandinavians was not quite peaceful migration but rather a territory takeover. Vikings arrived in the northeast of England in the 870s and settled there, taking control of the area, which then became known as the Danelaw. They intermarried with the local population, whose Anglo-Saxon language was mutually understandable with the Norse language, and as a lasting relic northern England retains many Norse place and family names. In 1042 the Danelaw reverted to English rule, though the descendants of the Scandinavian settlers were by then anglicized, and they remained. One last *landnáma* was attempted in 1066, when Norwegian King Harald Hårdråda invaded England. He was defeated by Anglo-Saxon King Harold II, himself of Scandinavian descent, at Stamford Bridge (Richards 2005, 6). Later that same year the Anglo-Saxon King Harold was defeated by yet another Scandinavian descendant, William the Conqueror, Duke of Normandy, in the Battle of Hastings, and England became a Norman kingdom with an imported French-speaking Norman nobility, like its king of Scandinavian descent.

The Northmen's forays as Vikings were thus ended, and 1066 is considered the closing date of the Viking Age (Krause 2005, 248). The tenth-century conversion of the Danes and Norwegians to Christianity was a factor in moderating Viking behavior. In Sweden the new religion did not fully take effect until the twelfth century (Robinson 1992, 73). With Christianization, the process of medieval nationhood began for Denmark, Norway, and Sweden.

Language

The Vikings spoke not a unified language but closely related dialects of Old Norse, a Germanic language which is the ancestor of Danish, Swedish, Norwegian, and Icelandic. The first three languages have changed considerably since Viking times, while Modern Icelandic remains so similar to Old Norse that today's Icelanders can read the old sagas with relative ease (see Chapter 6).

Old Norse (often used interchangeably with the term Old Icelandic, since the written record is mostly from Iceland), with its Scandinavian daughter languages, represents the North Germanic branch of the Germanic language family. East Germanic, represented by Gothic and other related languages, is now extinct; while German, Dutch, English and all other existing Germanic languages belong to West Germanic. Beginning in the twelfth century, the written tradition of Old Norse includes Skaldic (court) verse, the popular Eddic verse, prose sagas, historic writing, religious works, and even a linguistic analysis of Old Icelandic (Robinson 1992, 73–76).

Old Norse, like the other Germanic languages of its time, showed a case system, in which nouns and adjectives had a different form depending on whether they appeared as the sentence subject, the direct or indirect object, or a possessive. Its verbs were conjugated, like verbs in Modern German.

Vocabulary was similar to that of other Germanic languages, and Old Norse was understandable to speakers of Anglo-Saxon and Old Saxon. Even today, many Old Norse words will seem familiar to speakers of English. Examples include *armr* 'arm', *fótr* 'foot', *hanga* 'hang', *standa* 'stand'. Further, quite a few Modern English words, such as "knife," "window," and "bag," were borrowed from Old Norse during Viking settlement of northeastern England.

A little bit of Old Norse (twelfth century)

Hinn er sá vill saeði sínu, tha ferr hann út.
That one who to sow wants with seed his, then goes he out.
Ok meðan hann er á veginum, tha fellr sumt niðr î hjâ veginum,
And while he is on the way, then falls some down on next to the way,
ok koma fuglar at ok eta that.
and come birds to (there) and eat it.
("The Parable of the Sower and the Seed," from the Bible, Matt. 13.3-8,
    twelfth century; Robinson 1992, 77; interlinear translation mine)

Runes

Runes, alphabetic symbols which avoided curves and horizontal lines for easy carving on wood and stone, were used from the mid-first century for Old Norse and other Germanic languages; the overwhelming number of carvings have been found in Scandinavia. The "alphabet" of the runes is called *futhark*, from the sound values of its first six symbols. They were used for prosaic inscriptions as well as for ritual or magic (their name in Old Norse, *run*, is 'secret' or 'mystery'). The ultimate source of these runes is not known, but some linguists have suggested that they were invented in what is today Denmark, where most of the runic inscriptions have been found; others suggest that they were borrowed and developed from North Italic or Etruscan writing systems. Old Icelandic literary sources ascribed the invention of the runes to the god Odin (Robinson 1992, 94).

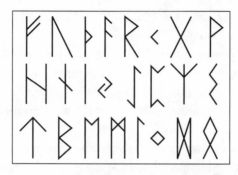

The 'older futhark', or runic alphabet of twenty-four symbols, used in the northwestern Germanic territories primarily before 550 AD, was named after the sounds of the first six symbols of the top line: f, u, th, a, r, k. After 800 AD, runic inscriptions used the 'younger futhark', a similar but smaller alphabet of sixteen symbols.

The End of the Western Roman Empire

In 476 AD, almost exactly 100 years after the recorded beginning of the *Völkerwanderung*, Romulus Augustulus, last Roman Emperor in the West, was deposed by Odoaker, "son of the king of the Skiren, an obscure Germanic people from the eastern European steppes," writes Krause (2005, 173). Odoaker declared himself King of Italy, putting an end to the Western Roman Empire which for 400 years had governed what are today France, Spain, and Italy, as well as parts of what are today Britain, Hungary, Switzerland, Belgium, and Germany. The Eastern Roman Empire in Constantinople, renamed the Byzantine Empire after the fall of the Western Empire, continued until the defeat of its last emperor in 1453.

Not only the size of the migrations but also their centrality to subsequent cultural developments have been questioned by some anthropologists (see, for example, Lucy 2000, 158–159). Nonetheless, the fact of the Germanic peoples' movement into and invasion of lands throughout and beyond Europe is accepted. Reckoned into the *Völkerwanderung* are the migrations of the Alamanni to France, the Vandals and the Suabians to Spain, the Visigoths to the city of Rome and to southwest France, the Burgundians to central Germany, the Vandals to North Africa, and the Angles, the Jutes and the Saxons to Britain (this last dated to the fifth century in the ninth-century *Anglo-Saxon Chronicle*, though again anthropologists are now skeptical;

see Lucy 2000, 157–158). The last major Germanic tribal movement came in 568, as the Langobards conquered northern Italy. The Germanic world then reached northward and southward from the fjords of Norway to the Italian Abruzzi, and eastward and westward from the mountains of Galicia in Asia Minor to the River Elbe in what is today Germany (Krause 2005, 181). But then the Germanic peoples stopped their wanderings:

> mostly in the fourth, fifth and sixth centuries, Goths and Vandals disappeared as separate peoples, Burgundians were established in southeast France, Lombards in northern Italy, Alemanni and Bavarians in southern Germany, Angles and some Saxons in Britain, and West Franks in northern Gaul. Lombards and West Franks gradually gave up their Germanic languages in favour of Romance ones. The Viking raids, the settlement of Iceland, and the Norman conquest of Sicily and England were the last episodes in this movement of Germanic peoples. (Chambers and Wilkie 1984, 20)

In the Frankish Kingdom the Germanic rulers and the Germanic peoples retained their hold through the coming Middle Ages:

> The stabilizing force that emerged as the Germanic world at last came to rest was the Frankish Empire. Beginning with Clovis (king 481–511) and culminating in Charlemagne (king 768–814, crowned emperor of the West in 800), the Franks, by conquest or peaceful annexation, gradually drew together under their dominion all the Germanic peoples of continental Europe. (Chambers and Wilkie 1984, 20)

In what is today Italy, Spain, the Slavic territories, Asia Minor, and north Africa, however, the Germanic peoples of medieval times shared the fate of the earlier migrating peoples in our story, who remained in place but lost power, their peoples and their cultures gradually dissolving into new peoples and new cultures.

If the Germanen had not won the decisive battle at Kalkriese, there might have been other effects on Europe into the Middle Ages and beyond. The Roman *limes*, the wall built by the Romans to serve as the border between the Empire and free (uncolonized) Germania, was the first sign of the east–west division. In medieval times this border demarcated the "old" Christian lands in the Roman colonies to the west and the more newly converted lands in the central and eastern parts of Europe. In the Reformation, the "new" lands were to convert to Protestantism while most of the "old" lands would remain Catholic.

The Germanen under Roman Rule

Intending to colonize all of Germania, the Romans constructed settlements which were apparently meant to be the kernels of future cities. At Waldgirmes an der Lahn in Hessen, built around 4 AD, for example, recent archaeological excavation has uncovered not only Roman administrative buildings but also Germanic dwellings, pottery ovens, and marketplaces. The Germans were being Romanized (Krause 2005, 95). *Pax romana* 'Roman peace' provided not only safety, but also profit for both Romans and Germanen. The Romans hoped it would pacify and civilize the tribes so that, even if not colonized, they would no longer pose a threat to the Empire. For their part, the Germanen were a stiff-necked people. Though they allowed themselves to be pleased by the public safety, the peaceful contacts, and the trade to be had from the Romans, they did not give up their weapons, sensing that these might help them acquire the riches and power of the Roman Empire (Krause 2005, 95–97). The settlement at Waldgirmes, like others in the eastern territories of non-Roman Germania, was abandoned after the Romans' loss at Kalkriese; but German-Roman contact was far from over.

In Roman territory west of the Rhine, Caesar Domitian in 83 AD ordered the commencement of construction of the limes as a wall with watchtowers and gates, intended less to repel invaders at the border between the Empire and Germania than to control trade and collect import and export taxes (Krause 2005, 131). The building continued over a long period and ultimately reached from the River Rhine in the northwest to the river Danube in the southeast, extending across the territory of four of today's German federal states—Rhineland-Palatinate, Hesse, Baden-Württemberg, and Bavaria.

From the inception of the limes, through its long construction until its abandonment by the Romans in 260 AD, its gates were locations for trading settlements as well as toll-collection centers. Modern excavation of Roman latrines along the limes shows that the soldiers on duty in the Rhine area during this time enjoyed the fruits of Mediterranean cuisine, including grapes, olives, almonds, figs, and even Indian pepper (Krause 2005, 86–87). Little wonder that the Germanen, even if they rejected Roman rule, were eager to share Rome's culinary goods and other by-products of its prosperity. They seemed drawn to these outposts of the Empire, building village-like settlements around the gates of the limes where they could trade with the Romans and partake at the margins of the Empire's benefits.

As time went on, the trade in Roman weapons, coins, glass, silver cutlery, fine cloth, and jewelry brought the Germanen prestige and pleasure, as they learned to use these accoutrements. The Romans in turn valued the intricate metalwork and the amber that trade with the Germanen brought. They learned more about the barbarians, though some of what they learned only made them happier to be Romans. For example, "the Romans were horrified that the Germans cooked with lard," writes Lucien Musset. But as soon as they could, the Germanen "quickly adopted Mediterranean recipes," he adds (1975, 15).

Germania east of the Rhine remained free and noncolonized by Rome, but Rome was present. Whole clans of tribesmen signed on for Roman military service and returned some years later to their families in their home villages with Roman products in their bags. The Roman Empire, source of these luxury goods, remained a tantalizing goal for Germanic warriors (Krause 2005, 118).

The Religion of the Germanen

The Germanen did not take up the Roman pantheon but kept their own many gods and goddesses (and a few borrowed from the Celts) until they were Christianized. *Nerthus*, Mother Earth, was a "people's goddess," who dwelt on earth in a wagon pulled by cows; other goddesses represented fertility, protection, and fate. *Wotan* (in some tribes called *Odin*) was the god of war and death; *Donar* (later *Thor*) had a hammer with which he struck the lightning and thunder; *Diu* was the god of the heavens. *Odin*, *Thor* and *Diu*, among others, survived into later times among the Vikings; not all the early Germanic gods and goddesses did so.

The Goths were to convert to Arian Christianity in the fourth century, as the Roman Empire was converting to Roman Christianity; the Franks, Alamanni, Anglo-Saxons and Frisians were Christianized between the sixth and the eighth centuries. By the end of the ninth century only the Scandinavians remained pagan; their conversion was not completed until the eleventh century.

The Germanen Overwhelm the Empire

At the end of the fourth century the Germanen broke through and destroyed Roman fortifications on the Rhine and the Danube. In 402 AD the Roman garrisons were finally withdrawn as the Saxons and the

Franks Germanized the area from present-day Maastricht to Boulogne (Lockwood 1972, 97–98). Meanwhile the Franks spread beyond Paris and renamed Gaul, calling it *Frankenreich* 'Franks' empire' (cf. Modern German *Frankreich* 'France'); Roman influence lived on, however, after the Roman Empire was gone:

> In the West the Roman political structure, mortally wounded, lingered on for some time before eventually disintegrating, but the Roman social structure succeeded in imposing itself from within on the new kingdoms founded by the (Barbarian/Germanic) conquerors. . . . It is doubtful if medieval Europe would really have differed very radically from Roman Europe had it not been for the succeeding waves of invasion. (Musset 1975, 29)

At the dawn of the Middle Ages the Germanic Odoaker was on the throne of Rome, the Roman Empire gone in all but name. In a bit of historical irony, its influence continued to be felt even in postmedieval times in the "Holy Roman Empire," which from 962 to 1806 officially designated most of the territories now known as Germany.

The Germanic Languages, ca. 800 AD

Since written records of Germanic languages (except for Gothic and English) are rare before the eighth century, much of what we think we know about the Germanic dialects during the premedieval Roman Empire must be speculative. The five tribal confederations suggested by archaeological evidence dating to about the beginning of the Christian era, however, do provide some links to later developments of the German language. The five are: the *North Germanen* in Scandinavia (later Norwegians, Danes, and Swedes); the *East Germanen* between the Oder and the Vistula (the Goths, the Vandals, and the Burgundians, recently arrived from Scandinavia); the coastal *North Sea Germanen* (Frisians, Angles, and Saxons); the *Weser-Rhine Rivers Germanen* (chiefly Franks); and the *Elbe River Germanen* (Alamannen, Bavarians, and Lombards). The dialect names below reflect these five divisions only loosely (Chambers and Wilkie 1984, 22–24), and a direct linguistic line from the tribes to the modern dialects almost certainly does not exist.

Sometime before the ninth century, a consonant shift began in the south and moved to south-central Germanic-speaking territory; even today the resulting sound difference is used by linguists to classify the

Germanic languages (excluding Scandinavian) into High and Low Germanic (see chapter 3). Some of the dialects were only partially affected by this shift and are classed as Middle German.

North Germanen (Scandinavians) and their languages are discussed in chapter 3. The languages of the East Germanen are extinct; their major historically documented language, Gothic, is discussed below in this chapter.

The North Sea Germanen

North Sea Germanic is represented by *Old Saxon* and *Old Frisian*. Old Saxon was spoken from the Zuyder Zee to the Elbe in the north and to the Harz Mountains region on its southernmost border; a group of modern dialects known as Saxon are spoken in eastern Germany. Old Frisian was spoken in coastal areas of Holland and the northwestern islands of Germany, in the areas where modern Frisian is spoken today as a minority language. Saxon (a "founding dialect" of English) and Frisian both have many features in common today with English, though these are not always immediately noticeable to English speakers. The following samples of older dialects and their translations into English are from Robinson. All date to the ninth century or later; written records of Germanic languages except for Gothic dating to earlier times are sparse, consisting for the most part of a few words embedded in Latin text. By this time the tribal organizations had passed into history and the tribal peoples were blended into medieval life, their original languages assimilated or mutated.

A bit of Old Saxon:

> *Fadar ûsa firiho barno,*
> Father our of people's children,
> *Thû bist an them hôhon himila rîkea,*
> you are in the high of the heavens kingdom,
> *Geuuîhid sî thin namo uuordo gehuuilico.*
> hallowed be your name with every word.
> *Cuma thîn craftag rîki.*
> Come your powerful kingdom.
> (from the Lord's Prayer, in the *Heliand*, ca. 830;
>   Robinson 1992, 112)

The language of the Germanic Franks, Franconian, survived in four variants: Low Franconian, the ancestor of Dutch and Flemish, spoken in the area that is today southern Holland and Flanders; Middle Franconian, spoken around the German cities Cologne, Trier, and Coblenz; South Rhenish Franconian, spoken in Alsace (a province of today's France, on the west-central border of Germany); and East Franconian, spoken around the German cities Würzburg and Bamberg.

A bit of Old West Low Franconian:

Hebban olla vogala nestas hagunnan hinase hi(c) (e)nda thu w(at)
    (u)nbidan (w)e nu
All the birds have begun nests except for you and me—what are we
    waiting for?
(eleventh century; a note found in England in the binding of a Latin
    manuscript; Robinson 1992, 205)

Elbe River Germanen

This is represented by Alemannic (spoken in Swabia, Alsace, and large parts of Switzerland) and Bavarian (spoken south and west of the Lech River and eastward to the Danube at Linz, covering Bavaria in Germany and all of Austria).

A bit of Old High German

Das hôrtih rahhôn dia uueroltrehtuuîson
That heard I tell the pious (people)
Daz sculi der antichristo mit Eliase pâgan.
that would the Antichrist with Elias battle.
(Bavarian; ninth century, from *Muspilli* 'End of the World';
    Robinson 1992, 228)

Roman Views of the Germanen

Roman historians wrote quite a bit about both the Germanen and the Celts in the first century BC and the first century AD, when significant contacts between the Empire and the tribes first occurred;

Roman and Greek historians' descriptions are tinged by stereotypical expectations of the "barbarians" and are often based on hearsay rather than direct observation, whereas later artistic images in sculpture are often based on the iconography of power and empire (Ferris 2000, 182–83). Apparently they found the barbarians both fascinating and terrible and, since the Germanic languages did not have a written form until four centuries after Christ, the Roman descriptions are virtually the only ones that have survived. These descriptions present the Germanen as "savage, uncouth, uncivilized peoples," but also "noble, simple peoples unspoiled by sophisticated lifestyles" (Wells 1999, 100). The observations of the Roman writers cannot be taken as fact, as modern archaeology and anthropology have shown.

These Roman descriptions of Germanic barbarians are as colorful as they are unreliable. Germanen were said to be like wild animals, simple, straightforward, and lazy; frightening others but themselves easily frightened by the new and the strange (Wolfram 2005, 14–17). The cool climate of Germania, the Romans believed, could not steam off the emotional fluids of their large bodies. Wine, not native to their culture, was unnatural and even dangerous to them, since it might exacerbate their impetuousness. Still, Tacitus, writing in 98 AD (never having observed Germanic life directly, but repeating information from earlier writers), praised them for their marriage customs, which he found more moral than the Roman customs. Germanen did not countenance adultery, he noted approvingly, and young men avoided premarital sex—although on military grounds rather than moral ones (they believed it would sap their strength). The Romans believed the Germanen, while quick to take up weapons, had little persistence in battle and no long-term goals.

The Romans reckoned as beautiful both the Germanen and the Celts: tall, blond, and slim, although disgustingly dirty, since they bathed in cold rivers and used butter to dress their hair (unlike the Romans, who enjoyed steamy baths in marbled halls and smoothed olive oil on their hair and skin; Wolfram 2005, 15). The Greek historian Strabo, who completed his *Geography* between 7 and 23 AD, wrote that "The Germans, who, though they vary slightly from the Celtic stock in that they are wilder, taller, and have yellower hair, are in all other respects similar, for in build, habits, and modes of life they are such as I have said the Celti are" (1917, VII, 1/2, 290). Strabo reports that the Germanen learned from the Celts how to make lye soap that lightened or reddened (already fair) hair. The yellow hair proved intriguing to the Romans, and increasing contact between

Romans and the Germanen fueled a fashion among Roman women for blond wigs worn over their own dark hair. The height differential between Italic and Germanic peoples was real enough, though not as dramatic as the Roman perception of it, which was likely drawn from battlefield impressions of particularly tall and fierce Germanic warriors. Archaeology reveals that male Germanen in classical times averaged 180 centimeters in height (5'9"), the women 160–165 centimeters (5'2 ½"–5'4 ½"), both sexes about 4 centimeters (1.57") taller on average than their counterparts among Italic Romans of the same era (Wolfram 2005, 17).

Julius Caesar, like Strabo, found the Germanen wilder, larger, and less cultured than the Celts. He wrote about them starting in 58 BC in *The Gallic Wars*, his narrative of his campaigns in Gaul. Since the Romans had not succeeded in colonizing the Germanen, Caesar considered them impossible to subordinate (Wolfram 2005, 9). However, the Romans, who rarely learned to speak or even to recognize the languages of the barbarians, were often unable to differentiate Celts from Germanen. In fact, the same difficulty has plagued modern researchers, since the Germanic and Celtic languages of early Roman times left few written traces (cf. Wells 1999, 108–109 ff.). Like other barbarians, the Germanen were for the Romans the not-Greeks, not-Romans, who slurred and mumbled (that is, they spoke neither Greek nor Latin, or at best spoke them badly), and were unreasonable and incapable of following rules. The barbarians insisted on their 'freedom,' which the Roman writers viewed as chaos, and which they contrasted unfavorably with the disciplined, orderly pax romana fostered by Rome (Wolfram 2005, 12).

Germanic Life and Society

Many Romans inaccurately believed the Germanen were nomads or half-nomads, living from cattle-raising and hunting and having no knowledge of agriculture; even Strabo makes this error (1917–32, VII, 1/3, 291). However, even long before Roman contact, the peoples of temperate Europe, including the Germanen, were agricultural, with sickles, yokes for cows, and ploughs (Wells 1999, 35). After Roman contact, many of the Germanen quickly adopted as much of the Roman lifestyle as they could afford. Life in the Germanic territories at this time was, however, often enough not peacefully rural, but violent; war was frequently waged between the tribes, and when Germanen went over to Rome, they did so often to escape from this tribal strife (Wolfram 2005, 20).

Ideally, disputes among the Germanen were taken before the *Ding* (lit. 'thing' or 'matter'), the highest court, which judged according to laws given by the gods. After a case was presented, a vote was taken, the "nays" mumbled, the "yeahs" expressed by spear-poundings, the chieftains exercising strong influence in the decisions (Krause 2005, 88). Some crimes, such as adultery (an offense only for women), treason, desertion, or cowardice in battle, were punished by death. Lesser offenses, including murder, could be made good by payments of horses or cows, some of which went to the chieftain, some to the complaining victim. Even capital punishment could sometimes be bought off. Some of these tribal rules were preserved in Latin in manuscripts dating from the fifth to the ninth century, but they provide little more than one- or two-word snapshots of these early languages.

Germania and the Roman Empire

In the early centuries of pre-Christian times, some of the Germanic tribes were colonized by Rome while others became Romanized even if they remained politically independent of Rome, but by 400 AD the situation had reversed. The Roman Empire, as it became less democratic, more autocratic, and more Christian, was more like the Germanic tribes. The Germanic tribes in turn gradually moved into Roman territory and even "confederated" their kingdoms into the Empire. Finally, the Romanized, Christianized Germanen actually became the Roman Empire. Patrick Geary writes:

> The Germanic world was perhaps the greatest and most enduring cre-ation of Roman political and military genius. That this offspring came in time to replace its creator should not obscure the fact that it owed its very existence to Roman initiative, to the patient efforts of centuries of Roman emperors, generals, soldiers, landlords, slave traders, and simple merchants to mold the (to Roman eyes) chaos of barbarian reality into forms . . . they could understand and, perhaps control. (1988, vi)

By 400 AD, Germanen were at the top of the Empire. The Roman Era was over, and the Germanic languages had survived. These languages were to take another turn in the medieval era that was about to begin, as we will see in chapter 3.

Timeline: From the Battle of Kalkriese to the End of the Western Roman Empire

Year (AD)	In Germanic Territories	In the Rest of the World
6		Judaea a Roman province
9	Arminius, leader of the *Cherusci*, destroys Roman army at Kalkriese	
10		Earliest mention of the Battle of Kalkriese, in Roman poet Ovid's "Sorrows"
14		Death of Roman Emperor Augustus, under whose rule the Roman Empire reached its greatest geographical extent
ca. 30		Crucifixion of Jesus
43		Romans invade Britain; London founded
79		Mt. Vesuvius erupts, destroying Pompeii
90	Roman provinces west of the Rhine founded: *Germania inferior* (Lower Germania, capital Cologne) and *Germania superior* (Upper Germania, capital Mainz).	
95		Roman historian Tacitus describes the Goths in his *Gotones*
98		Tacitus completes *Germania*, his history of the Germanic peoples
150		First mention of the Saxons in the works of the Greek geographer Ptolemy
160	Earliest rune found at Vimose, Denmark	

Year (AD)	In Germanic Territories	In the Rest of the World
200		Bishop of Rome becomes first Pope
229		Greek historian Cassius Dio completes his eighty-volume *History of Rome*, including a detailed account of the Battle of Kalkriese
257–268		Germanic invasions: Goths invade Black Sea area, sack Athens, Sparta, and Corinth; Franks invade Spain; Alamanni and Suevi invade Upper Italy
270–275	Franks destroy Trier and other cities in Gaul	Marcomanni cross the Danube; Roman Emperor Aurelian defeats them and the Alamanni, rebuilds the walls of Rome; Vandals arrive in Pannonia (Hungary); Roman troops start to withdraw south of the Danube; the Romanian language starts to diverge from Latin
350	Ulfilas invents the Gothic alphabet and translates the New Testament into Gothic	
360		Books begin to replace scrolls; Picts and Scots cross Hadrian's wall and attack Roman Britain
376		Large group of Goths come to the Danube and ask Rome for asylum

continued

Year (AD)	In Germanic Territories	In the Rest of the World
383		Rome, unable to defend its large empire, begins evacuation of its legions from Britain
400		First records of Japanese history
406	Founding of Burgundian Kingdom at Worms	
429	Picts and Scots expelled from southern England by Angles, Jutes, and Saxons	Vandals establish kingdom in northern Africa
433		Attila becomes ruler of the Huns
436	Burgundian kingdom in Worms destroyed by Huns	Last Roman troops leave Britain
470		Huns withdraw from Europe; flowering of Maya civilization in Mexico
476	Gaiseric, king of the Vandals, sells eastern Sicily to Theodoric, king of the Visigoths	Fall of the Roman Empire: Germanic Odoaker deposes Romulus Augustulus, last Roman emperor in the West, and declares himself King of Italy; traditional date for beginning of Middle Ages

3

A Fork in the Road

High German, Low German

600 AD: Idorih

The warrior or smithy working in about 600 AD to inscribe a lance with the name *Idorih* certainly had no notion that the inscription would make linguistic history. That is what happened, though, when linguists of a much later age saw "Idorih" as the earliest written evidence of a new Germanic sound shift.

The inscription was a new version of an old name, *Idorik*, the *-rik* ending (meaning 'king') common in Germanic names. The *-rih* ending of the lance inscription is thought to be a consequence of a new sound shift and hence the earliest recorded word in High German. Most historians of German believe it gives us a date for the Second Sound Shift (in German, *die Zweite Lautverschiebung*), which divided Germanic languages into two streams (inevitably, however, there is not full agreement among linguists on this matter; Ernst 2005, 79).

The lance, found in Wurmlingen, Germany, with its inscription scratched in runic characters, is the earliest written evidence of a second sound shift that divided Western Germanic languages into two branches: High (southern dialects, in "high," mountainous territory), and Low (northern, flat- or lowlands). These branches were to give rise to the modern West Germanic languages: High, to

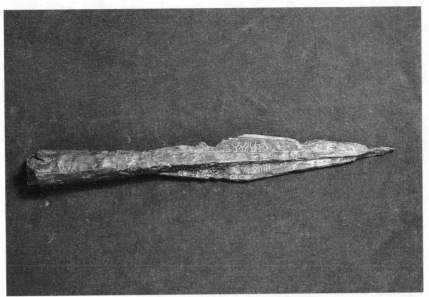

This lance with runic inscription 'Idorih', dated to ca. 600 AD, was found in Wurmlingen, Germany. The inscription represents the earliest written evidence of the Second Sound Shift. By permission of Württembergisches Landesmuseum, Stuttgart.

Modern German and Yiddish, Low to Modern English, Modern Netherlandic, and Afrikaans.

It may be the earliest *written* evidence, but even earlier oral evidence exists. That oral evidence is *Etzel*, the name of Attila, the leader of the Huns, as it is recorded in the Old High German epic poem *Nibelungenlied*, written in the early thirteenth century but describing events that happened many centuries earlier, during the *Völkerwanderung*. Attila, who died in 453, was known to the Germanic people by that name during his lifetime, but "Attila" would only have mutated to "Etzel" if it had already been part of the Germanic language before the date of the Second Sound Shift. The Second Sound Shift probably took place, then, during the centuries between 500 and 700 AD.

The Second Sound Shift

Starting in approximately 500 AD in the Alps, and moving northward during the next two hundred years to what is today central Germany (its ultimate boundary, called the Benrath Line), a language-wide consonant change, now called the Second Sound Shift, affected Germanic dialects (there was as yet no single German language). Those dialects whose consonants were changed, entirely or in part, by this sound shift are known as High German (because of the mountainous or high landscape of the region); those that were not changed by it are known as Low German. Only the family of West Germanic languages in England and on the European continent (such as German, Yiddish, and Netherlandic) are so designated; the Scandinavian languages belong to North Germanic and are not included.

The Second Sound Shift affected the consonants of High German in three ways, as outlined below in a simplified account. More details of the sound shift as it occurred under various phonological conditions are found in Stedje (2001, 59–62) and other standard histories of the German language. The shift affected the *sound* of words, not necessarily their *spelling*, since many varieties of Germanic were not written at the time of the Second Sound Shift.

It is noteworthy that the consonants affected by the Second Sound Shift, *p*, *t*, *k*, and *d*, had been major actors in the First Sound Shift a couple of millennia earlier. For this reason some linguists have classified the Second Sound Shift as part of a "chain" pulling (or being pushed) through the entire history of the Germanic languages (relevant discussions are in Chambers and Wilkie [1984, 112]; and, on the two sound shifts as evidence for a new grouping of the Germanic languages, in Robinson [1992, 262–263]).

Theodiscus, Diutisk, Deutsch: German Takes a Name

Not until 786 does the Latin word *theodiscus* (the ancestor of the word *Deutsch* 'German') appear in print. It is in a communication from George von Ostia, nuncio of Pope Hadrian I, ordering Church decisions in England to be read out *tam latine quam theodisce, quo omnes intellegere potuissent*, 'in Latin as well as in the people's language [*theodisce*], so that all can understand.' Here, *theodiscus* refers to the Saxon language of England, but the word was used in von Ostia's home in the kingdom of the Franks, as well as in Rome, for all the Germanic languages (Ernst 2005, 86). The first use of the word *diutisk* in a German-language text appears in the tenth century (Stedje 2001, 66). *Diutisk* became *Deutsch*, denoting a language and its speakers. Finally German, still a family of closely related languages rather than a single language, had given itself a name.

1. The three unvoiced consonants *p*, *t* and *k* became *pf*, *ts*, and *kch*—a throat-clearing sound which is retained today only in the South Bavarian and High Alemannic dialects, not in Modern Standard German. Examples of *kch* given below are *Altbairisch* 'Old Bavarian' and are taken from Roelcke (1997, 79).

This change occurred under three conditions:

- when the *p,t,k* are in initial position, as in
  - English 'pound' → German *Pfund*;
  - English 'tame' → German *zahm*;
  - English 'corn' → Old Bavarian *kchorn*;

- when the *p,t,k* follow a consonant, as in
  - English 'carp' → German *Karpfen*;
  - English 'swarthy' → German *schwarz*;
  - English 'work' → Old Bavarian *werkch*;

- when the *p,t,k* are "geminate," that is, a doubled consonant that is pronounced for an audibly longer time than the corresponding single consonant, as in the Old Saxon examples that follow. Note that consonant doubling in Modern German, by contrast, simply indicates a preceding short and lax vowel.
  - Old Saxon *skeppian* → Old High German *skepfen*;
  - Old Saxon *settian* → Modern German *setzen*;
  - Old Saxon *wekkian* → Old Bavarian *wekchan*;

- Finally, *p,t,k* shift to *f,s,x* medially (in the middle of the word) and in final position.* Examples include:
  - English 'open'→ German *offen*;
  - English 'ship'→ German *Schiff*;
  - English 'eat' → German *essen*;
  - English 'that' → German *das*,
  - English 'make' → German *machen*,
  - Dutch 'ik' → German *ich*.

2. The voiced consonant *d* became *t* or *tt* in High German. Examples:
  - English 'daughter'; German *Tochter*;
  - English 'deep'; German *tief*;
  - English 'bed'; German *Bett*.

3. In what Stedje calls a "possible further chain reaction" (2001, 61), the Germanic *th* (Þ, an old Germanic character named *thorn* after the initial sound of that word) shifted to *d* in High German. English is the main Low German language which has retained the *th* sound in modern times, Netherlandic having lost it to a subsequent sound change. Examples:
   ○ English 'brother'; German *Bruder*;
   ○ English 'thing'; German *Ding*.

*This shift did not take place in instances of *p,t,k* that had been doubled in the process of gemination two hundred years previously, around 300 AD. In West Germanic gemination, all single consonants except *r* after a short vowel and before *j* were doubled.

Life in the Early Middle Ages

By about 500 AD the village communities of Germanic tribal times, with their free farmers and craftsmen, had mutated into the world of feudal obligations, in which the tillers and other workers were outright dependents of their local patrons (Prinz 2005, 323–344). Between the early sixth and the ninth centuries there was little change in living conditions throughout Europe except for that brought about by the natural cycle of the weather and the crops and the man-made cycle of wars. Landowners let their land be cultivated by peasants, who were obligated to give a percentage of the crop to the landowner; princes permitted landowners, peasants, and craftspeople to take refuge behind castle walls in case of invasions; and peasant, soldier, and landlord owed loyalty and service to those higher in the social hierarchy, up to the prince or king.

In the German-speaking territories of this time, as in Europe overall, varied food sources were available to the upper echelons, that is, the nobility and the clergy. Cattle and sheep provided dairy products; swine, both wild and domestic, provided meat; fish was available in coastal or lake areas; and cereals were grown throughout German territory (though today's German staple, the potato, native not to Europe but to South America, was not commonly eaten anywhere in Europe until the seventeenth century). Considerable trade with the Mediterranean meant that even citrus fruit was sometimes available. In higher-class kitchens, the art of assembling these comestibles was cultivated, as the

Mediterranean cookbooks dating to classical times in early medieval monastery libraries indicate. The peasants made do with porridge, bread, and the occasional scrap of soup meat or fish.

Difficulty lay in the logistics, however: particularly in times of war, supply lines were interrupted, distribution problems resulted, and loss of population meant fewer people to till the land and herd the animals. Serious episodes of hunger and general want interrupted periods of sufficiency.

In the eighth century there were approximately two million German speakers, all but the top echelons illiterate. The feudal aristocracy, from kings to minor nobility and landowners, along with the clergy, monks, priests, nuns, and higher church officials, were the upper classes, making up about 10 percent of the population. These groups were for the most part literate (or at least partly able to read, in Latin or German), though probably less so for the upper-class laity than for the clergy. The farmers and craftsmen were illiterate, and since for the most part they worked from dawn until dusk, they would not have had the time to read in any case.

The ninth-century spread of crop rotation mitigated the exhaustion of the soil, alleviated food shortages, and supported population increase, so that cities began to grow out of villages and trading centers. Life expectancy, for those who did not die in infancy, was about forty years.

Family organization continued the pattern established by the Romans, in which the *paterfamilias*, head of the family, had legal guardianship over the entire household including minor children. There were some refinements made by Church law: the head of the family no longer had the power of life or death over the household members, whether related by blood or not. Other groups were also treated as family, with a titular head: a noble or landowner with slaves or other household dependents, and the abbot or abbess of a monastery or a nunnery had the same authority (called *Munt*, modern German *Vormund*) as a father over those in his or her care.

Women, though in general under the control of husbands or fathers, were not completely unprotected by the law. For instance, harming women was punishable, particularly while they were pregnant. Abortion was permitted for the first forty days of pregnancy (Roman and Islamic medical sources available to the literate in Europe provided instructions for both birth control and abortion), but it was punishable as murder thereafter. Widows might inherit their husband's property, and daughters their father's, in the absence of a son of legal age to assume guardianship. The high death rate of young men in battle and other conflicts meant in practice that women were active financial actors in early medieval society. Ninth-century Alemannic legal records indicate that about 30 percent of real estate was owned by women (Prinz 2005, 328).

Legal marriage was at first practiced only by the upper-class population, since its main purpose was specification of inheritance and property rights. Slaves or dependent workers might be members of the households of others but were not able to marry legally and head their own households until Church intervention in the ninth century made this possible.

Monasteries and Convents

One acceptable way for women (either widows or unmarried daughters without brothers) who inherited wealth to invest it was in the founding of a convent. Often the foundress became abbess, setting the "rule" of the house (with, of course, Church permission). Both nuns and monks, at least in some cloisters, lived a life not only of prayer and contemplation, but also of scholarship, studying primarily the Bible and Church tracts but also texts of classical humanities, philosophy, mathematics, and science. The monasteries and cloisters thus became the repository of learning in the Middle Ages. Since the printing press had not yet been invented, the cloistered monks and nuns copied manuscripts by hand and sometimes translated them into German; and some wrote their own books, usually in Latin. Two examples are the monks Otfrid of Weißenburg, who in 865 wrote *Otfrids Evangelienbuch*, a retelling in Old High German of the New Testament; and Notker Labeo of St. Gallen, who in the tenth and eleventh centuries translated church and secular texts into Old High German. The convents provided an opportunity for some nuns, usually those who had been born into and educated by wealthy families, to translate and write as well. Two German nuns, Roswitha of Gandersheim (935–973) and Hildegard of Bingen (1098–1179), gained recognition in their own time, continuing into ours, for their writings, though they wrote in Latin, not in German. Hildegard is known for her theological writings and liturgical songs (currently available online and as CDs); Roswitha is known primarily for her plays. The theme of Roswitha's drama *Theophilus*, a pact with the Devil, was subsequently taken up several times in German literature, in recent centuries by Johann Wolfgang von Goethe (*Faust*, 1832) and Thomas Mann (*Dr. Faustus*, 1947).

Eighth-Century Germanic Languages

Up to this time the Germanic forerunner of Old High German was only a spoken, not a written, language; royal as well as church business was carried out in Latin, and in the main only the clerical class could read and write. The Germanic tongues were referred to, if at all, by their tribal names: Franconian, Bavarian, Saxon, Alamannic (this spelling used for the premedieval tribe and its dialect, "Alemannic" used for dialects of medieval or later times). By 770 AD a welter of written texts document post-Second-Sound-Shift Germanic, which would be known to later ages as Old High German. The language of these texts marks out a direct path to today's German. During the same period, Germanic languages not affected by the sound shift continued their development into other languages: Old Low Saxon (ancestor of today's Low German dialects), Old Low Franconian (ancestor of Dutch/Flemish), and Anglo-Saxon (Old English). The pool of West Germanic languages that was split by the Second Sound Shift into two language streams remains separated fourteen hundred years later: High German, made up of Modern Standard German as well as Yiddish and some southern dialects of German; and Low German, made up of Dutch/Flemish, English, Frisian and some northern German dialects. As was mentioned earlier, Scandinavian languages are considered North Germanic, a separate branch of the family, and are not included in this division.

German of the seventh and eighth centuries was still not a unified language (Eggers 1963, 30–31), and neither Old High German nor its successor Middle High German (beginning around 1150 AD) was ever standardized. Naturally, no one now living has ever heard Old High German or Middle High German as it was spoken in its own time. Both have come down to us solely in written form, and therefore we know them only as literary languages, with a few exceptions (see below). For both Old High German and Middle High German, a varied and artistically skilled body of texts survives.

High German was spoken in areas of Germany south of the "Benrath Line" that runs through central Germany, from approximately Aachen on the eastern Dutch border, moving eastward just south of Düsseldorf, to Frankfurt an der Oder; to the north of this line the languages were Low German. The line, roughly speaking, marks off the flatlands of the north from the hilly or mountainous terrain of the south. An area just to the south of the Benrath line, the Speyer line, marks the territory where only one part of the sound shift—represented by the Low German *Appel* (English 'apple') shifting to the High German *Apfel*—took place.

German dialects spoken south of the Benrath Line, but north of the Speyer line and only partially affected by the consonant changes of the Second Sound Shift, are counted as High German; only those completely unaffected by the sound shift are counted as Low German. A literary language, Old Saxon, was Low German; other Low German ancestors include Old Frisian and Old Low Franconian. Surviving texts in Old Frisian include approximately thirteen hundred texts consisting mostly of legal documents. Old Frisian's daughter languages are Saterland Frisian and North Frisian, minority languages in Germany; and West Frisian, an official language alongside Dutch in the Netherlands. Old Low Franconian survives as an interlinear translation of a Latin psalter; its daughter language is Modern Netherlandic (Dutch/Flemish and Dutch's daughter language Afrikaans). Of the early German written languages only Old High German is a direct ancestor of modern German.

Old High German, 750–1150

Old High German consisted collectively of dialects with somewhat shifting borders. These dialects were quite similar, though, and were surely mutually intelligible. An example is provided by these samples of the first words of the Lord's Prayer (English: "Our Father, who art in Heaven") in four dialects of Old High German (Stedje 2001, 68):

Alemannic, 8th century: *Fater unseer, thu pist in himile*
Bavarian, 8th century: *Fater unser, du pist in himilum*
East Franconian, 825: *Fater unser, thu thar bist in himile*
Rhenish Franconian, 9th century: *Vater unser, thu in himilom bist*

Charlemagne (German *Karl der Große*) used German to carry out his program of Christianization, and so the Lord's Prayer, the Confession of the Faith, and the confession of sins had to be translated into German. Also Christian concepts for which there had been no words in pagan times had to be brought into German: the tribal world had not spoken of *Feindesliebe* 'love of the enemy'; nor had the pagan Germanen, who worshipped their gods outdoors rather than in temples (Ernst 2005, 82), needed words for *Kloster* 'cloister', *Mönch* 'monk', or *Kirche* 'church'. German compound words were coined to express the new church concepts: Latin *regnum caelorum* 'kingdom of the heavens' became Old High German *himilrîhhi*; Latin *oratorium* 'oratory', a prayer room, separate from the main church, became Old High German *betahûs*, 'prayer-house'.

The earliest surviving Old High German book is the *Abrogans*, ca. 765, an alphabetical Latin-German glossary in Bavarian dialect, whose name is taken from the first Latin word in its list. The oldest known heroic epic is the fragment *Das Hildebrandslied* (the manuscript dated ca. 830 but probably originating 400 years or so earlier), about two warriors, a father and a son, unknowingly fighting each other . The oldest known historical poem is *Das Ludwigslied* (881 or 882), in West Franconian dialect, celebrating the Frankish King Ludwig's victory over the Normans at Saucourt.

In 842 two of Charlemagne's grandsons, Ludwig der Deutsche (Louis the German) and Karl der Kahle (Charles the Bald), allying themselves against their brother Lothar Kaiser, undertook a bilingual public oath of mutual support, in an Old High German dialect (Rhenish Franconian) and Old French (the first written evidence of that language; Eggers 1963, 41). The dual-language ceremony before both their massed armies was in its own time an attempt at unifying peoples, but for our time the oath is a demonstration that both a Germanic and a Latinate language were spoken in the Frankish kingdom. The Latinate language was Old French, a daughter of Latin and the ancestor of modern French (Robinson 1992, 227). The beginning words of the Franconian version of the oath were: *In godes minna ind in thes christanes folches* . . . ; in Old French: *Pro Deo amur et pro christian poblo* . . . , both meaning 'in love for God and for the Christian people . . .'.

This oath sworn by two kings represented not ordinary speech, but a dignified formal register of language, the kind most frequently found in the documents left behind from these early medieval times. Old High German writing was for the most part aimed at the cultural upper classes—clergy and nobility. It hardly represented what was spoken on the farms and in the streets by the ordinary folk.

At least two surviving Old High German documents do, however, represent the language of the common people. The *Cassel Glosses* (ninth century) and *Paris Old High German Conversations* (ninth and tenth centuries) make use of a casual register, even street language and obscenities, in translating conversational (also casual and obscene) Latin into the German of the time (Wells 1987, 65). For example, the *Cassel Glosses* tell us what to say to the barber in Latin: *Tundi meo capilli* (cut my hair), and in German: *Skir min fahs*. In *Paris Old High German Conversations*, the German spelling becomes unconventional, apparently replicating idiomatic pronunciation: Latin: *unde uenis, frater?* 'where do you come from, brother?'; German: *Guane cumet ger, brothro?* (*ger* evidently replicating street pronunciation for the expected *ir*; *brothro* apparently slang = 'bro'). The obscene verb *serten/serden* "is hardly attested again until the fifteenth-century *Fastnachtsspiele*," writes C. J. Wells (1987, 65), but it appears here in the request *Gauathere, latz mer serte* 'Darlin', let's screw' (all translations mine).

Yiddish: A New Branch of High German

Yiddish (from German: *Jüdisch* 'Jewish') must have begun its life no earlier than 801, in the Jewish settlement established at Charlemagne's new capital of Aachen. By Charlemagne's time the Western Roman Empire was history; government and Church life were recorded in Latin writing, but the common people spoke their own languages. After the Aachen settlement in 801, what may have started as a mercantile patois of Germanic, Aramaic, and Romance (early versions of French and Italian, languages of the kingdoms from which many of the Jewish settlers had come) developed on a Germanic base to become a specifically Jewish version of the urban dialects of twelfth- and thirteenth-century Germanic Rhineland, specifically Cologne and Frankfurt. Since its ancestors underwent the Second Sound Shift, Yiddish is, like them, classified as a form of High German.

The earliest recorded settlement of Jews in Roman-Germanic territory had been at Cologne (Latin *Colonia*) in 321 AD. Jews were Roman citizens and earned their living from agriculture, trade, industry, and money-lending (Duden 1992, 5–17). They would have brought from their homeland in Palestine their native language, Aramaic, since Hebrew had ceased to be spoken in everyday life, becoming instead a ritual religious language. They may have spoken Latin or its local variant with their non-Jewish fellow citizens, the Germanen and Celts, among whom they lived and worked.

However, these very early years of Yiddish can only be speculated on, for the oldest surviving written evidence is a Yiddish blessing in a Hebrew prayer book (*Mahzor*) from 1272. *Gut tag eem btaga s'vayr des*

Mahzor in bes keneses trage 'A good day will come to the person who brings this Mahzor to the synagogue', it reads. The Jews of the Rhineland wrote their Jewish-German in Hebrew characters and borrowed many words from Hebrew. *Taytsh* was the name they gave to the Rhineland's Germanic language, *Ashkenaz* the name they gave to these Germanic areas, after Ashkenaz, son of the biblical Gomer (Genesis 10:3), who was said to have migrated north from his homeland. *Taytsh* could also mean "non-Jewish German," and indeed the Jewish and the non-Jewish varieties were almost certainly largely mutually understandable, writes Max Weinreich:

> The basic difference between Yiddish and German has no direct bearing on the question of whether a German and a Jew, say in the year 1000 in Cologne, could communicate. Communication was possible even nine hundred years later, when Yiddish and German were most certainly independent linguistic systems. (Weinreich 2008, 350)

A medieval Jewish-German literature for education and entertainment arose, so popular among Jewish women (who at that time usually did not receive instruction in Hebrew) that a cursive script of Yiddish was developed for women's literature and was named *vaybertaytsch* 'women's German' (Duden 1992, 11).

By the tenth century, Jews had established communities throughout Frankish and German territories, living uneventfully with their European Christian neighbors and speaking the local languages. During the First Crusades in the eleventh century, however, harsh anti-Jewish doctrine promulgated by the Church in Rome replaced the tolerant policies of earlier emperors, and Christians responded by subjecting Jews to the most terrible persecutions, torturing and killing them by the tens of thousands. Persecutions of Jews continued in Western Europe for the next several centuries, culminating in the fourteenth century at the time of the Black Death, which struck virtually all of Europe between 1347 and 1351. Christians slaughtered Jews, blaming them for the plague even though Jews died of the disease in equal proportion to Christians. The surviving Jews of the Germanic territories fled in a "mass emigration" to eastern Europe, particularly Poland, where the rulers (for example, Kazimierz III, who reigned from 1333 to 1370) practiced religious tolerance (Duden 1992, 10). Jewish-German continued to be the lingua franca of the central and eastern European Jewish diaspora, though it quite unsurprisingly began to take in considerable vocabulary from Polish and Russian.

Yiddish was, and remains, primarily a Germanic language: its grammar and syntax, as well as 75 percent of its vocabulary, are Germanic. The remaining 25 percent is made up of words borrowed from Hebrew, Slavic, and Romance languages. The Romance elements have not yet been fully traced and dated; these probably stem from Latin or its daughter languages French and Italian. The Romance vocabulary is central, making up important parts of the lexicon of religious ritual. Examples include *bentsn* ('bless', from Latin *benedicere*) and *orn* ('pray', from Latin *orare*; König 1994, 89).

A Language or a Dialect?

The language-dialect distinction is not a firm one and is often made on cultural or political rather than linguistic grounds. Weinreich's much-quoted, humorous but not entirely unserious remark, "a language is a dialect with an army and a navy," illustrates the point. Yet Yiddish, while it has never had armed forces, has been considered from early times a language rather than a dialect, on the basis of factors including its cultural separation from German, its large percentage of non-German vocabulary, its substantial differences in syntax and pronunciation from German, and its distinct writing system.

By the twentieth century, Yiddish had developed western, eastern, northern, and southern varieties. Prior to World War II an estimated six million of the eight million Jews in eastern Europe were native speakers of Yiddish, and one million native speakers of Yiddish lived in the United States. Today there are about three million Yiddish speakers worldwide, most of them in Russia, the United States, and Israel. It is increasingly a language of the generation born before, during or immediately after World War II, infrequently learned by their children. Like other minority languages that are shrinking in numbers of mother-tongue speakers, it continues to provide folk wisdom, idioms, songs, poems, and jokes to its communities of origin, serving as an in-group identifier. In the United States, phrases, gestures, intonations, and pronunciations characteristic of Yiddish have been borrowed into English to such an extent that the in-group identification function of Yiddish is threatened as these are increasingly used by both Jewish and non-Jewish Americans, who are sometimes unaware of their linguistic origins. Examples include *klutz, maven, bagel, schmooze,* and *chutzpah*.

When Yiddish is spoken or when its writing in the Hebrew alphabet is transliterated into the Latin alphabet, those who know

The name of the American Yiddish-language weekly newspaper *Forverts*, written in Yiddish, which uses an alphabet based on Hebrew.

German often understand quite a bit of it. An example is provided by the listing of author, title, and publisher of a book published in New York in 1973: *Max Weinreich. Geshikte fun der yidisher shprakh. Yidisher Visnshaftlekher Institut* (German: *Max Weinreich. Geschichte von der jiddischen Sprache. Jiddisches Wissenschaftliches Institut* (Stedje 2001, 106).

Modern German has borrowed quite a few words from Yiddish, which, though suppressed during the Third Reich because of their association with Jews, have returned to common usage, especially in the casual register of spoken German. These include *Schlamassel* 'mess'; *Schmiere stehen* 'stand watch'; *blechen* 'shell out'; *pleite* 'broke'; *mies* 'lousy'; *schofel* 'shabby'; *Moos* 'dough' [money]; *malochen* 'slave away' (Stedje 2001, 106; König 1994, 89; my translations).

How the Days of the Week Got Their German Names

The Germanic tribes from early times measured time not in days but in nights, which accounts for usages such as the archaic English "fortnight" (fourteen nights) and Modern German *Weihnachten* 'Christmas', literally 'holy nights', explains Dennis Green (1998, 236). Until their contact with the Romans, the tribes had no names for either the days or the nights. After Roman contact, the Germanen borrowed on an as-needed basis the names of the days from the Romans for secular trading purposes. For example, "payment or delivery had to be made by a certain day, fines or taxes were to be met by a fixed time-limit" (Green 1998, 236). During the reign of Augustus (27 BC–14 AD) the seven-day week had been introduced, as Green writes, "with support from the Jewish population, but also influenced by Chaldaean astrology . . . [which] associated the seven days with the seven planets and, in turn, with the gods attributed to these planets" (Green 1998, 240). The Germanen in time simply substituted their own gods and goddesses for the names of the Roman gods after which the days were named. However, in the seventh century some of the names were

Table 3.1. Latin to German: Days of the Week

English	Latin	Modern German	Comment
Sunday	*Solis dies* (sun's day)	*Sonntag*	direct translation
Monday	*Lunae dies* (moon's day)	*Montag*	direct translation
Tuesday	*Martis dies* (Mars's day)	*Dienstag*	Roman *Mars* was equated with *Tiu*, mutated to *Tues-* and *Dien-*
Wednesday	*Mercurii dies* (Mercury's day)	*Mittwoch*	Germanic "Midweek"; English *Wednesday* mutated from *Wodan*, equivalent of Mercury
Thursday	*Jovis dies* (Jove's day)	*Donnerstag*	Roman *Jove* = Germanic *Donar*; English name *Thur*
Friday	*Veneris dies* (Venus's day)	*Freitag*	Roman *Venus* = Germanic *Fria*
Saturday	*Saturni dies* (Saturn's day)	*Sonnabend* (north Ger.)	"Eve (i.e., day before) of Sunday"; "Sabbath"; English version retains reference to *Saturn*

altered by Christian missionaries, as seen in Table 3.1 (after Ernst 2005, 85).

The alterations were motivated by religious considerations. Irish and Anglo-Saxon missionaries to the Germanen, as part of their effort to convert them to Christianity, set out to counteract the still strong popular belief in the Germanic gods by keeping their names out of the calendar. *Sonntag* 'Sunday' and *Montag* 'Monday' were deemed harmless, since the Germanic tribes did not worship the sun or the moon, and these days remained a direct translation from Latin. Mercury, the Roman god whose name was in the Latin *Mercurii dies* 'Wednesday', however, was equated with *Wotan*, the chief Germanic god, still considered too powerful in the Germanic population to be in the Christian week. While his name had been preserved several centuries earlier in the Anglo-Saxon *Wodensdag* (becoming English

'Wednesday'), the Germans instead received the colorless *Mittwoch* 'midweek', deemed safer. *Jovis dies* 'Thursday', in Latin 'day of Jove' (also called *Jupiter*, god of the sky), remained named for *Donar* (English *Thur*, Scandinavian *Thor*), Germanic god of thunder, and came into modern German as *Donnerstag*. The day of the Roman goddess of love, *Veneris dies* 'Friday', remained in German *Freitag*, after Venus's Germanic equivalent *Fria (Freya)*. Saturn, Saturday's god, was neutralized (possibly because of his association with the Roman *Saturnalia*, festival of debauchery) in north Germany as *Sonnabend* (eve of Sunday) and in south Germany as *Samstag*, a derivative of a Greek word for Sabbath. English, though, retained the Saturn connection in its *Saturday* (Ernst 2005, 85).

The Early Influence of Latin

In the second and first centuries BC the tribal languages of the Germanen borrowed about five hundred words from Latin, most of them still present in Modern German. The Germanic tongues borrowed from Latin names for things that the Germanen lacked in their own culture: Roman-style administration, spices, household tools, building materials other than wood, commercial concepts, and fruits not native to Germania (the Germanen originally knew only the apple). Not only the sounds and the spelling changed through history; sometimes the meaning of the Latin shifted as well after the word was borrowed into German. Several centuries later, from the Middle Ages and into the Renaissance, Latin became the European language of learning and was the source of many additional words borrowed into German (and into other European languages as well) in the fields of theology, natural science, and philosophy.

Table 3.2 shows some examples of those approximately five hundred early Latin borrowings into German, all of them preceding the Second Sound Shift, given here in both Old High German and their Modern German equivalents. The words in this "first Latin wave" (Stedje 2001, 55–56) were subsequently affected by the Second Sound Shift. Where there are English equivalents in the table, they do not show the consonant changes, because English is a Low German language and did not undergo the Second Sound Shift.

Their regular and predictable consonant changes are additional evidence for establishing the date of the Second Sound Shift. The fact that these Latin borrowings were sound-shifted dates the sound shift to sometime after the Germanic tribes' first contact with the Romans,

Table 3.2. Latin Words that Entered German before the Second Sound Shift

Latin	Old High German (ca. 500–1050)	Modern German
planta 'plant'	*pflanza*[a,b]	*Pflanze*[a,b]
campus 'field'	*kampf*[a]	*Kampf*[a] 'battle'
pilum 'arrow'	*pfil*[a]	*Pfeil*[a]
piper 'pepper'	*pfeffar*[a]	*Pfeffer*[a]
sinapis 'mustard'	*senaf*[a]	*Senf*[a]
strata 'road'	*strâza*[a,b]	*Straße*[b]
tegula 'brick, tile'	*ziegal*[b]	*Ziegel*[b]
moneta 'coin'	*muniza*[b]	*Münze*[b]
prunum 'plum'	*pfruma*[a]	*Pflaume*[b]

[a] *Shows the shift from Latin p to Germanic pf or f*
[b] *Shows the shift from Latin t to Germanic s, ß or z*

in the closing pre-Christian and the early Christian centuries. Latin words that were borrowed into German during medieval times or later (many of them in the course of Christianization of the Germanen) do not show Second Sound Shift consonant changes. A sound shift has an end as well as a beginning; the Second Sound Shift was by then complete and no longer affecting German words.

What Causes Sound Shift?

We saw in chapter 1 that the First Sound Shift, a systemic shift from one set of consonants to another set, occurring in every single word of the language, differentiated Germanic from its mother tongue, Proto-Indo-Germanic. In this chapter we investigated Old High German, the language that resulted when another such sound shift occurred in the southern dialects of continental Germanic. Readers of this book may ask why German had a First Sound Shift and a Second Sound Shift, or even why sound shifts happen at all.

At least one part of this question was addressed by structural linguists when they studied language as a system and discovered that the sounds of a language are in some sense dependent upon each other. When changes occur in some sounds, other sounds change in concert, like the voices of a multipart choir as they sing a composition in a new musical key:

> . . . in the history of languages, items do not change independently. . . .
> This was the basic positive insight of structuralism. A classic example is
> that of vowel systems. However many vowel sounds a language has,
> they will tend to be . . . as distant as possible from each other. . . . If one
> vowel sound undergoes historical change, then it will often cause the
> others to move in a co-ordinated way, so that in the end optimal spacing
> will be re-established. The chains . . . can be extremely complex and
> last several hundred years. (Nettle 1999, 9)

There is no reason to think that consonants would not function in a similar way; if all the unvoiced stops (in German, *p, t, k*) become voiced (*b, d, g*), they will force the previous *b, d, g* to shift to something else, or they will become "overloaded," that is, the speakers will not be able to use these sounds to differentiate words from one another. For example, if the unvoiced *t* in "tire" becomes voiced, the word will be pronounced as "dire," leaving a need to find a new way to pronounce "dire." Hence, once a process of shifting begins, it is to be expected that further shifts will occur as well.

But what initiates the change? To understand this we must move from viewing language as a system to understanding language as a social artifact. Both of these ways of analyzing language are valid and will yield insights about how language developed and how it works.

Describing how language functions in more than one way, Daniel Nettle writes that languages "are obviously not natural objects. . . . Nor are they deliberate human productions . . . , since people do not intentionally create their languages." However, although speakers are not aware of most of the rules of their language, "languages are still the consequences of speakers' actions, just not the outcome of their intentions." Nettle calls this combination of the messages speakers wish to convey and the mechanisms they have at their disposal "biological evolution or . . . cultural evolution, or more likely . . . some combination of the two. . . . a structural, a social, and an economic phenomenon" (1999, 13–14).

Language may contain random variations that, accumulating and combining as time passes, become noticeable, perhaps in the same way as children grow into adults, with changes that are imperceptible minute by minute or day by day but perceptible over months and years. Particularly in tribal languages with small populations, a small random change could be picked up by enough people to become a universal shift. Furthermore, tribal organization, like many other forms of society, provides "big men" (typically influential politically or militarily) and "big women" (typically influential socially), whose opinions are pacemaking for the group, and whose use of language may also be considered worthy of emulation by the whole tribe.

Substrate Hypothesis, Again

As in the case of the First Sound Shift, linguists have introduced into discussions of the Second Sound Shift various substrate hypotheses (that is, influence on Germanic from other languages spoken previously in ultimately Germanic territories). For example, Celts and Illyrians in the south and southwest were militarily and socially overwhelmed by incoming Germanic tribes, but these Celts and Illyrians may have (perhaps through sheer numerical superiority) influenced local pronunciation of Germanic, writes Eggers (1963, 33). Eggers also quotes other writers who attribute causative influence on the Second Sound Shift solely to Celts, noting that this shift occurred only in areas once ruled by Celts (90).

The twin factors of assimilation and dissimilation may also cause sound change. For example, a language group may ally with another, and its members may tend thereafter to shift certain pronunciations of their own language subtly toward sounds of the allied tribe's language, to emphasize their new alliance. Conversely, members of a tribe that is absorbed by a more powerful neighbor may choose to exaggerate pronunciations of their own language so as to emphasize differences in the languages. Foreigners who move to a new country and acquire a new language, for example, may respond in either of two possible ways: If they are able, they may studiously imitate the native speakers as closely as possible. Alternatively, even if they become quite proficient in the vocabulary and structure of the new language, they may cultivate their native accent and pride themselves upon their distinctiveness. William Labov's study of accents on the island community of Martha's Vineyard documented this phenomenon (1993, passim). He found two distinct linguistic reactions from permanent residents to summer visitors to the seafront island. Those who resented the transient tourists who arrive every summer and leave every fall adopted a strong version of the local "island" accent, whereas those who considered the tourists a positive factor in the island's life spoke in a more mainland standard accent.

For the time being we cannot give a final answer as to the causes of the Second Sound Shift. To summarize, we have hypothesized that random changes in language production or language learning could have accumulated and started a trend to consonant shifting; that idiosyncratic pronunciation on the part of a single dominant tribal member could have spread to an entire tribe and perhaps from there to a region; that substrate influence, perhaps from Celtic speakers of Germanic, could have influenced the pronunciation in the southern region of Germanic; and that social identification or differentiation with neighboring tribes could have caused the systemic sound shift, or spread a sound shift that had already begun. Languages do not remain static through time, and the nature of language means that changes are likely to turn out to be systemic, rather than affecting just individual words.

It is clear, though, that the Second Sound Shift represented a central event in the history of the German language: the division it created in the German dialects was a first gesture pointing toward the standardization first of written German, and then of spoken German. An account of the events that set the standardization in motion appears in the next chapter.

Timeline: From the Beginning of the Middle Ages to the Protestant Reformation

Date (AD)	In Germanic Territory	Elsewhere in the World
477	Saxon settlement of Sussex, England	
481	Childeric I, king of the Salian Franks, dies, is succeeded by son Clovis I, founder of Frankish Merovingian dynasty	
493	Clovis I marries Burgundian Princess Clothilda, who converts him to Christianity; the Frankish kingdom becomes Christian	
495	Saxon settlement of Wessex, England	
507–534	Franks conquer the realms of the Visigoths, the Thuringii, and the Burgundians	

Date (AD)	In Germanic Territory	Elsewhere in the World
510		Provence (southeastern France) goes to the Italian Ostrogoths (until 563)
534–555	Toledo becomes capital of Visigoth kingdom of Spain; after destruction of Ostrogothic kingdom, Provence becomes part of the Frankish kingdom; Arthur, (legendary?) king of the Britons, killed in the Battle of Camlan	Eastern Romans (Byzantine Empire) conquer the Vandal kingdom in North Africa, the Ostrogothic kingdom in the Black Sea area; plague in Constantinople spread by rats all over Europe (542); disastrous earthquakes worldwide (543)
558	Chlothar I, son of Clovis I, reunites the Kingdom of the Franks	
568	The *Völkerwanderung* ends	Langobards conquer north Italy
570		Birth of Mohammed, founder of Islam
633	Spain becomes a kingdom of the Visigoths	
636	In the Frankish kingdom, differentiation between French and Germanic languages appears	
711	Visigothic empire in Spain conquered by the Arabs.	
712–720	Seville (Spain), Sardinia (Italy), conquered by Arabs	
732	Charles Martell of Frankish Court defeats Arabs at Tours and Poitiers and stops their westward advance	

continued

Timeline (continued)

Date (AD)	In Germanic Territory	Elsewhere in the World
750	Hops used for the first time in Bavaria in making of beer	Culmination of medicine, astronomy, mathematics, optics, and chemistry in Arab Spain
770	First texts in Old High German language	
792	Beginning of Viking Era in Britain: Danish pirates attack and plunder north English monastery Lindisfarne	
800	Coronation of Emperor Charlemagne (German: Karl der Große), King of the Franks; Norse invasion of Germany; writing of High German poem *Hildebrandslied*; Norse discover Faroe Islands	Machu Picchu, Peru, founded
814	Death of Emperor Charlemagne	Arabs take over Indian numerals, using zero to multiply by ten
840	Danish settlers found Dublin and Limerick	
850	Yiddish language begins to develop from Rhenish German dialects	Arabian goatherd Kaldi credited with discovery of coffee
859–861	Norsemen sack Mediterranean coast to Asia Minor, Paris, Toulouse, Cologne, Aix-la-Chapelle, and Worms; Norsemen discover Iceland	
866	Danes found kingdom in York, England	

Timeline (continued)

Date (AD)	In Germanic Territory	Elsewhere in the World
871		Alfred (the Great) becomes King of (non-Danish) England
900		Norse discover Greenland; Medieval Warm Period in Europe (until ca. 1200)
973	Death of Otto I, founder of Holy Roman Empire of the German Nation	
1000	*Beowulf* written in Anglo-Saxon English; Danegeld, tax to buy off Viking attacks, first collected in England; Arabs and Jews become court physicians in Germany	*The Pillow Book* written by a woman at the Imperial Japanese Court; Leif Ericson travels to Nova Scotia
1050	Old High German superseded by Middle High German	
1066	Battle of Hastings: England conquered by Normans (originally Scandinavian), from Normandy, France	Appearance of comet later called Halley's Comet
1095		Pope Urban II proclaims First Crusade
1100	Anglo-Saxon (Old English) superseded by Middle English; start construction of Stavanger (Norway) Cathedral	Probable date of colonization of Polynesia from South America
1123		Death of Omar Khayyam, Persian poet and astronomer
1145		Pope Eugene III proclaims Second Crusade

continued

Timeline (continued)

Date (AD)	In Germanic Territory	Elsewhere in the World
1176	Construction begins, Strassburg Cathedral	
1191	*Das Nibelungenlied*, Middle High German historical poem	
1202		Mathematician Leonardo Pisano Fibonacci introduces Arabic numerals in Europe; first court jesters at European courts
1203	Wolfram von Eschenbach, *Parzival*, Middle High German epic poem	
1204	Founding of Amsterdam	Jewish philosopher Moses Maimonides dies
1210	Gottfried von Strassburg *Tristan und Isolde*, Middle High German	
1229		The Inquisition in Toulouse forbids Bible reading by laymen
1248	Construction begins, Cologne Cathedral	
1252		The Inquisition begins to use instruments of torture
1271		Marco Polo journeys to China (until 1295)
1291	League between Uri, Schwyz, and Unterwalden, eventually leading to Swiss state	End of the Crusades
1300	Hanseatic League rises to prominence in North Sea coastal cities	Begin Little Ice Age in Europe (until 1850)
1315–1322	Catastrophic famine in Northern Europe	

Timeline (continued)

Date (AD)	In Germanic Territory	Elsewhere in the World
1337		France and England begin the Hundred Years' War (until 1458)
1347–1351	Middle High German gives way to Early New High German	Black Death kills 10–20% of the population of Europe, including England
1375		Robin Hood appears in English popular literature
1386	Heidelberg University founded	
1388	Köln (Cologne) University founded	
1389	First paper mills in Germany	
1409	Leipzig University founded	
1431	First German peasant revolt at Worms	Joan of Arc burned at the stake in Rouen, France
1440		Cease wine cultivation in England after decades of severe cold weather
1453	Gutenberg and Johannes Fust print the 42-line Mazarin Bible (in Latin) at Mainz, using movable type	
1466	Johann Mentel prints first translation of Bible into German at Strassburg	
1474		William Caxton prints the first English book
1483	Birth of Martin Luther	
1489		The symbols + (plus) and – (minus) come into use;

continued

Timeline (continued)

Date (AD)	In Germanic Territory	Elsewhere in the World
1492		Ferdinand and Isabella of Spain finance the voyage of the Italian Christopher Columbus to the New World; he sails from Palos, Spain, to the Bahamas, Cuba, Haiti
1495		Da Vinci begins work on "The Last Supper"
1502	University of Wittenberg founded	
1517	Martin Luther posts his 95 theses on Roman Catholic Church reform in Wittenberg; beginning of Protestant Reformation	Coffee comes to Europe

After Grun 2005.

4

Bible German and the Birth of a Standard Language

1522: September Testament

No holy book has had more secular influence in Germany than Martin Luther's translation of the Bible into German. The Good Book in German appeared as hundreds of partial or complete editions revised or supervised by Luther between the first appearance of the New Testament in September 1522 and his last edition of the complete Bible in the year of his death, 1546. It was Germany's first mass-market publication, aimed at every Christian in the land, and it soon became the best-seller of the German sixteenth-century publishing world.

In the fourth century the Latin Vulgate, Saint Jerome's translation of the Greek Scripture into Latin, provided a Bible in the lingua franca of the early Christians, but in the intervening twelve hundred years the Latin of the Vulgate Bible had ceased to be spoken or understood by anyone but the clergy. The Roman Church in fact discouraged the laity from reading the Bible and actually forbade translation of it into vernacular languages, though this edict was not consistently enforced. The Bible remained essentially inaccessible to all but the clergy, and it was to be interpreted only by the Church hierarchy. By contrast, the reformer Luther considered the sole authority in matters of faith to be not the Church, but the Bible. Accordingly, he believed that Scripture should be available to ordinary Germans in their own language. But how to do this in a Germany with no single standard language but rather dozens (or hundreds, depending on how they are counted) of dialects, some not easily understandable to Germans in different regions?

Luther's solution was to make a translation that would vault over the dialects, a Bible that would speak God's word to every German in every region. And so it was: his teachings and his Bible translation reached a wider audience than any German publication ever had. People all over the German territories read this Bible if they could read, listened to others reading it aloud if they couldn't, and for the first time heard God speaking German. The spread of printing made available thousands of copies in German and transformed the German language from a collection of local household and marketplace dialects to a supraregional language that commanded respect and attention. Ultimately it became the standard of its land. From virtually the moment of its creation, the Luther Bible and its language were propelled into prominence by the force multipliers of technology, politics, culture, and demography: a perfect German storm.

The History of European Printing

Gutenberg's printing press, invented in 1440, appeared in Europe on the coattails of a constellation of social developments favorable to its growth. These included the effects of the fifteen new universities founded in the German-speaking territories in the fifteenth century (the five oldest were founded in the fourteenth century; Chirita 2003, 178), the increase in literacy in Germany that had occurred at the turn of the fifteenth into the sixteenth century, and the relatively low price and easy availability of paper in Europe (Clair 1976, 1–8). Thus the demand for academic works, the popular market, the materials, and the technology were in place for an explosion of printing activity throughout Europe, but especially in Germany, the home of the printing press.

Although printing with movable type was known in China as early as the eleventh century, Johann Gutenberg (full name Johannes Gensfleisch zur Laden und zum Gutenberg) reinvented it in Europe four centuries later, apparently independently of the Chinese achievement. Though no single book or piece of printing with Gutenberg's name on it remains, evidence of Gutenberg's professional activity survives in written records showing his invention by 1440 of a complete printing press (Clair 1976, 8).

Born to a patrician family in Mainz, and relocating probably in 1428 (Ing 1988, 32) to nearby Strassburg (now in France; then in German territory), Gutenberg was a goldsmith and metal expert. For his printing press he formulated a malleable but hard metal alloy for the printing plates, and with it repurposed a wine press, part of the local viniculture of Mainz since Roman times. Gutenberg printed on both vellum (sheepskin) and paper, but the latter met with more commercial success. Paper had been known in Europe since the twelfth century, having been brought from China by the Arabs (there was a paper mill in Baghdad as early as 794). By the fifteenth century it had become easily obtainable, inexpensive, and far more feasible for mass copying than its costly forerunner, vellum.

Also pushed out by market forces was the "block book," popular in the 1460s, in which every page, both letters and illustrations, was painstakingly carved out of a single block of wood. The wood blocks wore out after only a few pressings. The more practical metal soon replaced the wood blocks.

The Gutenberg Bible

The Gutenberg Bible, also known as the "Mazarin Bible" (named for a cardinal by that name) appeared in 1455 or 1456 in the 48-line-per-page version (Clair 1976, 17). Of the surviving copies, twelve are located in Germany (the most in any single country), eleven in the United States, one in Japan, and the remaining twenty-four elsewhere in Europe.

These Bibles, and Gutenberg's Latin Psalter with its ornamented and colored capitals in red, light purple, and blue, look very much like the hand-illuminated manuscripts of an earlier time. Gutenberg, a Roman Catholic who lived before the Reformation, continued to print, until his death in 1468, Psalmbooks, canticles, Creed books, prayers, and liturgy, mostly in Latin. In its time the Gutenberg press made "the most beautiful books ever printed" (Clair 1976, 18). By the end of the fifteenth century, printings were issued from fifty cities in Germany, including Strassburg, location of the printshop of Johann Mentelin, who in 1466 printed the first complete Bible in German. Not until well into the next century, however, did the printed book cease to be an imitation of handwritten medieval manuscripts and begin to develop a unique style and look.

Book printing was just coming into its own as a craft and an art in the early decades of the sixteenth century, when Luther's 1522 *Septembertestament*, his first German translation of the New Testament, appeared in print. Where medieval professors and students, if they could afford it, had hired a copyist to write out a desired manuscript for them, printing made available a mass-produced book relatively cheaply. Universities began designating a *stationarus* (so called because he had a fixed, or stationary, booth or stall at or near the university) to stock and sell approved books. The publishers soon began to differentiate books from each other by title pages, which bore the name of the author, the date, and the city of publication. Within the pages, more blank space was provided to facilitate silent reading; the medieval habit of murmuring while reading had arisen partly out of necessity, since the continuous text without breaks made it easy to lose one's place. And where manuscripts were designed to be read from beginning to end, the study of canon law and scholasticism created a need to consult books as references, not just as complete narratives; therefore printers began to provide indices and concordances (Gilmont 1998, 10–15). A printed book was no longer just a machine-made copy of a manuscript.

The Numbers

By the sixteenth century, a typical print run of a nonliturgical book was about 1,000 to 1,500 copies, liturgical books and Bibles (which represented about half of all books) somewhat more. For example, the first edition of the Luther Bible in 1522 ran to 3,000 copies; also produced with a print run of 3,000 was the Hebrew Bible of 1566, printed expressly to be sold to North African Jews. Luther's works were especially popular; his 1520 pamphlet *An den christlichen Adel deutscher Nation* 'To the Christian nobility of the German nation' sold 4,000 copies within the first five days of its printing (Clair 1976, 122–123). One hundred thousand copies of Luther's translation of the New Testament were printed in Wittenberg alone during his lifetime.

Book fairs were a prominent feature of the German scene, and the European scene in general. A very early German book fair was the one in Leipzig, begun in 1165. In Frankfurt, the center of Catholic publishing, the first book fair, mostly in Latin, took place in 1530, though Frankfurt's fair was to be eclipsed subsequently by Protestant book fairs in other cities where most publishing was in German.

Social Effects

The spread of printed books greatly influenced culture and politics in Europe. News of scientific discoveries, once transmitted only by personal correspondence, could now be spread through the printed word in thousands of copies, fostering scientific discourse throughout the European continent. There could be many more copies of printed works than hand-copied ones; and the cost of printed books was a fraction of the cost of manuscripts, making it possible for the laity too to be informed of science. While books of science and learning continued to be written in Latin, which was still Europe's lingua franca for the educated classes, writing in the vernacular grew more common, contributing to the rise of Europe's national languages such as German, French, and English.

By 1500 about 10 percent of the German population was literate, higher in the cities. Ability to write one's own name was often the definition of the term, although for many, their name was the only thing they could write; and how much they could read cannot be reliably established from this fact. Nonetheless, thousands of people in Germany thought themselves sufficiently literate to purchase books, especially the Bible. As printers and authors began to consider their main market to be the common people, rather than only the learned clergy and upper classes, they increased their production of works in the people's language—German. Though Latin was to dominate the printed book trade for another fifty years or more, the growth in German-language publishing during the sixteenth century was considerable. In 1513 fewer than a hundred German books were printed; by 1519 about two hundred fifty, in 1520 almost six hundred, in 1523 over nine hundred—a ninefold increase in ten years. One important factor was the prolific creation of new German universities in the previous century. The five oldest, founded in the fourteenth century (Prague, Vienna, Heidelberg, Cologne, and Erfurt) were joined by fifteen new ones in the fifteenth century. The cost of a printed book, although high by modern standards, was low enough to make their purchase practical for prosperous city folk and farmers.

Readers

The population of Germany had doubled to twenty million between 1470 and 1600 and by 1600 from one-third to one-half of the population could read (Flood 1998, 85). Even if the literacy of the public was sketchy by modern standards, the availability of so many printed books and a growing reading public combined to increase both printing and reading even further. The religious reformers soon got the idea that their writings were a major tool for making converts, and since public reading aloud was the norm, the common people, especially in the Protestant-leaning free cities of central and northern Germany, could hear the message even if they could not read it themselves (Flood 1998, 79). There were colorful stories of how the Protestant message got out to the working people: Luther's hymns, for instance, were sung by a door-to-door clothmaker in Lübeck in 1529; young men sang them at travelers' inns in Brandenberg in 1524; Lutheran propaganda pictures were printed and passed from hand to hand (Flood 1998, 83). Pamphlets—unbound and cheaply printed brochures in German, essentially arguments, usually on religious subjects, aimed at the general public—were widely distributed. Luther's Bible translation was extremely popular, as contemporary Catholic writer Johannes Cochlaeus observed with dismay: "Even tailors and shoemakers, even women and other simple folk who had ever learnt to read a bit of German, read it with great eagerness as though it were a fount of truth. Some clutched it to their breasts and learnt it by heart" (Flood 1998, 90).

The Catholic Church was slow to recognize the value of printing. As late as 1590 some Catholic clergy were still refusing to pray from a printed book (Flood 1998, 24), and after the invention of printing many of these particularly opposed printed religious material in local languages. The 1244 Council of Toulouse had forbidden translations of the Bible into national languages, and in 1485 the Archbishop of Mainz repeated the injunction, although it was afterward not generally enforced. In the sixteenth century the Church banned all writings of the excommunicated Martin Luther, including his German Bible translations. The ban, however, appears to have been as good as powerless before the tide of public demand for the Luther Bible translations and religious pamphlets and for the crude and vulgar Protestant propaganda cartoons aimed at the Pope, other Catholic authorities, and (after they disappointed Luther by rejecting his efforts to convert them to Lutheranism) the Jews of Germany.

Martin Luther

Martin Luther, born in 1483 to the Luder or Ludder family, prosperous but of humble origins, changed his name during his education for the Augustine monkhood, as was the fashion for educated young men of the time: "Luther" is a play on the Greek *eleutherius* 'freedom' (Nestingen 2003a, 240). Well educated in Greek, Latin, and Bible studies, Luther finished his training as a monk and, after completing his doctorate, moved to the position of Doctor in Bible at the University in Wittenberg. He found pleasure in writing (first in Latin, then in German) and loved to dispute with other theologians in the German public sphere newly created through the invention of printing and its wide distribution of written commentary. His bold challenges to the Roman Church caused him to be excommunicated and cast out of the Augustine order. But Luther, remaining in his university professorship at Wittenberg until his death in 1546, continued his activities as a writer and theologian and ultimately became the founder of a new Christian church, eventually called "Lutheran." In the process—and here lies his importance for the biography of German—Luther laid the foundations for a standard German language.

Open Conflict with the Church and Internal Exile

In the famous ninety-five theses (actually ninety-five statements of an argument) posted on the church door at Wittenberg in 1517 and sent speedily around Germany thanks to the technological magic of printing, Luther rejected the Church's sale of indulgences, certificates of forgiveness of sin. Indulgences had become big business, a way to finance the needs of the Church and, more than occasionally, the personal needs of the priests who sold them. Luther demanded that Christians be told that such penances and indulgences counted for nothing with God.

For the ninety-five theses and his other writings against the Roman church, Luther was excommunicated by Pope Leo in 1521. In the Holy Roman Empire, Church oversight controlled secular authority, and so Luther was called to account before a panel of government officials at the Imperial Diet of Worms and given one last chance to renounce his words. He refused, saying "I am bound by the Scriptures I have quoted, and my conscience is captive to the will of God. I cannot and will not recant anything, since it is neither safe nor right to go against conscience" (quoted in Nestingen 2003b, 46). In the night after his testimony, before his almost certain condemnation to death (Ozment 2004, 74), Luther was spirited away by agents of his princely protector, the sympathetic Elector Friedrich, to a remote castle in Wartburg. Here, in knightly garb and under the false name "Junker Jörg," Luther spent ten months (May 4, 1521, to February 29, 1522) of internal exile. Wartburg Castle was, as

Will Durant notes, "itself a sober punishment . . . a gloomy chamber equipped with bed, table, stove, and a stump as stool" (1957, 363).

There Luther was plagued by hallucinations of the devil and his demons, and once, according to legend, he threw a bottle of ink at a vision of the devil (a faded ink stain on the wall of Luther's study is still pointed out to tourists at the castle). But regardless of the hardships, Luther was advised by Friedrich's minister to stay in hiding for a year while Emperor Charles cooled off. In the event, Charles, having in the Edict of Worms declared Luther an outlaw, apparently made no effort to find him. "Luther's many readers gave pause to civil and church authorities," writes Nestingen (2003b, 38). Luther was by that time so popular that neither he nor his printer, Hans Lufft, could keep up with the demand for his works. At Wartburg Castle the popular author, excommunicated former monk, and outlaw Luther settled down to passing the time with a project: translation of the New Testament into German, using as his central text the 1516 edition of the Greco-Latin New Testament published by the Humanist writer Erasmus of Rotterdam (Füssel 2003, 29).

As a 20-year-old student at Erfurt University, Luther had read a Latin Bible, apparently for the first time, and found in it both comfort and pleasure. In the monastery he followed this interest and once, in a low mood, requested a Bible. The Latin Vulgate Bible he received, bound in red leather, became a constant guide and he soon made it the center of his spiritual interests—anything but a standard expectation at that time and place (Kaufmann 2006, 64), in which the Bible was more of a source of ritual than of personal devotions. And so it was that Luther's Bible translation during his year-long exile at Wartburg did not result from an impulse of the moment, but was a theme of his spiritual life and a long-planned project. This translation, so attuned to the language of the people, was to be Luther's finest cultural achievement, deeply influencing the development of spoken and written German and "lifting the veil between the Apostles and the man in the market, the mother at home, and the child in the streets by giving them a common language" (Arndt 1962, 86). That was Luther's aim, but his Bible translation was to have reverberations in the secular language as well.

Martin and Katharina Luther

In 1525, at the age of 42, Martin Luther married 26-year-old Katharina von Bora, a former nun of aristocratic but impoverished origins. Katharina, who had been given to the church at the age of 10 by her widowed and newly remarried father, had two years earlier left the Cistercian cloister at Nimmschen in Saxony in a dramatic escape aided by Luther himself. Along with several of her sister nuns, Katharina had decided to leave the convent, something that could be done only by stealth. They contacted Luther asking for help; he arranged with a herring purveyor to smuggle them out among the fish barrels (Nestingen 2003b, 63). To rescue the young former nuns from an uncertain fate as unmarried women without family to protect them, Luther and his colleagues searched out marital matches for them. But Katharina would not accept any of the matches they found for her; eventually she expressed a preference for Luther himself. The surprised reformer, who had until then considered himself a confirmed bachelor, assented. "One thing is sure," writes Nestingen, "love had nothing to do with it, at least not in the beginning. In the sixteenth century, . . . couples got married and then came to love one another, if they were going to—and that is just what happened between Martin and Katie" (Nestingen 2003b, 63).

The Luthers had six children and, to all evidence, a loving marriage. Their home became a sixteenth-century student hostel and think tank for like-minded theological activists and intellectuals, many of whom were long-time active consultants in his frequent revisions of the Bible translation. The highly competent Katharina (called *Käte* in German, a name usually translated into English as "Katie") kept house, managed the family finances, cooked, grew a vegetable and fruit garden, raised pigs, and brewed beer for visitors and family, while raising the couple's six children as well as four orphans, including her nephew. In addition, having received an education in the convent, she discussed theology with her husband and advised him in his work. In his correspondence, Luther commented throughout their entire married life on her virtues and on his love for her.

The marriage of a former monk to a former nun was viewed harshly not only by opponents of Luther and his reformation, but even by some of Luther's allies. After Luther announced his plans to marry, his close friends and associates, such as Philipp Melanchthon and Luther's lawyer Hieronymus Schurff, expressed concern that the marriage would harm the cause. Indeed, "in the hands of Counter-Reformation opponents Luther's marriage became a convincing argument for the monk's depravity," writes Heiko A. Oberman (1992, 281). However, Luther and the Reformation succeeded in spite of this criticism, and Luther's wife continues to be much admired by present-day Lutheran theologians (Nestingen 2003b, 62–67). The Evangelical Lutheran

Martin and Katharina Luther, wedding portraits; studio of Lucas Cranach the Elder, 1528. Lutherhaus, Wittenberg, Germany. Photo: Holly Hayes. By permission of Sacred Destinations.

Church of America sponsored a documentary film about her life (transcript at Evangelical Lutheran Church of America 2001), and she is commemorated every December 20 in the Lutheran Calendar of Saints as a "renewer of the church." Though Katharina is known to have written many letters to her husband, earlier ages did not consider them worth saving, and none of these or any other first-hand commentary of hers has survived.

Life in the Sixteenth Century

By the beginning of the sixteenth century, paganism was long gone, the Germanic tribes had been absorbed into Christian Europe, and the Church and its Pope in Rome ruled over the spiritual life of all Christians in Western Europe—including what are now the countries of France, Spain, Italy, Portugal, Belgium, Holland, England, Sweden, Norway, Denmark, Iceland, and Germany. The local languages, including dialects of German, were spoken in the marketplaces, on the farms, and in homes, while Latin was the language of the Church and the lingua franca of the royal courts of Europe. In the Germanic world, ruled by the Holy Roman Empire in Rome and its local representatives, the legal centers called *Kanzleien* 'chanceries' began to use a version of the local German dialects as a means of written communication. German was not yet a unified language, but the chancery scribes had found ways to reconcile the dialects so that memos and directives could be understood within broad regions, if not universally across all the Germanic territories. In centrally located Saxony, Luther's home state, this scribal language was referred to as *Kanzleideutsch* 'chancery German'; to the south, in the Austrian Imperial court, another scribal language, *Gemeindeutsch* 'common German', was developing. The two supradialectical versions, both High German varieties, had much in common and "exercised significant influences upon each other, but were for a time rivals" before *Kanzleideutsch* won out (Barbour and Stevenson 1990, 48). However, a serious linguistic divide remained between north (Low German) and south (High German).

Two rebellions in the Germanic regions brought the common people out of their small world and into the larger world of European events. These were the Protestant Reformation, begun in 1517 with Luther's ninety-five theses posted on the Wittenberg Church door; and the Peasants' War of 1524–1525, centering on economic and religious issues. The Protestant Reformation led almost immediately to a crack in the Roman Church of Europe and eventually to a Continent-wide split resulting in two branches of Christianity: Protestantism and Roman Catholicism. Though it began as largely a war of words rather than of violence, the Reformation was to serve later as the excuse for bloody Continent-wide, religion-based conflict. The Peasants' War (1524–1525), played out in southern, western, and central Germany, was a regional prelude to the series of Continent-wide religious wars following upon the Reformation. Europe's most massive popular uprising until the French Revolution, the Peasants' War ultimately failed when the authorities brutally crushed it.

The Reformation

Martin Luther's 1517 posting of his ninety-five theses against the Church of Rome on the church door at Wittenberg, Germany, began the Protestant Reformation. Luther's putting of Scripture, rather than

Church authority, at the center of Christian practice had been anticipated in earlier attempts at reformation, specifically in England (by John Wycliffe, d. 1384) and Czechoslovakia (by Jan Hus of Prague, burned at the stake in 1415). These calls for reform, however, had been unsanctioned by any authority, as opposed to Luther's Reformation, which was supported by many princes in the Germanic territories. Ultimately this and other social factors gave Luther's reform a far greater impact in central and northern Europe than the earlier reforms, and for this reason Luther is generally recognized as the founder of the Protestant Reformation.

The young Luther, as a Catholic monk, scholar, and preacher, had a religious vision that drove him to attempt reform of Church corruption rather than to found a new church; but his rejection of Church hierarchy and his Bible-centered theology put him beyond compromise with the Roman Church. He was excommunicated, left his orders as an Augustinian monk, eventually married, and became the leader of a new branch of Christianity. "Lutheranism," as it was first called sarcastically by Luther's opponents, became the leading representative of the Protestantism that in relatively short time split the European Christian world in two—in general, Northern Europe became Protestant while Southern Europe remained Catholic. Germany reflected this split, and even today it tends to be Protestant in the north and Catholic in the south. However, this distinction has been blurred by the mobility of the population, so that there are many Protestants in the south, Catholics in the north; and by the increasingly secular nature of German society—about a third of the population is not affiliated with any religion. Even among those who are declared church members there is considerable religious nonparticipation—less than 10 percent of the population attends any religious service regularly. The Catholic and Lutheran churches are state religions, with about 30 million members each; about two million Germans are Muslim, and about 35,000 are affiliated Jews (Country Reports 1997–2007).

But the Reformation was not only a religious movement; it was also part of a secular rebellion of some of the European principalities against the Holy Roman Empire. The princes, as well as the urban populations, wanted to loosen the grip of Rome. In the "free cities" of central and north German territory there was at least some self-governance even though it was, overall, subject to the sovereignty of the rulers. Because of their greater freedom of action, city dwellers considered themselves superior to the landed nobility and the subservient peasants around them. The rising skilled classes—the bakers, shoemakers, printers, and builders—wanted self-determination, and they saw Roman rule, secular and religious, as an impediment (Ozment 2004, 66). Luther's call for sovereign Christian communities without papal influence spoke to their wishes in both civil and religious matters. And Luther's "belief that the essence of religion lay in an inner experience was in . . . a mystical tradition in no way purely German, but especially rife in Germany from the fourteenth century onwards because nowhere else were political and social conditions such that the only freedom left to the common man was the inner freedom of the spirit," writes Geoffrey Barraclough (1963, 368).

Some of the princes of the German north were drawn to Luther's reforms for religious reasons, others for reasons of state. The Saxon Elector, Frederick the Wise, became Luther's first powerful patron from religious conviction as well as for political advantage.

Luther's role in the merging of religious and secular protest was not entirely benign, however. Luther began as a friend of the peasants and supporter of the Peasants' Revolt, but by 1525 he feared it would lead to anarchy. His pamphlet *Wider die räuberischen und mörderischen Rotten der Bauern* 'Against the murderous, thieving hordes of peasants' used strong language to call for the authorities to put down the revolt. The princes needed only a little encouragement to do just that, and the revolt was not only suppressed, but suppressed brutally. A similar change occurred in Luther's views concerning the Jews, whom he began by admiring and hoped to convert to (Lutheran) Christianity. But toward the end of his life he became increasingly harsh and even enraged as he realized that his conversion efforts had not succeeded; the Jews preferred to stay with their own religion.

Luther against the Jews

By the 1540s, near the end of his life, distracted and choleric, obsessed with the Devil and convinced of an imminent second coming of Christ, Luther dispatched the subject of the Jews in vulgar and harsh terms which modern sensibilities find almost incredible in a man of God. His 1543 pamphlet *Von den Juden und ihren Lügen* 'On the Jews and their lies' has been taken in modern times as evidence that Luther was a forerunner of the Nazi anti-Semitic racism of four centuries later. Hateful and anti-Jewish as this pamphlet was, Luther's ideas on the subject were not quite the same as those of Nazi anti-Semitism, however. Luther considered Jews a religious group rather than racially or ethnically distinct from or inferior to Christians, and he considered a converted Jew to be "a brother or sister in Christ," though he "did not regard Judaism as a legitimate religious alternative" (Nestingen 2003b, 104–107). However that may be, it is undeniable that the Nazis in the twentieth century co-opted Luther's pamphlet as a kind of argument from authority, quoting his statements to support their campaign against the Jews. Though Nazi ideology rejected belief in God, and had far from benign intentions toward Christianity, the Nazi government did not shy from using religious documents or religious authority to bolster its own position.

In an inexcusably late acknowledgement, the two major Lutheran groups in the United States finally, four centuries after the fact, repudiated Luther's anti-Jewish writings (Lutheran Church-Missouri Synod 1983; Evangelical Lutheran Church in America 1994). In 1998 the Lutheran Church of Bavaria, Germany, also officially repudiated Luther's anti-Jewish writings and utterances and distanced itself from every expression of anti-Judaism in traditional Lutheran theology.

The Impact of the Reformation

Modern historians differ in their assessment of the secular impact of the Reformation. Some have stressed its eventual success in triggering internal reform of the Catholic Church in the form of the Counter-Reformation, and in encouraging in the German people a spirit of anti-authoritarianism. Others see in Luther's writings rather a defense of accommodation to authoritarian rule, impeding German unification of the principalities and hence German nationhood. The German-speaking regions (with the rather large exceptions of Austria and Switzerland) were not to become a unified state until 1871, far later than other European nations.

Following the Reformation, the Holy Roman Empire split along religious lines. The north, the east, and many of the major cities, including Strassburg, Frankfurt, and Nuremberg, became Protestant, while the south and west largely remained Catholic (though in the sixteenth century Austria first became predominately Protestant then was re-Catholicized by the Habsburgs). Religious conflicts in various parts of Europe for a century eventually resulted in the Thirty Years' War (1618–1648), which devastated the Empire.

The Thirty Years' War

Thirteen wars fought from 1618 to 1648 in the German-speaking territories are now named the Thirty Years' War, as if referring to a single event. Together, these wars caused the death, directly in battle or indirectly through plague and starvation, of an estimated 20 to 45 percent of the German population (Schmidt 2003, 88–89); by comparison, German population losses in each of the two world wars of the twentieth century were about 10 percent. Almost all of the military powers of western Europe were involved, and the final peace agreement (following ten attempts) changed the political face of Europe—France emerged as the chief Continental power, the Netherlands and Luxemburg emerged as independent states.

The German principalities, however, remained as they had been, small states in a Holy Roman Empire, albeit one seriously weakened by the war. This is not to say, however, that the peoples of the German territory were unchanged. On the contrary, everyday life was marked for decades, and German national memory for centuries, into our own time, by the battlefield deaths, the destruction, barbarity, and chaos of repeated invasions and plundering of the countryside and villages, as well as the desolation, starvation, disease, and economic failure of the postwar period. During that conflict Germany "became an involuntary battlefield on which militarily superior nations settled their conflicts and increased their assets," writes Steven Ozment (2004, 107), adding that although the German people "endured most of its pain and sacrifice," neither they nor their leaders were in control of the conflict or of the terms of its resolution.

State and Religion

The foreground of the wars was religious, but the background consisted of the usual issues of political and financial power: Protestants and Catholics in Bohemia and Germany jockeyed for position on the European continent as Catholic rulers sought the return to Catholicism of territories that had become Protestant. Smoldering hostility between Catholics and Protestants in the Hapsburg Empire and Eastern Europe escalated into armed conflict. Sweden's Lutheran king, Gustav Adolf, intervened in 1630 on the Protestant side, ostensibly to prevent the re-Catholization of the Baltic Prussian states that were neighbors to Sweden, and soon war spread throughout Central Europe. Historians have suggested that religious motives were not Gustav's real priority—rather that he intended to take control of German territory, or even to become Kaiser of the Holy Roman Empire (Schmidt 2003, 50). In any event, Sweden was a central actor in the battles of the next thirty years, becoming for a time a major European power before fading from international view.

All the armies of the Thirty Years' War were not only violent but also vicious to soldiers and civilians alike, slaughtering, raping, and otherwise brutalizing their way across central Europe. Sweden's forces were especially rapacious throughout Catholic Germany, plundering, burning, and destroying livestock, croplands, and dwellings, and looting Catholic churches and stripping them of gold altars and artwork. They used barbaric techniques of interrogating, punishing, and sometimes just torturing both combatants and noncombatants in their path. In Catholic areas of Germany today this behavior is memorialized in sardonic turns of phrase such as *hinter schwedischen Gardinen* 'behind Swedish curtains', meaning in prison, or the ghastly *schwedischer Trunk* 'Swedish cocktail', buckets of liquefied cow dung forced down peasants' throats. The latter was recorded along with other brutal techniques in Grimmelshausen's 1668 novel of the Thirty Years' War, *Simplicius Simplicissimus*. Far from forgotten, the *schwedischer Trunk*, among other memorial historical events, is still reenacted (symbolically!) at the yearly festival of Rakoczyfest in the German city of Kissingen, one of the places in which Swedish troops committed it on the local population. Detailed source studies of Grimmelshausen's novel have determined that the author drew on both personal experience and published accounts of the Thirty Years' War, and that he stayed "remarkably close to historical facts," so that the novel is considered a reliable and realistic narration of the war (Schulz-Behrend, introduction to Grimmelshausen 1993, xxi).

In sixteenth-century Europe, religious and political issues could not easily be separated, since the two major Christian confessions of the time—Catholicism and Lutheranism—were part of the states' power structure. Catholic monarchy drew its fundamental justification from religious authority, while on the Protestant side, Martin Luther had preached that Christian duty called for loyalty to the ruler: two apparently opposing stances that in practice had the same endpoint, that is, theological justification for earthly rule. However, religion was only one factor in the shifting alliances the war produced. For example, Catholic France entered the battle in 1632 on the side of the Protestants in order to protect itself from the incursions of Catholic Spain. The fighting was generally on German soil, with the German peasants, whether Catholic or Protestant, the heaviest losers.

As if the Thirty Years' War did not provide enough upheaval to the continent, seventeenth-century Europe saw a series of additional conflicts in France, the Netherlands, Catalonia, Andalusia, Portugal, and Naples. Some historians describe these as a "general crisis of the seventeenth century," others, particularly Marxists, as a transition from feudalism to capitalism (Schmidt 2003, 9). The smaller harvests and widespread hunger caused by the "Little Ice Age" of lowered temperatures starting in 1570 were one impetus behind social reorganization and its concomitant upheavals. In Eastern Europe the societies were refeudalized, peasants once again becoming serfs tied to the land owned by large landowners, and this situation lasted into the twentieth century (Schmidt 2003, 10). As is usual with such large-scale restructuring, many lives and livelihoods were disrupted and people were displaced from their accustomed habitats. The optimism that had characterized the sixteenth century vanished in the seventeenth in the face of new social pressures, including commercial competition, business failures, hunger even in the middle class, poverty, and religious conflicts.

Demographic pressures contributed to the European tensions. Population in the Germany of 1618 had grown, necessitating the use of marginal land for agriculture (Vasold 2003, 19). This marginal land grew even less productive when climate change brought falling temperatures. Farmers could barely grow enough for their own families and had little excess to sell. The resulting grain shortages caused prices to rise. Craftsmen such as shoemakers, tailors, and construction workers lost income as most of their customers put what money they had into food and not shoes, clothes, or buildings. In the same market, however, landowners, millers, bakers, and butchers grew prosperous. Class differences were widened, and currency manipulators made the situation worse, causing inflation.

The population of Germany at the end of the Thirty Years' War in 1648 was about twelve million—three to four million fewer than it had been in 1618. The majority of the deaths in seventeenth-century Central Europe were the result of the plague, not of weaponry directly. There is no question, however, that war was the ultimate cause, by bringing across Europe thousands of soldiers who lived in the open with little or no sanitation. One result was the near starvation of the local populations; another was the spread of diseases, including those referred to as the plague. The large numbers of refugees fleeing the armies meant that many people sickened and died away from their homes, causing the death toll in some localities to be greater than the recorded population.

Plague, 1633–1635

The worst plague years in seventeenth-century Germany were 1633–1635 (Vasold 2003, 13–23), but the disaster was not spread evenly across the country. The northwestern part of Germany was hardly affected, but losses were heavy in the *Pestgürtel* 'plague belt' (Vasold 2003, 21) from the southwest to the northeast, that is through Baden-Württemberg, Franconia, Thuringia, and Saxony to Pomerania. It was the worst pestilence in Central Europe since the thirteenth and fourteenth centuries.

An example is provided by the town of Nördlingen in the year 1634, in the eye of the war-storm; first the Swedish troops of Gustav Adolf arrived, welcomed by the Protestant population, but then the Kaiser's Catholic army, fortified by Spanish troops, laid siege to the city. The resulting defeat of the Swedish army cost the lives of 350 soldiers, but that number was dwarfed by the thousands of civilians who died in the plague that arrived on the battle's heels. Between 1627 and 1640 the number of households in Nördlingen shrank by half. Nürnberg, to take another example, with a population of 50,000 in 1620, lost 18,000 in 1634/1635 alone and did not number 50,000 again until the year 1845. This pattern was repeated in many German cities. Large areas of Germany were decimated, some towns and rural areas completely depopulated (Vasold 2003, 21).

Plague follows wars. Epidemics thrive on the conditions of war: large numbers of strangers flowing into areas where local people lack resistance to new bacteria; unsanitary living conditions caused by lack of latrines; rats, endemic to wooden houses and barns, breeding fleas that spread to humans, especially those who are not bathing or changing clothes often; and near-starvation lowering resistance to illness. A final touch is the lack of well people to provide elementary nursing care to the spiraling numbers of the sick.

Postscript: War's Aftereffects

Many commentators have ascribed the dysfunctional political culture of Germany during the twentieth century to aftereffects of this brutal war. Henry Kissinger, calling the Thirty Years' War "the most violent, most brutal and most destructive war of history," blamed French First Minister and Cardinal Richelieu (1585–1642) for hindering the unification of the German territories by two centuries, fostering a bickering and provincial politics there which ultimately caused the worst tragedies of the twentieth century (Vasold 2003, 22–23). During the seventeenth century, Germany had became Europe's battleground and graveyard, absorbing by far the greatest numbers of casualties of any of the warring countries.

The final truce, the 1648 Treaty of Westphalia, gave over to Sweden parts of Pomerania on the Baltic coast, and to France, the regions of Alsace and Lorraine. Further, it guaranteed freedom of minority worship, but only in areas where it had existed before the conflict. "Every hope and project inspiring the wave of revolutionary ardour which swept Germany at the beginning of the sixteenth century had been disappointed. A movement which began as a reaction against foreign intervention, and the internal weakness which permitted foreign intervention, resulted in its last phases in foreign intervention on a scale hitherto unknown," wrote Barraclough (1963, 372). The Peace of Westphalia was and is widely interpreted as a Protestant victory, but its cost to Germans as a people and to the future of the German nation and to Europe itself were so great that "victory" seems a misnomer.

By the seventeenth century, religious wars would rage over all of Europe, with Germany at the geographical center. In 1618–1648 the conflicts reached their peak in the Thirty Years' War and ended by splitting Europe and realigning its national boundaries. The 275 years between the Reformation (begun in 1517) and the French Revolution (1789–1792) became a period of such unbroken conflict in Western Europe that some historians consider it as one unit—the "long sixteenth century" (Goertz 2004, 11).

The feudal organization of the Middle Ages was gone; peasants were no longer beholden to a lord, and cities and their citizens were more independent of central control, both economically and in some ways politically. Their own elected city councils took some powers that had been previously held by dukes and princes. In other ways, though, ordinary life went on much as it had in the Middle Ages. Common people counted on the folk wisdom they garnered from traditional pictures, gestures, rituals, rumors, folk sayings, and folktales. Their humor and fun came from church festivals and was bolstered by beer drinking, noise making, brutality, and humor centering on jokes about excrement and sex, possibly survivals of earlier pagan fertility rites (Goertz 2004, 221). This medieval sense of humor still reigned as the printing press enabled the widespread distribution of illustrated pamphlets arguing political and religious questions of the day.

Religious reformers made the most of vulgar illustrations, apparently considering them merely an amusing and effective appeal to the popular mind. One Protestant pamphlet included a drawing of a pig dressed as the Pope running through a church while dropping excrement. Catholic pamphleteers drew upon the same inventory of barnyard images to impugn Luther and other Reformation figures. In other ways, too, the medieval style was still alive in the early sixteenth century. Not only the common uneducated people, but also the educated elites, were still believers in the rankest superstitions. For example, Luther's friend and adviser Philipp Melanchthon, a theologian and diplomat who belonged to the "enlightened avant-garde of his times" (Goertz 2004, 224), declined to participate in the parliament on days when the stars were unfavorable to him, or if a bad sign had come to him in a dream.

Social Control

The world of the sixteenth century was only beginning to emerge from the medieval *Verordnungsfreudigkeit*—pleasure in excessive regulation. These regulations had controlled styles of clothing (social class was to be visible) and behavior at festivals ("free" behavior might lead to mass uprising). The clergy were agents of the state, and they enforced social values (Goertz 2004, 227) such as respect for one's "betters" and premarital chastity.

An unanticipated consequence of excessive regulation is that it may end in encouraging the behavior it is meant to discourage. For example, Church persecution of witches (stronger in Protestant areas than in Catholic ones, and by the seventeenth century stronger in Europe than on the American continent) began as an attempt to wean Christians from belief in witchcraft, which was rooted in pagan religion, but it ended in actually fueling that belief.

So it happened in the sixteenth century: multiple and strict regulations against everyday pleasures (particularly as these are difficult to enforce) only encouraged popular resistance. The religious reformers, who were to become the Protestants, campaigned against the medieval regulations supported by the Roman church and the Holy Roman Empire and thereby enjoyed a populist advantage—the reformers stood against hated convention, for the individual and for a German way of life rather than a Roman one.

After the Reformation, the Protestant clergy were free to marry; as a result, in Protestant territories, Christian social ethics became centered in marriage and the family. Whereas the medieval Catholic church had denounced female sensuality as a danger to men, Luther argued that "God's vital presence" animated the [marital] sexual drive (Goertz 2004, 229). This change in one blow raised the status both of women and of married sex. The Reformation did not, however change the patriarchal organization of society, since women remained subject to their husbands, as Luther underlined in his 1529 pamphlet on marriage, *Traubüchlein* 'marriage booklet' (Goertz 2004, 229).

Finding a Language Fit for the Bible

Martin Luther's genius as an accomplished writer and speaker, a reformer who spoke for ordinary people rather than the church hierarchy, found its ideal outlet in translation of a people's Bible in a supraregional German language.

But Luther could hardly have created, even in consultation with his many associates, a unified German language to replace the High and Low folk dialects of the sixteenth century. Rather, to spectacular effect, he combined two varieties of German, one spoken and one written, which were already well positioned to communicate to both sides of the High German–Low German divide. To allow the German Bible to speak as plainly as the common people, Luther used the everyday German of his home district, Meissen-Upper Saxony, borrowing idioms, folk sayings, and vocabulary from the language of the marketplace, the farm, and the home. In Luther's Wittenberg, in east-central Germany, the High German of the south and the Low German of the north had already collided and were creating a middle ground. Luther listened and consulted, seeking the most authentic but also the most widely understandable translations for the Bible's Greek, Hebrew, and Latin, sometimes asking consultants and friends obsessively about which of a pair of High and Low words was more likely to be understood among a wide German audience.

But Luther's home dialect wasn't polished enough, or universal enough, to carry his Bible translation alone. For spelling, grammar, and word order, and for appeal to the intellectual elite as well, the scholar Luther turned to the writings of his local Imperial government office for the language it used to communicate with other chanceries. In the Imperial *Kanzleideutsch* Luther found an institutional German of laws and memos that was already becoming the accepted form of German writing and was replacing both Latin and the Low German dialects of the north. Low German was losing its former preeminence as the economic importance of the Baltic cities of the Hanseatic League declined, yielding by default to the High German of the less cosmopolitan central and south German states (Keller 1978, 375–77).

In combining these two forms, Luther may have been simply making a shrewd gesture to the marketplace, for he was writing for a national, not a regional, audience. But the consequences went far beyond the marketplace: his Bible translation broke new ground in sixteenth-century German writing. Luther rejected his age's Latinate style of convoluted syntax and learned vocabulary and created for the first time in German a dignified written style based on oral traditions rather than scholarly debate.

The People's Bible

In one stroke, the Luther Bible advanced the goal of a universal German language further than the chancery efforts had. In fact, as Füssel writes, "The Bible often being the only book in the household, it was frequently used as a primer" (2003, 46). The same could definitely not be said of chancery correspondence.

Luther's sure touch in stylistic and translation matters transmuted two workaday language varieties into a new German, direct and expressive. The earthy, plain-spoken language of east-central German tradesmen and peasants and the grammatically careful, but dry as dust written language of chancery memos now married and begat a German language colorful enough for the common reader as well as dignified enough for the Bible. This new German vessel for Scripture now took a place of honor alongside the linguistic pantheon of Greek, Hebrew, and Latin, the languages of the Bible.

By the last quarter of the sixteenth century, the written language throughout Germany was the High German of the Luther Bible, and it became the mother to the Standard High German which is the spoken and written language of the German-speaking countries today. The many dialects of High and Low German, meanwhile, remained as regional spoken (but not usually written) variants, up to our own time (Keller 1978, 377). As it happened, not quite every German reader in every region could immediately understand the Testaments' prose, clear and idiomatic though it was. In South Germany the Testaments were sold with Middle German/Upper German glossaries, and for North Germany, Low German editions were made (Füssel 2003, 46). Nonetheless this "people's Bible" marked a leap forward toward a standard German language.

Artful Artlessness

Luther's translation was a masterpiece of style that appealed to the ears of the uneducated as well as to the minds of the scholars. This quality was one the Luther translation had in common with its forerunner, the Latin Vulgate Bible, St. Jerome's fourth-century translation from the Greek *Septuagint*. What Daniel Sheerin writes of the Latin Vulgate might be said as well of Luther's German translation twelve centuries later: "The (apparent) artlessness of Scripture, its popular, subliterary character, . . . came . . . to be viewed as an advantage, a medium peculiarly suited to its message, a vehicle of an unexpected and peculiar eloquence" (Sheerin 1996, 139). The Christians of the fourth century, most of them illiterate and few of them native speakers of Latin, used Latin as an oral lingua franca, and a simple direct style had been effective in communicating the Christian narrative among them. However, the rhetorical power of the Latin Vulgate was lost on the Christians of Luther's Germany, few of whom could either read Latin or understand it when it was read out in church. In setting out to put the Bible into the living idiom of German Christians, Luther was embarking on a renewal of the power of biblical language for his own time and place. To that end, he turned every word and phrase over in his mind, evaluating it for authenticity (Arndt 1962, 78).

Luther's artful artlessness hit the mark. Those butchers and their customers, market women, housewives, tradesmen, and craftsmen showed an immediate enthusiasm for owning, reading, or hearing Luther's new German Bible translation. The first edition of Luther's New Testament numbered 3,000 (large for its time) in the relatively new technology of the printing press. *Das Neue Testament Deutzsch*, or the *Septembertestament*, as it came to be called, sold briskly at one guilder (two months' salary for a schoolmaster, or the price of a calf), necessitating a second, revised edition; the *Dezembertestament*, the first revision of the *Septembertestament*, appeared on December 19, 1522 (Füssel 2003, 38).

Not only the educated elites, but also ordinary Germans, even the loyal Catholics among them, soon wanted to read and own a German

Bible. The Roman Church met the Catholic demand with its own versions of the Luther translation. The most prominent example is the 1527 edition edited by Hieronymus Emser and published by Wolfgang Stöckel. Based on Luther's *Dezembertestament*, even using the same Lucas Cranach woodcuts that had appeared in it, this edition included an epilogue by Emser advising laymen against reading the Bible, which he recommended for scholars only. The 1534 Johannes Dietenberger edition was likewise based on Luther's translation, although with marginal notes on "Luther's false interpretations" (Füssel 2003, 52).

Luther's Bible was not actually a single book, nor was it only Luther's. The Old Testament, first published in six parts in 1534, was, like the New Testament, revised numerous times by Luther before his death in 1546. "In all, 430 partial and complete editions were produced between 1522 and 1546," writes Stephan Füssel (2003, 46). Luther was a meticulous translator and revised constantly. And while he was definitely the "genius in charge" (Robinson 2004, 232), there was a team of co-translators, particularly for the Old Testament of 1534, which, unlike the New Testament, was written in Hebrew, in which Luther was inexpert. Luther's brain trust of Bible scholars and Greek and Hebrew experts included Johannes Bugenhagen (Wittenberg's town priest, Wittenberg University lecturer in theology), Justus Jonas (Professor of canon law), Caspar Creuziger (Professor of theology and philosophy), Philipp Melanchthon (Professor of Greek and Latin), Matthäus Aurogallus (Professor of Hebrew), and Georg Rörer (pastor, deacon, and Luther's secretary).

A Sixteenth-Century Best Seller

Luther's German Bible may be described as the incubator of the infant modern German language, while its nursemaids—the printing press, the German princes, the cityfolk, and the peasants of Germany—guarded and nourished it. The sheer numbers of copies printed and sold, and the even greater numbers of ordinary German people who read, or heard someone read, the Luther Bible were unprecedented at the time.

Luther was no newcomer to the publishing scene; as a writer, preacher, and theological scholar, he had been highly visible and even dominant in Germany's public culture for some time. The *Septembertestament* was to be a best seller, and both the translator Luther and the printer, Melchior Lotter of Wittenberg, were canny enough to anticipate that. Lotter started setting up the type for this

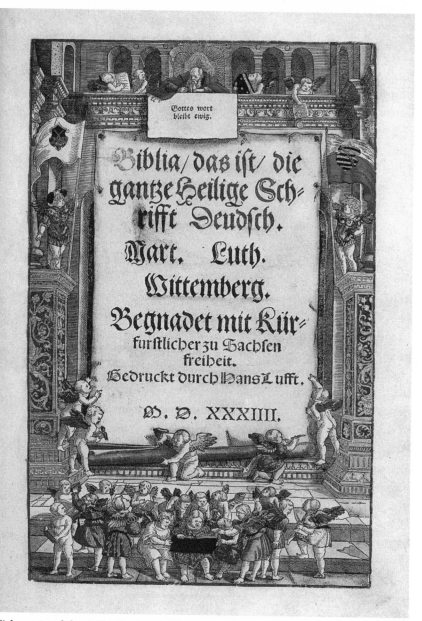

Title page of the 1534 Luther Bible, Lutherhaus, Wittenberg, Germany.
Photo: Holly Hayes. By permission of Sacred Destinations.

first edition of Luther's New Testament translation on May 5, 1522, and ran double shifts to get the first print run ready in time for the Leipzig book fair of September 29 to October 6 (Flood 1998, 49). It sold fast, as did subsequent print runs of the Old Testament and, from 1534, Luther's translation of the entire Bible, Old and New Testaments, in all of its many editions. By the time of Luther's death in 1546, 100,000 copies of his complete Bible translation had been printed in Wittenberg alone, at least 500,000 in all of Germany. Furthermore, the popularity of the Luther translation remains almost undiminished into the modern era. In the subsequent four and a half centuries, many newer German Bibles have come and gone, but Luther Bibles, from reprints of the 1534 edition to the 1984 revised, modernized-spelling edition, are still sold in almost every bookstore in Germany; and the 1984 edition is the central text of the Evangelical Lutheran Church of Germany (EKD: Evangelische Kirche Deutschlands 2007).

Bootlegged Luther Publications

So popular were the Luther translations and his other writings that they were quickly stolen and reprinted by (non-Protestant) printing houses across Germany, as Church resistance to printed material in German weakened. Luther, who never made any money from his writings (he lived from his university earnings), was unconcerned about profit (all profit went to the printing houses in any case) but was appalled that the unauthorized printers sometimes copied carelessly, left out entire columns or even deliberately rewrote his words. He devised a mark of quality to be stamped on authorized editions—a sign of the Lamb with chalice and a flag with the cross, next to the Luther rose, the Luther family coat of arms. Under some of these signs appeared the statement "Let this sign be a guarantee that these books have passed through my hands, for wrong printing and corrupt books now abound" (in German, *Dis zeichen sey zeuge/das solche bucher durch meine hand gangen sind/den des falsche druckes und bucher verderbens/ vleyssigen sich ytzt viel*; Flood 1998, 53). In response Saxon Elector Johann Friedrich, at Luther's request, granted Lufft, the publisher of the first complete Bible translation of 1534, exclusive reprint rights within Saxony.

Loosening the Ties to Rome

The German territories, a patchwork of thousands of principalities, duchies, and chanceries of the Holy Roman Empire, were ruled from Rome, home of Church and Empire. The imperial supreme court (the *Reichskammergericht*) had in 1495 made the law of Rome supreme in every matter, even local ones; the nobility as well as the citizenry of the

The Luther Lamb and Rose: Martin Luther's copyright mark. Courtesy of the Richard C. Kessler Reformation Collection, Pitts Theology Library, Candler School of Theology, Emory University.

sixty-five imperial cities chafed under the lack of local control. But how to rebel, when rebellion against Rome might mean rejection of God, an all but unthinkable idea in the sixteenth century? Both the princes and the burghers welcomed the coming of a religious reformer, Martin Luther, who told them to seek God in the Bible, not in the doctrines of the Church, and in so doing to bypass Rome. As Steven Ozment writes: "Local grievances against the Roman Church and a desire for communal sovereignty attracted urban populations to Protestant reforms" (Ozment 2004, 66). Luther's reformation-turned-rebellion garnered secular as well as religious support. "Clearly," as Nestingen writes, "things were stirring":

> Germany had been for centuries a boondocks, a region useful to the southern Europeans for its resources and manpower but backwards and out of touch. Luther's protests had released long-term, festering resentment among the Germans, and those social, political, and economic forces had now coalesced around him. . . . Luther had been caught up and carried along in forces bigger than himself. (Nestingen 2003b, 41)

Luther understood these forces, and he did not disdain politics. Ozment writes: "During his formative years, from 1518 to 1528, Luther was as devoted to German nationalism and civic reform as he was to the restoration of biblical Christianity" (Ozment 2004, 77). He was supported in both by his prince, the Saxon Elector Friedrich; however, Friedrich and his fellow German princes walked the path of nationalism carefully. For example, a portrait of an angry Luther made by Cranach at the request of the Saxon court was deemed by it too provocative and was replaced at the court's request by a new Cranach etching of Luther as a saint. Luther was content to comply with these court-sponsored public-relations image campaigns so long as his spiritual message remained (Ozment 2004, 77). The princes stayed on message too. At the April 1521 Diet of Worms to which Luther was called to defend himself against charges of heresy, these rulers of the not-yet-Protestant German "estates" (as the territories in the Holy Roman Empire of the time were called), including Elector Friedrich's Saxony, presented Emperor Charles V with a "national laundry list of political, economic, ecclestiastical, and spiritual complaints." The religious reformer and the political dissenters were prepared to speak with one voice (Ozment 2004, 78–79). As it happened, neither Luther nor the estates got what they wanted right away, but their time would soon come.

Other German Bibles

In the last half of the fifteenth century, 30,000 different titles were published in Europe, of which only 15 percent were published in the vernacular languages, including German (Füssel 2003, 15–26). At least eighteen High German, four Low German, and four Dutch Bibles were printed up to the year 1518 (Grietsch, 2003, 62). The first known complete German-language Bible, based on a now lost century-old Bavarian translation, was printed and issued by the Strassburg printer Johann Mentelin. In a style that was to become common for pre-Luther German Bibles, the Mentelin Bible was a literal translation of the Vulgate, difficult for German speakers who did not know Latin grammar, and was intended not for the reading public but rather for clergy who needed help with their Latin.

These early German Bibles never reached a wide audience, both because they were not very readable and because of the Church's position that Bible reading was for the priests, not the common people. In the fall of 1522, however, everything about German Bibles and Bible reading was about to change with the appearance of Luther's *Septembertestament*; most of those pre-Luther translations were to disappear quickly.

In 1500 one in every three hundred German speakers possessed a partial or complete printed, pre-Luther German Bible; by 1546 one of every thirteen German speakers (Stedje 2001, 123), or, put another way, every fifth household (Ernst 2005, 166) owned a complete or partial edition of the Luther Bible. The drawing power of a readable Bible in German, plus the prestige of its translator, the famous writer, preacher, and reformer Dr. Martin Luther, must have been considerable. More Germans than ever could read, but Luther, who believed it was every Christian's duty to read the Bible, aimed to increase their number even more. In his 1524 letter "to the Councillors of all cities in German lands, that they build and maintain Christian schools," he calls for universal education for both boys and girls, including not only Bible reading, but also study of the ancient Greeks and Romans, languages and history. Luther was not only a religious reformer, but also a classical humanist.

The humanist scholar was never satisfied with his work. Fresh revisions of his New Testament were completed several times a year by the compulsive editor Luther and were as quickly published by his authorized printer—as well as by any number of unauthorized ones. Publication of Luther's Bibles was lucrative, but the profit was garnered entirely by the printers and booksellers, since Luther, on the evidence of surviving account books, never requested or received any royalties (Grietsch 2003, 71), living entirely on his income as a professor. By 1534 Luther's translation of the Old Testament appeared and was promptly forbidden by the Church, as all of Luther's previous writings already were. A less effective prohibition can hardly be imagined; he was the most popular writer of his time, author of about one-third of the published works in Germany between 1530 and 1599 (Arndt 1962, 93).

By the end of the sixteenth century, German printers, with the exception of those in Cologne (in a firmly Catholic region) and Switzerland (with its own brand of German, *Swytzerdüütsch*, and its own brand of Protestantism, Calvinism), replaced their many local printers' standards for German spelling and usage with common standards for *Ostmitteldeutsch* 'East Central German' or *Kanzleideutsch* 'chancery German.' The German Bible, the most common book in German households, became within a hundred years also Bible German, the common written language of Germany (Grietsch 2003, 71).

Translation as an Art

Luther had firm ideas about how Bible translation should be done and was dismissive of earlier attempts, which he considered inadequate and clumsy. In his 1530 letter on translation, he insisted on everyday

German. For Luther, translation of the Bible was not about elegance, or attempted elegance, in language, but about communicating the word of God:

> "Don't ask the letters of the Latin language how to speak German . . . rather ask the mother at home, the children in the street, the common man at the market. . . ."
>
> (*man mus nicht die buchstaben jnn der lateinischen sprachen fragen/wie man sol Deutsch reden . . . /man mus die mutter jhm hause, die kinder auff der gassen, den gemeinen man auff dem marckt drumb fragen. . . . [Sendbrief vom Dolmetschen]*)

Luther's decision not only to translate from the Latin Vulgate (the usual process for earlier translations), but to consult the earlier Greek version and, for the Old Testament, the Hebrew, meant a major undertaking in an age with few lexicons. Luther attempted to replicate each biblical phrase in all its reverberations. He viewed his task as spiritual communication with his readers, attempting to render exactly what he read in the original and to transmit it in all of its dimensions. "Luther possessed a particular feel for the narrative quality of the originals," writes Winfried Thielmann, arguing further that Luther situated each utterance into its religious context, searching for the proper effect even of single words such as prepositions and adverbs, discussing these with the like-minded associates who flocked to visit him at Wartburg Castle (2007, 219–225). Erwin Arndt writes:

> Seldom has a writer or poet of the early centuries penetrated through his work so deeply into the essence of language as did Martin Luther. . . . But through it all Luther's main interest was not even language itself; rather his first priority was the content. . . . From the beginning his compulsion for universal comprehension was a basic characteristic of Luther's German language creation. (Arndt 1962, 7)

Though it seems not to have been his aim, Luther's Bible translation turned out to be an artistic accomplishment, resulting in a beautifully realized religious document—and it ended by enriching, even ennobling, the German language. As Orrin Robinson writes, Luther "broadened irrevocably the range of registers and functions for which German, rather than Latin, was the preferred linguistic vehicle" (Robinson 2004, 232). Now German could leave behind its inferior standing as a poor second to Latin; it had been tried and found fit to express the word of God.

Luther's Bible spoke to the common people, but in a language common only on the surface. Rather, Luther's was an extract of German. He called expertly upon rhetorical devices long known to literature. For example, alliteration, a mainstay in old Germanic poetry, takes its place in "Stecken und Stab" (Psalms 23, 5), "zittern und zagen" (Mark 14, 33); rhyme in word pairs such as "Rat und Tat" (Proverbs 8, 14). He coined words, such as *Feuereifer* 'fiery eagerness' and *Herzenslust* 'heart's joy' (examples quoted in Kaufmann 2006, 73). These novel combinations of Germanic-rooted words sang themselves off the page into the readers' and listeners' understanding, a far cry from the Latinized and bureaucratic mouthfuls sent out from the chanceries.

Universal comprehension required at least some standardization, provided in large part by print shops; they developed a "house style" much as publications do today, settling on consistent spelling of words, or placement of verbs. Luther was in tune with these detailed standards and developed more of his own. Robinson writes that Luther was "obsessed with the right way to translate the Bible . . . and . . . also with the 'proper' way of writing and speaking" (2004, 233).

In Mansfeld (where Luther had spent his early childhood) and surrounding territories of central Germany where Luther lived and worked, the common people still spoke Low (North) German in the marketplace (Arndt 1962, 95). But in the population centers of that region, High and Low German were merging. In Wittenberg, where he preached for many years, Luther followed what he called *Gemeinsprachetendenzen* 'common speech tendencies' rather than a dialect of either Low or High German. In *Tischreden* 'Table Talk,' assembled out of colleagues' and students' notes on after-hours dining-table conversation, Luther is quoted as saying that he uses the language of the Saxon Chancery, which he claims was followed by all the princes and kings of Germany, so that both High German and Low German speakers can understand him. Arndt, however, finds that Luther here overstates the case for chancery German, which was not actually universal among kings and princes until much later (Arndt 1962, 96–97).

A particular strength of the Luther Bible translation is its use of vernacular phrases and metaphors. In a time when only the few written memoirs or diaries would have used the language of the common people, striking phrases found in the Luther translation cannot be placed with confidence in either the contemporary German language or credited to Luther as the originator. What we can know is that Luther's German equivalents to the originals are so apt that they have either become part of the language or remained so. A folk saying used by Luther in the sixteenth century was ensured a life of at least five hundred years—to our time—by virtue of being part of the Luther Bible.

Some examples appear in Table 4.1, alongside their equivalents in the Latin Vulgate and their descendants in the King James Version, which was strongly though indirectly influenced by the Luther Bible. The English Church reformer William Tyndale (1490–1536) visited Luther in Wittenberg in 1534 and used Luther's work as a model for

Table 4.1.   Proverbs from the Luther Bible Still in Use in Modern German

Latin Vulgate	Luther Bible 1534 (revised 1984)	King James Version (first edition 1611)	Verse
nolite iudicare ut non iudicemini	Richtet nicht, damit ihr nicht gerichtet werdet	Judge not, lest ye be judged	Matthew 7:01
Spiritus quidem promptus est caro autem infirma	Der Geist ist willig; aber das Fleisch ist schwach	the spirit indeed is willing, but the flesh is weak	Matthew 26:41
propheta in sua patria honorem non habet	ein Prophet gilt daheim nichts	a prophet hath no honour in his own country	John 4:44
beatius est magis dare quam accipere	Geben ist seliger als nehmen	it is more blessed to give than to receive	Acts 20:35
crescite et multiplicamini et replete terram	Seid fruchtbar und mehret euch...	be fruitful and multiply	Genesis 1:28
in terram quae fluit lacte et melle	ein Land, wo Milch und Honig fließt	a land flowing with milk and honey	Exodus 3:8
oculum pro oculo dentem pro dente	Auge um Auge, Zahn um Zahn	an eye for an eye, a tooth for a tooth	Exodus 21:24
non in solo pane vivat homo	der Mensch lebt nicht vom Brot allein	man doth not live by bread only	Deuteronomy 8:03

his own translation into English. The Tyndale translation was in its turn a strong influence on the King James translation.

Luther's decision to use the direct language of the people to bring the Christian message to the people replicates the practice of the second-century Christian fathers in putting the Scriptures into Greek. They chose vernacular *Koiné* 'Common' Greek, a supraregional version in its time, using not a literary style but a conversational style (Horrocks 1997, 91–95). The translation into Latin by St. Jerome, too, followed not the formal classical forms but the register of Latin as it was spoken in the fourth century. This unadorned style (Sheerin 1996, 137–156) is mirrored in the German version of Luther fourteen centuries later— no wonder, since, as a translator, Luther consciously modeled himself after the example of St. Jerome (Nestingen 2003b, 53).

Luther's emulation of the Vulgate's conversational style includes the use of *und* 'and' rather than subordinating conjunctions such as *weil* 'because' or *dass* 'that' to connect main clauses, giving a childlike quality to the story, which tumbles out as a series of assertions rather than an intellectual argument with cause and effect; frequent use of *denn* 'for', a coordinating conjunction indicating not a logical cause and effect but a weak connection between two units; and emphasis through repetition rather than through intensification or descriptive adjectives. Here is an example:

John 1:1–5:

> Im Anfang war das Wort, und das Wort war bei Gott, und Gott war das Wort. Dasselbe war im Anfang bei Gott. Alle Dinge sind durch dasselbe gemacht, und ohne dasselbe ist nichts gemacht, was gemacht ist. In ihm war das Leben, und das Leben war das Licht der Menschen. Und das Licht scheint in der Finsternis, und die Finsternis hat's nicht ergriffen.
>
> (King James Version: In the beginning was the Word, and the Word was with God, and the Word was God. The same was in the beginning with God. All things were made by him; and without him was not any thing made that was made. In him was life; and the life was the light of men. And the light shineth in darkness; and the darkness comprehended it not.)

The text relies on repetition and connection, independent clauses connected by *und* 'and' rather than dependent clauses explaining cause and effect. This format lends the narrative the quality of being told by, or to, a child, piling up detail upon detail without explaining or analyzing. The six uses of *und* in this short passage suggest a replication in German of the *kai* 'and' -style of the Koiné Greek of the New Testament. Narration, rather than cogitation, is emphasized with the repetition of the central nouns: *Wort* 'word', *Gott* 'God', *Leben* 'life', *Licht* 'light', *Finsternis* 'darkness'.

A choice had to be made at times between the northern word and the southern word (Luther's own dialect is best described as midway between south and north). Here he often had to evaluate whether the southern or the northern equivalent had already gained some currency outside of its own area. Often he reevaluated repeatedly, even after publication (this work was part of the endless revision that kept Luther occupied until the end of his life). For example, although Luther initially decided to follow southeastern practice and drop a final weak–*e* in both word roots and grammatical endings, in the end he brought back the unstressed–*e* in line with east-central German practice. Here we find that Luther's style choice affected even the grammar of modern German. The presence of the *Luther'sche*–e 'the Lutheran e' ultimately supported the preservation of the inflectional system (for example, subjunctive markers such as the *e* in *ihr habet* 'you might have') in standard High German (Robinson 2004, 235).

Because of the intervening time between Luther's last personally supervised Bible edition and our own, standard German has been subject to many other forces, including those from the major German writers of the Classical/Romantic period, the second Industrial Revolution, and two world wars. None of this should dim the significance of the Luther Bible translation for the development of a common German language.

Latin: The Beginning of the End

The steamroller of the now Bible-supported, universal German did not flatten the German dialects so much as it flattened Latin. The dialects survived as regional and familiar forms of mostly spoken communication; but from September 1522 the days of Latin were numbered in Germany, though it was to take more than a century for German to replace Latin completely in the universities and government.

The day of a new standard German language had dawned. Luther's Bible German, which would be known to later ages as

Early New High German, stretched and flexed by Luther to a height of majestic simplicity, moved beyond its regional beginnings; it gained status through its association with the Bible, it grew larger and more expressive through continued use in speaking and writing, and eventually it became the standard German for all public uses, written and spoken. In the Lutheran church, this new German instantly replaced Latin; as the Lutheran religion spread throughout Northern Europe, however, not German but the local languages were spoken in churches. In the Catholic church everywhere in the Western world, Latin remained at least partly the liturgical language until the Vatican II reforms of the twentieth century. More slowly but surely, German was to replace Latin in secular science, humanities, and government in all of Germany. The perfect storm had blown away the old Latin and left a clean slate for the new German.

Luther died in 1546 in Eisleben while traveling and was buried in the Castle Church in Wittenberg, where he had posted his ninety-five theses in 1517. His Bible translations, which had begun the process of modernizing, standardizing, and empowering a unitary German language for a German nation not yet born, continued to set the standard for writing long after his death. The next chapter will tell how the story continued when, 350 years later, the political identity of the nation caught up with the German language.

Timeline: From the Beginning of the Reformation to the First Industrial Revolution

Date (AD)	In continental Germanic territory	Elsewhere in the world
1517	Conventional date for the beginning of the Protestant Reformation; Martin Luther posts ninety-five theses on the church door in Wittenberg.	
1518		Spain grants license to import 4,000 African slaves to its colonies in America

continued

Date (AD)	In continental Germanic territory	Elsewhere in the world
1519		Hernando Cortes brings Arabian horses from Spain to the North American continent; he enters Tenochtitlan, capital of Mexico and is received by Montezuma, Aztec ruler
1522	Luther's translation of the New Testament	
1527	First Protestant university founded at Marburg	Pope Clement VII imprisoned by soldiers of Charles V of the Holy Roman Empire, ending the Renaissance; Protestant Reformation in Sweden
1529	The Lutheran minority at the Second Diet of Speyer protests against decisions of Catholic majority, earning the name "Protestants"	Portuguese colonize Brazil
1533		Henry VIII marries Anne Boleyn and is excommunicated by the Pope, declares himself Supreme Head of the Church of England. Their daughter, the future Queen Elizabeth, is born; first lunatic asylums founded
1534	Luther's German translation of the Bible (Old and New Testaments) appears	Jacques Cartier, on his first voyage to North America, sights Labrador

Date (AD)	In continental Germanic territory	Elsewhere in the world
1555	Peace of Augsburg, motto *cuius regio, eius religio* 'whose state, his religion', German princes could choose for their region either Lutheranism or Catholicism. Of the German states, only Bavaria chooses Catholicism.	
1559		Elizabeth I becomes Queen of England; John Calvin helps establish Presbyterianism as the official religion of Scotland
1567		Rio de Janeiro founded; two million South American Indians die of typhoid
1572	University of Berlin founded; population of Cologne 35,000, of Amsterdam 30,000	Population of Paris 300,000; London 180,000
1587	*Volksbuch von Dr. Faust* first printed in Frankfurt (translated into English 1588)	
1588		Thomas Marlowe, *Doctor Faustus*
1589		Galileo Galilei becomes professor of mathematics at University of Pisa; forks used for first time at French court
1611		King James Bible (English translation) is published

continued

Date (AD)	In continental Germanic territory	Elsewhere in the world
1618	Beginning of Thirty Years' War (until 1648)	Johann Kepler's third law of planetary motion
1620	Population density of Germany, 35 per square mile (at time of Julius Caesar approx. 6)	Pilgrim Fathers leave Plymouth, England, to sail on the *Mayflower* for North America
1626	First German production of Shakespeare's *Hamlet*, in Dresden	Dutch colony of New Amsterdam (New York) founded; Peter Minuit buys island of Manhattan from Indian chiefs
1630	Gustavus Adolphus of Sweden marches his army into Germany as part of Thirty Years' War	
1633	Outbreak of plague in Oberammergau (Germany) leads to vow to God to reenact passion play every ten years if plague abated	Galileo forced by Inquisition to abjure the theories of Copernicus
1648	Peace of Westphalia ends Thirty Years' War (Protestant victory); population of Germany has sunk from 17 million in 1618 to 8 million because of war, famine, and plague	
1665	The Prince Archbishop of Münster sells 7,000 of his subjects as soldiers	The Great Plague of London begins, killing 68,596; Caleb Cheeshateaumuck, first North American Indian to take an A.B. degree at Harvard

Date (AD)	In continental Germanic territory	Elsewhere in the world
1709		14,000 Germans from the Rhineland emigrate to North America; 100,000 Germans will follow during the next 100 years, 5 million during the 1800s
1714	Witch trials abolished in Prussia; Gottfried William von Leibniz publishes *Monadologie*	Battle of Storkyro ends Swedish domination of Finland, begins Russian domination; Peace of Baden: France keeps Strassburg and Alsace (formerly German)
1717	School attendance made mandatory in Prussia	Smallpox inoculation introduced in England
1720	Johann Sebastian Bach: "Brandenburg Concertos"	Spain occupies Texas; Swiss immigrants introduce rifles to America
1734	University of Göttingen founded by King George II	8,000 Protestants from Salzburg, Austria, settle in Georgia, U.S.A.
1754	First M.D. degree granted to a woman, University of Halle, Germany	King's College, New York (later Columbia University) founded
1775		American Revolutionary War (until 1783)
1789		French Revolution (until 1799)
1804	Napoleon Bonaparte crowns himself emperor of France; Austrian Empire founded by Francis I	
1806	Holy Roman Empire dissolved by the Treaty of Lunéville	

continued

Date (AD)	In continental Germanic territory	Elsewhere in the world
1810	University of Berlin founded	Napoleon annexes Hanover, Bremen, Hamburg, Lauenburg, and Lübeck
1834	Bavarian Franz Xaver Gabelsberger publishes his version of German shorthand	English mathematician Charles Babbage invents the principle of the "analytical engine," forerunner of the computer
1848	*Märzrevolution* 'March Revolution' in the German states (failed)	Revolutions in all the major European states except United Kingdom and the Ottoman and Russian Empires; in England, Karl Marx and Friedrich Engels publish (in German) *The Communist Manifesto* (trans. English 1850)

Table after Grun 2005.

5

The German Language
Gets a State

1871: High German Follows the Empire

Language follows power, and German was no exception. Power in the form of a brand-new German nation lured High German down from its birthplace in Martin Luther's central highlands to the flat and sandy northern plains of Prussia. In its new headquarters it kept its old grammar and its Second Sound Shift, but it learned some local words and took on a local accent. In fact, soon the neighbors almost forgot that High German wasn't Prussian by birth and simply accepted it as part of the new national plan.

It was in 1871 that the German states joined together at the instigation of Prussian Chancellor Otto von Bismarck to form a new nation, the *Zweites Deutsches Reich* 'Second German Empire,' its capital placed in the northern city of Berlin, not coincidentally also capital of the state of Prussia. High German followed the Empire and became the national language, making itself at home in Berlin and environs and pushing Prussia's native *Plattdeutsch* 'Low German' into secondary status. Luther's Bible translation had made High German the language of God; now the new nation made it the language of mammon too.

Well before 1871 High German had replaced Plattdeutsch as the status variety for writing. It now took its place as the status variety for speaking as well. No longer just the language of a collection of states left over from the implosion of the Holy Roman Empire, High German for the first time had a national address as well as a new purpose. It would be the means of communication of a modern, secular Germany, a *Kulturnation* 'nation of culture'.

Low German, both written and spoken, had continued to flourish in post-Reformation northern Germany, partly because the language of the Hanseatic League, the trade federation of Baltic free cities, was *Mittelniederdeutsch* 'Middle Low German'. The Hanseatic League, also known as the *Hansa* 'guild', was from 1358 the trade federation of Baltic and North Sea free cities including, among many others, the German-speaking cities of Lübeck, Hamburg, Bremen, and Rostock. The Hansa declined starting in the seventeenth century, finally breaking up in 1862. By the mid-nineteenth century, High German had replaced all forms of Low German in the manufacturing centers of northern Germany, and it was used for virtually all public writing. Low German continued to be the North's spoken language, in private dealings and even to a large extent in public affairs. Soon, however, High German would be so vigorous and comfortable in its new home that it would replace Low German as a spoken language for virtually all public uses. High German's conquest as the standard language of Germany was then complete.

It was a reciprocal relationship: the standard language provided the new Germany with a cultural focus, while the new nation in turn provided the German language with a modern nation-state home. German now took its place as a state language alongside its sister languages English, Norwegian, Danish, and Swedish in their respective states. However, its new role would bring some significant changes to the German language.

Setting the Stage: The German Confederation, 1815–1871

The Holy Roman Empire of German Nations dissolved in 1806, and with it any pretense to German unity. Napoleon created in its place the *Rheinbund*, 'Rhine Confederation', which lasted until his death in 1815. In that year the Congress of Vienna created the *Deutscher Bund* 'German Confederation'. The 234 German states of the Holy Roman Empire were pared down to just 39 (Thackeray 2004, 25). Still there was no German nation, nor any linguistic center for a spoken German language. High German served all the states as the standard for writing, but local dialects were spoken for all regional and local purposes. German dialects were found from the French border to the Polish one, from the shores of the Baltic to the southern edges of the Alps, in places called *Preußen* (Prussia), *Bayern* (Bavaria), and *Sachsen* (Saxony): old territories named after ancient tribes, not a modern nation-state like France, Spain, or Denmark. In the German states, *Kleinstaaterei* 'particularism'—territorial rather than national centricity—continued to dominate. This situation was to change by the time of the European and German Revolutions of 1848.

The Revolution of 1848

In Brussels, Budapest, Milan, Prague, Rome, and Venice, as well as in all the thirty-nine city capitals of the German Confederation and in rural areas, 1848 was the year of rebellions of peasants, workers, and the middle classes. Inspired both by the ideals of the French Revolution of 1789 and by American democracy, they hoped to replace aristocratic governments with more popular ones. "Europe in 1848–49 saw the mobilization and politicization of groups as never before. That politicization, in Germany as in other revolutionized areas, would be a major factor in the politics of all Europe thereafter," writes Robert D. Billinger, Jr. (2004, 8). In Germany particularly, one old problem that had plagued Germany since the Thirty Years' War was still at issue: national unity versus *Kleinstaaterei*. "It [was] manifest that abrogation of the rights of the princes, and of the privileges of the aristocracy which were vested in the principalities, was the first necessary step toward securing the welfare of the German people" (Barraclough 1963, 414).

For a time in the mid-nineteenth century it seemed that German national unity might take center stage. "After 1846 agrarian and economic crises set the larger stage for revolution," writes Ozment (2004, 171). Germany's "freedom movement" (Ozment 2004, 170) demanded elections; a voice in the courts, the civil service, and the military; the (male) right to vote; freedom of the press, speech, and religion; and trial by jury. Local parliaments throughout the German territories pressed for a national parliament which would write a national constitution. Meanwhile in the streets, the freedom movement's demonstrations were frightening the rulers and the aristocracy. Austrian emperor Ferdinand left Vienna in fear; Prussian King Frederick William IV offered concessions, but these were rejected and he was placed under house arrest by the revolutionaries.

Finally a national assembly convened on May 18, 1848, in St. Paul's Church in Frankfurt. The delegates were drawn from the ranks of upper-level civil servants and academics, all state employees who were idealistic in their aims but unwilling to risk their jobs by demanding too much. Their initial goal was a confederation of *Großdeutschland* 'Large Germany', including Austria, but leaving out the Austro-Hungarian Empire's non-German-speaking territories (such as Hungary). The Empire declined to comply, and the assembly opted instead for *Kleindeutschland* 'Small Germany' (without the Austro-Hungarian Empire) under Prussian Hohenzollern leadership (Ozment 2004, 172–173).

In December 1848 this Frankfurt National Assembly passed a Basic Rights Law containing fourteen articles protecting personal, political, and property rights and, borrowing from the French Enlightenment and the Napoleonic revolution, separating church and state in law.

The other European powers of 1848 did not recognize the Frankfurt National Assembly or its decisions; only the United States did so. France and England were not eager to see a potentially powerful German state in their midst; the major German states Austria, Prussia, Bavaria, and Hanover did not wish to see their power diluted by a national government. The Assembly offered the German crown to Frederick William IV of Prussia, but he refused it, saying he would not "pick up a crown from the gutter." In Saxony, the Bavarian Palatinate, and Baden, the revolution's demonstrations were violently suppressed by the authorities. Most of the Assembly delegates resigned, declining to "foster civil war" (Barraclough 1963, 415), having failed to gain much support from either the ruling classes or the middle classes. Proud nevertheless of their attempts, the delegates dubbed themselves *Achtundvierziger* 'Forty-eighters'.

Thus was the revolution in Germany and Austria defeated without reaching its goals. Historians are of two minds in evaluating the final results. Ozment emphasizes the positive: "For all its precedential value and bright future prospects, the Revolution of 1848–49 divided and politicized contemporary Germans. . . . The assembly's work had addressed progressively the most basic of German needs [and] would be remembered and revived when later parliaments resumed the search for the elusive German political mixture" (2004, 176–178). To Billinger, labeling the revolution a total failure would be to "overlook the strong liberal, democratic, and socialist political strands in German history that, inspired by the heroes of the 1848–49 Revolutions, continually arose to trouble conservatives, reactionaries, and fascists ever since" (Billinger 2004, 178). True enough, more than a century afterward the revolutionaries' name, Forty-eighters, was echoed in *Achtundsechziger* 'Sixty-eighters', the name the radical veterans of Germany's sometimes violent street demonstrations of 1968 gave themselves. The designation is still claimed by some politicians and many other Germans who took part in the student revolts of 1968, as well as by some who only stood and watched.

Emigration to America

Disappointment in the lack of immediate results from the 1848 revolution inspired a mass migration to the United States of Forty-eighters and their sympathizers. They expected to find in America the freedoms they could not gain in Germany. A German-English guide for newly arrived immigrants prepared by a German émigré pastor in Boston emphasized the democratic and egalitarian nature of the American society the immigrants were entering:

> The German emigrant . . . comes into a country free from . . . despotism . . . , privileged orders and monopolies . . . , intolerable taxes, [and] constraint in matters of belief and conscience. Everyone can travel . . . and settle wherever he pleases. No passport is demanded, no police mingles in his affairs or hinders his movements. . . . Fidelity and merit are the only sources of honor here. The rich stand on the same footing as the poor; the scholar is not above the most humble mechanic; and no German ought to be ashamed to [pursue] any occupation. . . ." (Ozment 2004, 171)

However, these German immigrants and their children, settling in Midwestern states such as Wisconsin, Minnesota, Ohio, and Michigan, brought their ideals with them. Many of them and their children lived to become the core of farmers' and laborers' rights movements that characterized regional and national politics in nineteenth-century America. Their own and their descendants' influence is still felt as part of the liberal (Blue) element of the U.S. Red state–Blue state divide of the twenty-first century.

Power Moves to Prussia

Unpromising agriculturally (it was known as "the sandbox of Europe") and in the seventeenth and eighteenth centuries economically depressed, Brandenburg-Prussia seemed at first an unlikely power center. But by the mid-eighteenth century Prussia (as it was known after 1806), located in the northeastern territories around Berlin and ruled by the Hohenzollern dynasty, became the most powerful of the German states. In the nineteenth century Prussia would "wrest control of the unification of 'small Germany' from an excluded Austria" (Fulbrook 2004, 71).

Starting with the eighteenth-century "Soldier King" Frederick William I, Prussia specialized in military power, spending 80 percent of state revenues in maintenance of the army. A contemporary witticism had it that Prussia was not a country with an army, but an army with a country (Fulbrook 2004, 77). After two centuries of astounding military success, Prussia was taken seriously by European rulers and military planners.

When Prussian Chancellor Otto von Bismarck came to power in 1862, he did not act on the Frankfurt Assembly's demands for liberal reform, nor did he sympathize with these demands; but he did act on its wish for a national confederacy dominated by Prussia. In 1871 he orchestrated the birth of a united Germany and of the second German Empire. Despite the defeat of the Revolution of 1848, the dissension and its expression that were practiced there were to become part of the way forward for Modern Europe and of the new German nation (Billinger 2004, 18). For his part, Bismarck had set a far different tone when he told the Prussian legislature that not speeches and majority votes would be his methods, but "blood and iron" (Thackeray 2004, 27). It was Bismarck's tone that was heard in Europe and America then and into the two world wars of the twentieth century. Dissension and expression, speeches and majority votes—these would have to wait until after 1945 to be the voice of Germany.

The German Constitution of 1871, with Chancellor Otto Bismarck as midwife, guaranteed the dominance of Prussia in the new nation: the Prussian king would rule the Second German Empire (the first had been the Holy Roman Empire; Gerhard 2004, 31). "The new Reich of 1871—whatever the theory—was in practice a Prussian Reich," comments Barraclough (1963, 422).

Language and State

Early in the nineteenth century, German was not the only language of Prussia, since a large proportion of the population were not even German speakers. Especially in the eastern regions, many spoke Polish, Lithuanian, or stateless Slavic languages such as Wendish. More languages came into Prussia as it sought to replace the population lost in the Thirty Years' War by inviting "useful religious minorities"

(Fulbrook 2004, 87) to settle. For example, the Protestant Huguenots (members of the Calvinist Reformed Church), expelled from France by the 1685 Edict of Nantes, settled in Berlin and left a French influence there that has lasted into the present.

All over the European Continent, French replaced Latin in international affairs. By the seventeenth century French was becoming the language of prestige, though not the language of everyday usage, even within the German territories. Although the common people in the German states spoke German in one form or another as their mother tongue, at that time French manners and French phrases attracted the attention of upwardly mobile middle-class Germans, even if they couldn't actually speak French. The German Confederation (1815–1871) had used French for international communication and for military and legal terminology. In the ruling and diplomatic circles of Europe, German got little political respect. Meanwhile, French was usually the first language among German aristocrats; some could barely speak German at all (Barraclough 1963, 406).

This situation would change after 1871, however. "The development of GSG [German Standard German] and its status are closely related to the notion and essence of German nationhood," comments Clyne (1995, 27). Florian Coulmas, writing about the national language as a source of legitimacy, explains:

> Germany lacked both the tradition of political unity which had moulded the French nation and the voluntaristic element of the new constitution which had created the American. Hence, in the German context the most promising path open to nation-building, as a reaction first to French cultural domination and later to military occupation, was that of a Kulturnation, one based on a common cultural heritage. To this end the language was an indispensable tool. Although the process of linguistic unification, which had been given a focus and pushed forward by the Reformation, was hardly complete at the time of the French Revolution, the German language was more likely than any other social feature to lend itself to the creation of a national myth. (Coulmas 1995, 57)

Pronunciation

The new German nation followed the lead of other European languages and put its linguistic center into its political center. Not just High German, but High German with a Prussian accent became the prestige language of the new state; the stamp of cultural recognition came with Theodor Siebs's 1898 work *Deutsche Bühnenaussprache* 'German Stage Pronunciation', which codified in detail the "correct" pronunciation for stage, and later, screen. It soon became the prestige pronunciation all over Germany (although not in Austria and Switzerland).

Where central and southern Germans, the original native speakers of High German, comfortably slurred or dropped sounds in their speech, northern Germans, whose home language was Low German, learned to speak High German in classrooms and through reading; and they pronounced all the letters in their precise North German accents. The careful diction of the northerner, or at least a good imitation of it, is to this day heard on radio, on television, and in films in all parts of Germany. The specifically North German accent is characterized by the following examples (from Clyne 1995, 29):

- *g* in certain positions pronounced as an *ich-laut*, for example in *fertig*;
- long vowels instead of the southern short vowels in *Art*, *Städte*, *Vogt*, *Behörde*, *werden*, *Pferd*;
- the *ich-laut*, rather than the hard southern *k*, in initial position, such as in *China*, *Chemiker*;
- dropping the *p* in initial position before *f* and after *m*, as in *Pflaume*, *Sumpf*; and pronouncing *ng* as *ngk*, as in *Angst*;
- short vowels instead of long vowels in some words, such as *Glas*, *Zug*.

Of specifically South German pronunciation habits, only the sound of *schp* and *scht* for initial spellings of *sp* and *st* remained in Siebs's guidelines. Today most Germans who are not language professionals, and many foreign learners of German, believe that North Germans speak the "purest" German (Stedje 2001, 156), or even, in a common-parlance redirection of the word "high," the "highest" German. In this urban legend, language purity has a specific home: it is Hanover, a northern city about sixty miles west of Berlin, which is reputed to have the "best" German in the land.

The Language of Bureaucracy

As happened with the chancery language of the sixteenth century, government administration was the engine of standardization. In 1871 the new German nation needed nationalized government communication, replacing the multiple standards of the old states; Kleinstaaterei had to be overcome in language as well as in politics. "Centralized bureaucracies for post and telecommunications, railways, law, education, and administration all needed corresponding linguistic standards," writes Wells (1987, 397). It was in the military that the need first arose, for it had previously used a French-based *Heeressprache* "soldiers' language" (Wells 1987, 397). By 1878 Emperor Wilhelm II had ordered a Germanization of military terminology, and the French-borrowed *Terrain* became German *Gelände* 'terrain', *Detachements* became *Abteilungen* 'detachments', *Avancement* became *Beförderung* 'promotion'.

Likewise, the Post Office got new Germanized forms for its previous French forms: *recommandiert* became *eingeschrieben* 'registered', *Billett* became *Fahrschein* 'ticket', *Couvert* became *Briefumschlag* 'envelope'. Many of the Germanized forms from this time have survived only as German officialese, while the foreign originals remain part of everyday speech. For example, *Personenkraftwagen* 'personal motor vehicle' appears in official documents, while the people speak of their *Auto* or *Wagen* 'car'. Meanwhile, these Germanizations were not accepted in either Austria or Switzerland, whose German speakers still retain their own largely French-based officialese (Wells 1987, 398).

Nevertheless, at the same time many new terms for political institutions continued to be borrowed from French and English, a result of German journalists' reporting on the French Revolution. These were sometimes translated literally (*Belagerungszustand* for *état de siège* 'state of siege'; *öffentliche Meinung* for *opinion publique* 'public opinion') or were created, like *Staatsbürger* for *citoyen* 'citizen'. English, too, became increasingly influential as the German government grew more democratic, resulting in the German words *Budget*, *Parlament*, *Defizit*, *Legislatur*. The German language itself was stretched to cover many new situations. Nineteenth-century political parties extended the meaning of three nonpolitical words in particular to describe themselves. These are still used in countless compound words describing political and nonpolitical groups: *Bund* 'federation', *Verein* 'unit', and *Partei* 'group of people with the same interests' (examples from Wells 1987, 403).

For the sake not only of communication and expression, but also of industrial efficiency, Germanization and standardization were necessary. In the old order, the aristocracy used French while the common people used their local dialect, and, since the two groups rarely talked to each other, that system sufficed. However, in the nineteenth century some of the aristocrats had become industrialists, and some of the peasants had become their employees, so they needed a common language. In addition, the common people became geographically mobile, so their home dialect was not enough. "Industrial production requires . . . a single standard language to reach all members of society who are drawn into the economic process. . . . including in particular the national labour market," writes Coulmas (1995, 58–59).

Linguistic Nationalism

It was perhaps inevitable that the rise of High German as the language of the powerful new nation-state would give rise also to linguistic nationalism, the idea that German was not just an equal of, but even better than, other languages. The German idealist Johann Gottlieb Fichte argued that German was superior to French, the daughter of Latin, a dead language with a dead tradition. German, he claimed, was more alive, more authentic, pure, representing the spirit of the Urvolk 'primeval people'. Fichte went so far as to declare that German was "a language shaped to express the truth" (Coulmas 1995, 61). The philosopher Wilhelm von Humboldt declared that language expresses the "national character" (Coulmas 1995, 62).

In the opening years of the nineteenth century, during the time of the German Confederation, a movement for linguistic purity was underway. The *Berliner Gesellschaft für deutsche Sprache* 'Berlin Society for German Language' (begun in 1815 and continuing until 1825) and subsequent linguistic purity groups asserted that foreign words harmed the German language and the German culture. "To purify the language was an act of national loyalty: indeed the words *Volk* and *völkisch* replaced *Nation* and *national* in certain contexts," writes Wells, describing another early nineteenth-century nationalist movement known as the *Deutsche Bewegung* 'German movement' (Wells 1987, 395–96). This movement, whose members included prominent writers, considered the German language to be an organism that, like a hothouse plant, had to be protected from the weakening effect of foreign elements. A perceived threat to German interests from foreign nations was extended to a perception that those nations' languages threatened German. The first to be targeted by the language purists were borrowed French words (*Französelei* 'Frenchifying'); as economic competition from England grew, borrowed English words were targeted. Examples of English influence identified then as harmful include not only many words now accepted, but also short-lived and comical expressions such as *Hemetex* for 'ham and eggs' or *Lehmanns Quatsch* for 'lemon squash' (Wells 1987, 395–396).

The similarity of some of these ideas to twentieth-century Nazi nationalist rhetoric is clear, though the Nazi purpose would be destruction of entire peoples rather than simply of foreign words. The linguistic purity movement, along with anthropological theories about race that flourished in the early twentieth century, provided a vocabulary and a frame of reference for later Nazi justification of xenophobia, war, invasion, terror, and genocide.

German as a Literary Language

Not the spirit of linguistic nationalism, but the ideal of universality had motivated the eighteenth and nineteenth century's great flowering of German letters. The works of poets and writers such as Friedrich Lessing, Johann Wolfgang Goethe, Friedrich Schiller, and Friedrich Gottlieb Klopstock were recognized in Europe and America not only as German literature but as world literature. "By the end of the eighteenth century there could be no doubt that German was one of the great literary languages of the world," write Chambers and Wilkie (1984, 50). The universalist ideals of Germany's eighteenth-century writers lived on during the German Confederation and into the post-1871 German national age. The work of these great writers was accepted both at home and abroad as art that transcended nationality, but Germany was understood as a special *Land der Dichter und Denker* 'land of poets and thinkers'—a formulation that was accepted abroad as well—particularly in the Germanophilic United States of the time (see chapter 6).

Throughout the nineteenth century, German scholars initiated serious study of the Germanic language and literature of the Middle Ages, and they established a fund of information and analysis that is still yielding insights today. The monumental dictionary of the German language, Jakob and Wilhelm Grimm's *Deutsches Wörterbuch*, begun by them in 1852 and completed by others in the twentieth century, is one example. The cultural authority brought to German by the great writers of the eighteenth century, and by scholars of the period following, provided a standard for clarity and precision in German prose writing. This seemed for a time set to replace the dense and clause-ridden Latinate style of German first opposed by the Humanists of the fifteenth century and their colleague, the monk and Bible translator Martin Luther. However, by the end of the nineteenth century the Latinate style was to prevail in nonliterary prose (Stedje 2001, 148).

This dense style moved from government and other bureaucratic documents to scientific and academic writing and to much of German philosophy. Some of the German literature of the twentieth century represented an attempt to reclaim directness and simplicity in German writing. Examples are the *Neue Sachlichkeit* 'New Objectivity' of the 1920s, and the works of writers of the *Gruppe 47* 'Group 47', begun in 1947. But in spite of these attempts, German writing overall since the second half of the nineteenth century has been highly accomplished, but also highly expressionistic (in literature) and dense and convoluted (in literary as well as nonliterary prose), not easily read by the uninitiated. In the first half of the nineteenth century, German philosophy in particular seemed to glory in difficult prose. "Fichte, Schelling, Hegel—each of the three remains to this day a byword for obscurity," comments Bryan Magee (1999, 32). The writing style of the philosophers, a prestigious jewel in Germany's cultural crown, was very influential. One result is the gap, much more strongly marked than in the Anglo-American tradition, between the written and the spoken language.

Intellectual Life in the Nineteenth Century

Germany during the years after the founding of the Second Reich was lively, productive, and influential in society and politics, not only within Germany but also across Europe and into America. "Liberal thinkers fanned the sparks of political change," writes Ozment (2004, 182). Philosophers Ludwig Feuerbach, Friedrich Hegel, and Friedrich Nietzsche electrified Germany and Europe with their academic arguments. Meanwhile, "closer to the street, reactionary intellectuals, with their own brew of romanticism, nationalism, racial theory, and Social Darwinism shaped a new-age chauvinistic culture . . . and fed a sociocultural revolt against the past that contributed substantially to Germany's twentieth-century catastrophes," writes Ozment (2004, 182).

One of these intellectuals, Karl Marx, had believed the National Assembly of 1848 would usher in a classless society. In that year, he and Friedrich Engels published the Communist Manifesto. Marx later moved to England and led the international Communist movement, exhorting workers to change their political situation by force. While the Communist revolution he hoped for did not occur in Germany, something happened which Marx might have approved of but did not foresee: reforms instituted first in the new German Reich actually looked in the end like a moderate form of Communism (Ozment 2004, 190–191); they were to provide a model for twentieth-century social welfare states all over Europe.

Meanwhile, as Steven Ozment writes, the *völkisch* 'folkish' movement viewed Germanness itself as a basic value. He continues, "German racial theorists took a first building block from Kant, who hypothesized a connection between geography, racial characteristics, and what he called a people's 'life force'" (Ozment 2004, 196). While these early racial theories were not for the most part directed explicitly against Jews, it was easy enough for racialists to extend them by imagining that Jewish culture had a power that threatened Germany because it motivated Jews to resist assimilation. The actual truth of the matter was that German Jews in the nineteenth and twentieth centuries were assimilating successfully and rapidly, and that this very assimilation was used by the Nazis as an argument first to separate them from German society and then to eliminate them.

One of the most prominent writers on this topic was Houston Stewart Chamberlain, son of an Englishman who had become a German. Chamberlain's 1899 book *Foundations of the Nineteenth Century* argued that the Teutons were the superior European race and that the Jews deserved no part in German history. When Chamberlain was on his deathbed, the young and struggling Nazi Party leader Adolf Hitler visited him and kissed the dying man's hands in tribute. "Although no one could have imagined it at the time, that kiss began the long descent of German racism into Jewish persecution and genocide," writes Ozment (2004, 197).

Social Democracy and the *Kulturkampf*

By the mid-nineteenth century the major European states were more secular than Christian, a situation of which the Roman Church took a dim view. Pope Pius IX's 1864 encyclical *Syllabus of Errors* condemned the separation of church and state, nonsectarian schools, religious pluralism, and toleration—all proud accomplishments in Prussia as well as in other secular European states. Further, the Pope declared papal infallibility in 1870, classifying kings as subject to the Pope in matters of faith and morals (Ozment 2004, 215). Meanwhile, the North German Confederation had challenged the Church's view of itself as supreme when it recognized in 1869 the equal rights of all German citizens, Christian or Jewish. The same recognition became the law of the Second Reich in 1871, when Chancellor Otto Bismarck proclaimed the emancipation of the Jews (Ozment 2004, 205).

In addition, Bismarck ended the traditional German cooperation with the Roman Church, maintaining that religion and state should be kept apart. The resulting conflict, called the *Kulturkampf* 'culture war' ended in a stalemate with the death of Pius IX and the succession of Pope Leo XIII, after which both the Church and the new German state backed away from confrontation (Ozment 2004, 217). The established churches in Germany—Lutheran and Catholic—continued their state-sanctioned existence within a substantially secular state, a situation that still exists today.

Daily Life in the German Reich

The *Gründerzeit* 'Founders' Time', the era of the start of the new German nation, soon developed its own style. "The former plain ways of the old upper class—dictated by the Prussian motto *Mehr sein als scheinen* 'Be more than you seem', and also a chronic lack of money— gave way to excessive pomp and nouveau riche ostentation in all areas of life," writes Hagen Schulze (1998, 157). This ostentatious style was to become an aggravating factor in the class struggles that were developing in the German Reich.

The transformation of Germany from an agricultural state to an industrialized one reinforced the class differences. By the end of the century the small towns of mid-nineteenth-century Germany had become large cities. By then railway links connected virtually the entire industrialized northwest, making all the more noticeable the contrasts with the still undeveloped eastern regions. Craftsmen and artisans throughout the country feared unemployment as their work became mechanized; the growing host of factory workers became central to the new labor unions and left-leaning political parties. In the cities, residential neighborhoods reflected economic divisions: leafy neighborhoods of large and comfortable villa homes for the haves, sooty apartment blocks for the have-nots. Ethnic and religious differences between the German majority and French,

Polish, Danish, and Jewish populations played out as political tensions.

A serious recession hit in the early 1870s, and farmers, workers of all kinds, and importers of foreign goods were particularly affected. The health, accident, disability, and old-age insurance schemes initiated by Bismarck softened the blows of economic downturns as well as those of Socialist and Communist street protests. Nonetheless, thousands of people who had moved from the poverty-stricken countryside into the cities in hopes of finding work found instead more poverty. In 1800 90 percent of the population of the German states lived in the country, while by 1871 more than half lived in cities of at least 5,000. In 1800 there were only two cities with populations of over 100,000; a century later there were 33 (Schulze 1998, 164).

Late nineteenth-century urban Germany aspired to achieve order above almost all else, perhaps because it made bearable this large-scale movement into densely populated cities. An ideal of mutual responsibility and duty, long traditional in the German regions, was maintained: city authorities were responsible for maintaining order and treating citizens fairly; correspondingly, citizens had a duty to obey them. Children were the responsibility not just of their parents, but of all adults; in turn the children had a duty to obey their elders. Visitors to German cities today may experience a modern-day application of this view at crosswalks, where adults who start to cross on red may be admonished by strangers, especially if there are children present, to "set an example for the children" by obeying the lights.

The standard of living of ordinary Germans had increased as the nineteenth century went on, and with it the population grew: Germany had 25 million people in 1816; by 1880 the population was 49 million. The Imperial Constitution of 1871 guaranteed all citizens *Freizügigkeit*, the right to change their place of residence, which, as C. J. Wells writes "must have significantly swelled town populations, again with social and linguistic effects" (1987, 346). Berlin dominated among the German cities, with a population in 1895 of 1,680,000, or 2,120,000 including its suburbs (Wells 1987, 346).

Compulsory education, which had already been the rule in pre-1871 Prussia, continued in the new Reich and reinforced the learning of High German, the language of speaking and writing in classrooms. Industrial employment contributed to the standardization as well, since workers moving to town from rural areas to take jobs would need to communicate in the standard language. Meanwhile, literacy increased markedly. Among recruits to the Imperial army and navy in 1876, 212 men per 10,000 were illiterate; in 1896 the figure was 15 (Wells 1987, 346).

Germany and Europe

The German Empire managed its internal issues with considerable success. It was viewed with mixed feelings, however, by its European neighbors. They regarded the new, powerful nation as a potential threat. The British statesman Benjamin Disraeli considered the founding of the German Empire "the greatest revolution of the nineteenth century, greater even than the French Revolution. . . . In his view the dangers for the future were incalculable" (Schulze 1998, 163). For a time, Bismarckian diplomacy succeeded in keeping these fears at bay as Germany strove to play the role of good citizen among the nations of Europe. In the coming twentieth century, however, World War I and its spawn, World War II, both instigated by Germany, would realize Europe's worst fears. Alongside the millions of dead soldiers and civilians of many nations, there would be another casualty. The cultural legitimacy of the language of the Dichter und Denker, German poets and thinkers, was to sustain a body blow that is still being felt both at home and abroad in the twenty-first century. We will see in the following chapter how this setback developed.

Timeline: From the Unification of Germany to the Beginning of World War I

Date	In Germanic Territory	In the Rest of the World
1871	Unification of Germany under Chancellor Otto Bismarck; Germany (pop. 41 million) replaces Great Britain (pop. 26 million) as Europe's primary industrial nation	Beginning of Second Industrial Revolution; Charles Darwin (England) publishes *The Descent of Man*
1876	Bayreuth Festspielhaus opens with first complete performance of Wagner's *Ring des Niebelungen*	Alexander Graham Bell (U.S.) invents the telephone

Date	In Germanic Territory	In the Rest of the World
1878	German historian Heinrich Treitschke begins anti-Semite movement; German engineer Karl Benz builds motorized tricycle	
1880	Cologne Cathedral completed (begun 1248)	Gilbert and Sullivan (England) publish *H.M.S. Pinafore*
1888	Kaiser Wilhelm accedes to throne of the German Empire (to 1918); Theodor Fontane publishes *Irrungen, Wirrungen*	Jack the Ripper murders six women in London; Fridtjof Nansen leads exploration party across Greenland on snowshoes
1893	Karl Benz builds a four-wheel automobile	Art Nouveau appears in Europe
1895	Sigmund Freud and Josef Breuer publish *Studies on Hysteria*, introducing psychotherapy; physicist Wilhelm Conrad Röntgen discovers X-rays	London School of Economics and Political Science founded
1898	German Count Ferdinand von Zeppelin builds an airship	H. G. Wells (England) publishes *The War of the Worlds*
1901	Nobel Prizes: Physics, Wilhelm Röntgen; Medicine, Emil Adolf von Behring; Wilhelm Maybach constructs the first Mercedes car; Thomas Mann publishes *Buddenbrooks*	Picasso's Blue Period (to 1905); U.S. President William McKinley assassinated by an anarchist
1905	Nobel Prize in Medicine: Robert Koch for work on tuberculosis; Albert Einstein formulates Special Theory of Relativity	First motor buses in London; Rotary Club founded (Chicago)

continued

Date	In Germanic Territory	In the Rest of the World
1908	British newspaper, *The Daily Telegraph*, publishes interview with Kaiser Wilhelm, whose reckless statements aggravate tensions between England and Germany	King Leopold II transfers the Congo, his private possession since 1885, to Belgium; Union of South Africa established
1912	Nobel Prize for literature: Gerhart Hauptmann; C. G. Jung publishes *The Theory of Psychoanalysis*	S.S. *Titanic* sinks, 1,513 drowned; Sun Yat-Sen founds Kuomintang (Chinese National Party)
1914	Archduke Francis Ferdinand, heir to the Austrian throne, and his wife assassinated in Sarajevo; World War I breaks out, eventually involving all the major European powers and the U.S.	Panama Canal opened; almost 10.5 million immigrants entered the U.S. from southern and eastern Europe between 1905 and 1914

After Grun 2005.

6

Postwar Comeback Times Two
A High Point, a Double Fall from Grace, and Recoveries

A "German Epidemic" Conquers America

"Sentimental? Yes; thank *Gott*, we Germans believe in sentiment, and keep ourselves young *mit* it." The speaker is Professor Friedrich Bhaer, suitor and future husband of Jo March, heroine of *Little Women* (1867), perhaps the most popular girls' novel ever written in America. Jo is visiting New York when she meets Professor Bhaer (soon to become "Fritz"). She is immediately charmed, writing home to her sister Beth, "I wish Americans were as simple and natural as Germans, don't you?"

Jo loves everything about Professor Bhaer—his sentimentality (her interpretation of his request that she call him "thou" as an equivalent of German *du*), his music (he likes to hum classical German *Lieder*), and his language—both his German-tinged English and his native tongue. Lurking in the hallway outside his room at the boardinghouse where both are living, she even listens in with delight as he gives German lessons. Jo knows enough German, though, to shake her head in dismay at his pupil's poor pronunciation. She seems to have been infected by the enthusiasm of the "German epidemic" that Theodore Parker (1810–1860), a New England preacher, abolitionist and Transcendentalist leader, wrote was "affecting men and maidens who have conspired to love everything Teutonic" (quoted in Doyle 2003, 51).

Like Jo's creator Louisa May Alcott, nineteenth-century America, especially literary New England, admired Germany, German ideas, and the German language. Freedom-loving, independent-minded German writers such as Goethe and Schiller, philosophers like Kant and Hegel, and creative musicians like Beethoven, Schumann, and Wagner all found wide appreciation in America. At the pinnacle of Germany's century-long flowering of arts and letters, eighteenth-century German writer Johann Karl August Musäus coined what was to become Germany's favorite sobriquet for itself: *das Land der Dichter und Denker* 'the land of poets and thinkers'. Soon Americans too were using the phrase.

The Germanophiles of America perceived German Romanticism, the artistic and philosophical movement of the early and middle nineteenth century, as anti-authoritarian, universalist, and sensitive. The resulting nineteenth-century "German epidemic" in America was a cultural and esthetic phenomenon, but it had a philosophical and political core.

Not only were German philosophy and literature enormously popular in nineteenth-century America—a forty-volume edition of Goethe's complete works in translation appeared in the United States between 1827 and 1830—but German-themed music had taken the New York arts scene by storm. The three most popular works of the New York opera at midcentury were Gounod's *Faust* (in 1859), Thomas's *Mignon* (in 1866), and Berlioz's *Mefistofele* (in 1868), all based on Goethe's writings.

Other factors, too, had favored the reputation of all things German in America. German immigrants, many or even most from Prussia, arrived in great numbers on American shores during the mid and late nineteenth century; 1.3 million of them were recorded in the 1860 census (Doyle 2003, 51). They were welcomed, particularly in New England, because of their Lutheranism (compatible with New England Protestantism), their social traditions (seen as advanced by progressive New Englanders), their support for education, their art, even their food (plain but tasty and nutritious), writes Doyle (2003, 51). They were perceived as hard working and cultured, at least partly because of Prussian compulsory education, which had a long tradition, predating the 1871 founding of the Second Reich.

But the aggression of Germany in 1914 sent shock waves right to the philosophical core of America's philo-German establishment. The cultural legitimacy that had been so effective after 1871 in establishing German as the national language of the new German Reich was consequently badly wounded abroad, not just in America, but in the entire English-speaking world, in response to the coming of the twentieth-century Great War instigated by Germany. American shock on the eve of World War I in 1914 was great when the much-admired Germany seemed to turn its back on its own humanistic cultural heritage to become the warmonger of the Western world.

The *Dichter und Denker* Go to War

How different the "German epidemic" in America would look fifty years after Theodore Parker named it. By 1918 public discussion focused on an evil *Deutschtum* 'Germanness', defined by Morton Prince as "a mystic paranoid ideal which has permeated the consciousness of the whole [German] nation . . . a system of mental, moral and political ideas organized about . . . the state and the German people as a super-race, superior to all others" (Prince 1918, 12–14). Five months before the end of what was then still called the Great War and not yet World War I, the *New York Times* reported approvingly the end of Deutschtum:

> *German Influence Dying in America*
> We judge from the cheering reports that come from all parts of Wisconsin that the end of Deutschtum's power in the United States is in plain sight. . . . .Deutschtum has in truth been a hydra-headed monster. Evil, cunning, sinuous, it has worked and plotted in our schools, using its language to inculcate moral treason in the unsus-pecting minds of children. (June 23, 1918, n.p.).

Because Germany and the United States were enemies in a bitter war, it was to be expected that average Americans would develop a dislike of Germany. It might not have been expected, though, that even America's intellectual elite would almost immediately stop loving the German language, German literature, German philosophy, and German opera—but that is what happened. On the long view, however, the love wasn't really lost—it just went underground. As it turned out, German–American friendship had deep roots.

The foundation of that friendship, laid in the eighteenth and nineteenth centuries, proved strong enough to survive two devastating world wars and the intervening low points such as those mentioned above. Today approximately 25 percent of Americans claim at least some German ancestry, and there is an undeniable mutual sympathy between Germany and the United States, and between Germans and Americans, which seems to transcend postwar political tensions.

German Cultural Capital Declines

Yet even the long-lasting German–American friendship and the shared DNA could not preserve into the twentieth century the high regard in which German language and literature were once held in America and the rest of the English-speaking world. During the post-World War I period, German immigrants in America took care not to be heard speaking their native language; German language teaching in the schools declined precipitously; and sauerkraut was renamed "liberty cabbage." In Great Britain it was common even for German Jews— already subject to enough discrimination just for their Jewishness—to disguise their German origins by changing their family names.

In the early to mid-nineteenth century, German scholarship had been in a leading position worldwide, explains linguist Ulrich Ammon, who quotes this 1869 statement by Thomas Huxley, prominent English biologist: "Ask the man who is investigating any question profoundly and thoroughly—be it historical, philosophical, physical, literary, or theological; who is trying to make himself master of any subject . . . whether he is not compelled to read half a dozen times as many German as English books" (2004, 159). More publications in the natural sciences were in German than in any other language during the early nineteenth century, although after the 1820s both German and French publications had begun a slow decline while English publications began to increase in number.

By the end of World War I, by contrast, scientists from Belgium and France organized a boycott of German and Austrian scientists, banning them from international science conferences from the end of the war until the mid-1920s, as Ammon reports, which they justified as a response to German scientists' support of wartime military actions (2004, 163). German scientists did eventually regain access to international conferences, but the German language had in the meantime suffered an apparently irreversible decline. The result, according to Roswitha Reinbothe, was that French was strengthened for a time as a European language of science; but, as she writes, "the hegemony of the French language at international associations and congresses was of short duration" (2006, 447); soon English became the dominant language of science, as it remains today not only in Europe but throughout the world.

However, despite all of this, after the November 11, 1918, armistice that ended World War I, the reputation of the German language and culture began slowly to recover, at home as well as abroad. The Weimar Republic, Germany's postwar democratic government, served as a magnet and a showcase for German creative energies and drew favorable attention from the European art establishment, though, it must be admitted, more in retrospect than in its own time. But the German language, in spite of the German-speaking world's considerable cultural output during the twentieth century, never quite regained its pre-World War I status. "Even today only German speakers recognise Brecht not just as a dramatist but as one of the great 20th-century lyric poets. . . . About the only branch of Weimar literature that broke out of the Central European enclosure was the anti-war fiction of the late 1920s, headed by Remarque's *All Quiet on the Western Front*," writes Eric Hobsbawm (2008, n.p.). The revival of German culture in its home country was not enough to restore its luster abroad and was not accompanied by the economic or political strength needed to bring back German's position as a language of modern, not just historical, *Dichter und Denker*. At home, satirist Karl Kraus had already mocked the *Dichter und Denker* with his 1909 rhyming anti-slogan *Richter und Henker* 'judges and hangmen'. The latter was made even more famous in the German-speaking world when postwar Swiss writer Friedrich Dürrenmatt borrowed it in 1950 for his Nazi war crime-themed literary mystery novella, *Der Richter und sein Henker* (translated in 1955 literally, with no hint of the wordplay, as *The Judge and His Hangman*).

The coming of Adolf Hitler and Nazism and the subsequent brutality of World War II and the Holocaust made Americans forget once again that there was anything admirable about the German language, or indeed anything German. Memory faded of the philosophical, humanistic language and culture that had so captivated nineteenth-century America. After 1933, the year of Hitler's ascendance to power, "German was not widely spoken in the West outside the transatlantic diaspora or read outside classical scholarship," writes Hobsbawm (2008, n.p.). After 1939 the harsh tones of soldiers— *Achtung! Hände hoch!* 'Attention! Hands up!' replaced in the popular mind the once well- known *Mignon's Song*. Its signature lyric, from Goethe's novel *Wilhelm Meister*, "*Kennst du das Land, wo die Zitronen blühn*" 'Know'st thou the land where the lemons bloom', had been set to music by Beethoven, Schubert, and the French opera composer Ambroise Thomas, among many others. It had been a favorite of Professor Bhaer and his sweetheart Jo.

But, Ulrich Ammon argues, the very real damage done to the worldwide status of German language and culture by two world wars was not the primary cause of the decline of German: "Germany was never a scientific center, nor was German a world language, to the same extent as the United States or English are today. In addition, the political basis of German prevalence was more fragile and problematic" (Ammon 2004, 159). Ammon believes that the decline of German and the rising prominence of English would have co-occurred even without the world wars, because of the economic preeminence of the United States, which was well on the way to being the number one economic world power even before World War I (Ammon 2004, 160). Nonetheless, the Nazi war machine drained resources, both economic and human, from German scientific enterprises. Of the thousands of scientists, professors, and other intellectuals expelled from Germany and Austria, most emigrated to the English-speaking world: the United States, Britain, and Australia. Even more were murdered in concentration camps during the twelve-year Nazi Reich. "The Nazi period stands out, among other atrocities, as a spectacular example of a country's scientific self-destruction," Ammon writes (164).

Nazism and the German Language

The hate and war machine of the Third Reich created a vocabulary largely designed both to glorify the state and to put the best face on genocide, suppression of free expression, and totalitarianism. After Germany's defeat, this Nazi lexicon went almost instantly out of use, leaving the modern language with a host of unacceptable words that, except in historical references, were and are no longer used even by current neo-Nazis, who often try to cloud over, at least for public consumption, their kinship to the historical Nazis. Among such words are *Führer* 'leader', the state title of Adolf Hitler (which is now used only in compounds), and *Endlösung* 'final solution', a euphemism for the wholesale murder of Jews. *Selektion* 'selection', a euphemism for the sorting of concentration camp prisoners into those to be killed immediately and those who will be forced into work, is not used in ordinary language, although it survives in scientific discourse, for example in *natürliche Selektion* 'natural selection'.

When rousing the crowds, however, the Nazis, far from using euphemisms, brought the German language to the boil. They used strong or aggressive-sounding words for ordinary situations, such as *Kampf* 'battle' for 'political or social issue'. Compound words with *Blut* 'blood' served to keep the Nazi slogan *Blut und Boden* 'blood and soil' (i.e., genetic origin and national territory) in the foreground of public awareness. Examples are *eigenblütig* 'same-blooded' and *Blutsverwandtschaft* 'blood relation'. Even the ominous Blut und Boden itself—used so often that it became a shorthand term for Nazi ideology—was truncated further in popular discourse to the comical-sounding *Blubo* (Seidel and Seidel-Slotty 1961, 78). Blut und Boden became a marketing campaign to popularize Nazi nationalism and racism: non-Germanic peoples (such as Jews and Slavs) were to be slaughtered or enslaved; territories believed by the Nazis to be rightfully German were to be conquered and appended to Germany. Given the widespread, and effective, takeover of the language by Nazi propagandists, it was inevitable that those who suffered from Nazi aggression, or even witnessed it from afar, would recoil from the German language too.

Nonetheless, after the Nazis were defeated in 1945, memories in the United States and England of the language of the Dichter und Denker stirred once again, their echo revived by the thousands of well-educated refugees from Hitler's Germany who had settled in English-speaking lands. "It was . . . Hitler who produced the community of refugees who came to play a disproportionately prominent part in the countries of refuge and to whom Weimar's memory owes so much. . . . In Britain émigrés transformed art history and visual culture," writes Hobsbawm (2008, n.p.). Much pre- and immediate postwar German immigration to the United States consisted of not only first-rank scientists such as Albert Einstein, but also artists, writers, and film actors and directors central to the development of the Hollywood film industry, as well as otherwise ordinary people—although they were understood as refugees from Germany, not representatives of it. Nonetheless, many educated even if not always prominent émigrès earned their living by teaching German language and literature in high schools and universities, and in the final analysis they mended the broken image of their native language and culture.

Postwar, the German language was again considered an appropriate object of study for young Americans. By the 1950s and 1960s German was once more a prestige language, but now its prestige rested on its past as a language of mathematics and science (even if not a dominant one) rather than of literature, and it owed this revival to Cold War concerns about competing with the Soviet Union and to the accomplishments, past and current, of German- and Austrian-born scientists, rather than to classical German culture.

Currently, study of German in the United States runs a poor third to Spanish (the hands-down winner) and French (itself a weak second; Furman et al., 2007). To be clear, though, cultural legitimacy is only one explanation for this trend. Latin American trade with the United States, as well as substantial immigration from Mexico and Latin America, are probably the driving forces of Spanish language study in the United States.

Ironically enough, a strictly domestic American event may have dealt another body blow to the European languages of science, German included. That was the decision in the late 1960s and early 1970s of many, perhaps most, American colleges and universities to eliminate the foreign language requirement. This action, taken not with the worldwide standing of English in mind but rather as a result of educational policy debates concerning the role of all required subjects in university education, resulted within a few years in a further reduction in the number of American scientists who were able to read European scientific publications. Ammon argues that this decision had the circular effect of encouraging scientists worldwide to publish in English in order to garner the greatest readership, while further encouraging American scientists to believe that reading foreign publications was not only difficult, but unnecessary (Ammon 2004, 164). "Under these circumstances," he writes, "only a miracle could have preserved the previous international standing of German as a language of science" (Ammon 2004, 165).

German Revives at Home

At the war's end in 1945 the German language had a major task of recovery before it. Not only Germans and Austrians, but also their language, experienced the opprobrium of a world shocked by the murderous behavior of the Nazis. The German language suffered loss of prestige even in Switzerland, neutral in the war, and in Luxemburg, which had been invaded and occupied by the Nazis—both of them multilingual countries whose peoples were eager to emphasize that they were not German. But life went on; Germans, Austrians, Swiss, and Luxemburgers spoke, read, and wrote in German.

In Germany, a *Stunde Null* 'zero hour' literary movement rejected the entire problematic German past and sought to begin again on a fresh slate. This movement led to *Gruppe 47* 'Group 47' begun in 1947 in the postwar ruins by Alfred Andersch, Walter Kolbenhoff, and others, as described by Kolbenhoff in his memoir (Kolbenhoff 2008, 100–102). The group sponsored informal writing circles and gave a yearly literary prize to writers such as Günter Eich, Heinrich Böll, Ilse Aichinger, Ingeborg Bachmann, Martin Walser, and Günter Grass, all of whom became literary lights of the German-speaking world in the following decades. These writers brought new voices to German literature, and after a time even the old German literary tradition could be seen to have survived, and in fact its survival provided encouragement to believe that German culture could once again be a point of pride. A new German literature arose, and the German language began to regain its prestige, at least at home, although not its previous strong position in the European tradition.

The postwar German literary revival was to play an important role in this recovery, serving as a denazification of the language through the works of exiled authors such as Thomas Mann. His novel *Doktor Faustus* (begun in 1943, published in 1947) updated to the Nazi years the Faust and the devil legend; it was read as a metaphor in which Germany sold its soul to Nazism. Since Mann, who had fled Nazism and emigrated to the United States, was living in California at the time of publication of the novel (translated into English and published in the United States in 1948), it almost certainly attracted more international attention than it would have if the author had been living in Germany. Mann, who as a young writer in Germany had won the 1929 Nobel Prize for Literature, now continued his writing career from America. In his new homeland his work was so popular that he even became a Book-of-the-Month Club author with his 1951 comic novel *Der Erwählte*, translated in the same year as *The Holy Sinner*.

Also effective in repairing the image of German culture abroad were the works of Heinrich Böll, who addressed from a moral point of view the topic of German individual behavior during the Nazi times in novels such as *Gruppenbild mit Dame* (1971, translated in 1973 as *Group Portrait with Lady*). Günter Grass also took as his topic the ordinary people of Hitler's Germany and earned a reputation in such novels as *Die Blechtrommel* (1959; translated in 1961 as *The Tin Drum*) and *Hundejahre* (1963; translated as 1965 as *Dog Years*), for demanding that his fellow Germans own up to their own behavior during the Nazi years. Grass, however, caused considerable controversy with his 2006 admission that he himself had been a recruit to the Nazi *Waffen-SS*, an elite wartime combat unit that preferred soldiers with a particularly strong ideological commitment to Nazism. For this near lifetime of silence on a crucial element of his past, Grass was judged harshly by many commentators, even some who had been his admirers, such as sociologist and *New Left Review* founding editor Norman Birnbaum, who concluded: "Grass treated himself with the indulgence he did not hesitate to describe as a moral defect in others" (2006, n.p.).

The German Democratic Republic, 1949–1989

The twentieth-century history of Germany provides a second example of totalitarianism: the communist German Democratic Republic (commonly referred to in the West as East Germany or the GDR), successor to the postwar Soviet occupied zone. The GDR left no more permanent traces in the German language than had the previous Nazi Third Reich, to which it was fundamentally opposed in an ideological sense; it ended nearly as disgraced by its own deeds as did the Third Reich.

The linguistic legacy of the GDR is both a garden-variety socialistic bureaucratese and a list of euphemisms intended to prettify its at best irritating and at worst noxious actions and policies. One prominent example is the term *Schutzwall* 'protective wall', the GDR government's name for the fortification at its border with West Germany (the Federal Republic of Germany). In the West, this was called simply *Die Mauer* 'the wall'. The GDR name derived from official insistence that its purpose was to keep the capitalistic West from invading, either as a corporate entity or through individuals acting for other states. In fact, no one was killed for attempting to enter the GDR. But an estimated 190 were killed attempting to exit the GDR at Berlin, and another 800 were killed attempting to exit at other points on the border.

A Marxist term favored by the GDR government on this theme is *Republikflucht* 'republic flight', the official name for attempting to leave the country (a crime punishable by a long prison term, in the event that the person fleeing was not fatally shot in the attempt). After the collapse of the GDR government and the unification of East and West Germany in 1990, Republikflucht and the "crime," it named, along with the term "Schutzwall," were dropped into the dustbin of history.

The wall itself, of course, was torn down, the job begun by enthusiastic amateurs and continued by West German bulldozers.

Governments attempting to control the language that was used to describe their misdeeds are fated to be mocked by the wit born of popular contempt. This fate came to the GDR during its forty-year existence, even before it was ushered off the world stage in 1989. For example, East German wits altered the Socialist cliché *Sozialistische Wertegemeinschaft* 'Socialist values community' by one letter, to *Sozialistische Wartegemeinschaft* 'Socialist waiting community', an ironic reference to the hours-long standing in line that characterized shopping of any kind in the GDR, including for basic groceries. And East German Party Secretary and head of state Eric Honeker was referred to in popular parlance as *Honi*, sounding much like English "Honey." Whether this was an expression of affection or mockery remained conveniently difficult to parse, since mockery would have invited Stasi retribution.

Tendencies in Contemporary German

The horrors of war and of the Nazi years, the postwar recovery of German society, the birth and death of the GDR, and the revival of the literary tradition were dramatic way stations in the life of the German language and its speakers. Even in times of stability, however, the language continues to change. The causes for the changes are the same in the twenty-first century as they were in the fifth millennium BC. Conditions of life progress and require speakers to coin new vocabulary to cope with them; outsiders come into the territory to trade, to make war, or to settle. The encounter often ends up changing the language of both the natives and the newcomers.

At the level of individual word modification or creation, particular tendencies seem to be especially congenial to the German language. These recur through time and continue to be productive in creating both casual and bureaucratic language.

Two opposite tendencies, compounding and shortening, have been evident in German for centuries. As an example of compounding, the domestic partner who is a spouse in all but name is the unwieldy *Lebensabschnittgefährte* (m.) or *Lebensabschnittgefährtin* (f.) 'life phase companion'. The opposite tendency, to truncate compounds, creates convenient nicknames. First names have long been shortened and then topped off with an *-i* to create an affectionate form: *Wolfi* for *Wolfgang*,

Moni for *Monika*. Truncation is also at work to make nonaffectionate short versions of serious, even deadly phenomena, as in the previously mentioned *Blubo* for *Blut und Boden*. Other examples are provided by the short forms for two dreaded but now defunct German secret police forces: *Gestapo* for the Nazi *Geheime Staatspolizei* 'secret state police' and *Stasi* for the East German *Staatssicherheitsdienst* 'state security service'.

Compounding, often by combining different parts of speech such as adjectives, participles, nouns, or verbs, proceeds as it always has. This is a tendency going as far back in the language's history as Gothic times. Today it has been adopted by the German advertising industry, creating such new words as *leichtflockig* 'light-fluffy' and *pflegeleicht* 'care-easy'. Adjectives often used as suffixes for the creation of trendy new combinations include *fertig* 'ready' (*Schrankfertig* 'cupboard ready', meaning arriving from the laundry folded) and *sicher* 'safe' or 'proof' (*Bombensicher* 'bomb-proof'). Also common are suffixes such as *-bar* '-able' (*undenkbar* 'unthinkable') and *-haft* 'ish' (*schulmeisterhaft* 'schoolmasterish').

Grammar is changing too; for example, the decline in use of the genitive case has been noted for at least a century. Functioning somewhat like the English possessive *'s*, the genitive was once used in scores of idioms which today are out of use; and the prepositions that originally caused their following noun phrases to appear in the genitive (*wegen des Wetters*) are now being used in the dative, at least in conversation (*wegen dem Wetter*). But the dative too now "faces competition from [accusative] prepositional objects: for example *jemandem schreiben* 'write someone [dat.]' is being replaced by *an jemanden schreiben* 'to write to someone' (Glück and Sauer 1995, 106). The traditional comparative adjective ending*–er* (*leichter* 'lighter') is now sometimes replaced with *mehr* 'more' (*mehr leicht* 'more light'), as in English, a change Glück and Sauer describe as "for the sake of emphasis" (1995, 109).

There are changes in word order too, in both speaking and writing: often, elements such as dependent verbs that, according to traditional grammar, must appear at the end of the sentence, do not. Additionally, in dependent clauses, for example after conjunctions such as *weil* 'because' and *dass* 'that', sometimes the verb appears in second position rather than in the grammatically prescribed final position.

Considerations of gender reference are complicated in German by the grammatical gender system. Thus, *der Arzt* 'the physician' is masculine, the derived form *die Ärztin* is feminine; there is no form for referring definitively to both male and female physicians, although, previous to late twentieth- and early twenty-first-century awareness of the need for nonsexist language, the masculine form played this role. This is true of all professional and nationality forms and many other nouns of agency (*der Raucher* '[male] smoker'/*die Raucherin* 'female smoker'), leaving no "generic" forms to indicate all persons of either sex in the specified category. Feminists argue that the masculine form cannot logically be both a reference to men only and a generic, and that the use of the masculine as a generic disadvantages women insofar as they are left out of the reference. They have suggested slashed forms to indicate inclusive gender, for example *Student/in* 'student', plural *Student/innen* or *StudentInnen* 'students', or the use of a neuter "generic" article, for example *das Student*. Very recently, gender-neutral neologisms have been coined to avoid the problem altogether, such as *die Studierenden* 'those studying'. These forms, however, have not gone much beyond the academic environment, and they are not completely accepted even there.

It is being debated whether these changes are features solely of colloquial speech (in the case of word order changes) or of academic language (in the case of gender-neutral nouns), which will not be taken up in the general language arena. Some of the changes, such as in word order, have begun to appear in the written media, arguably an indicator of long-term survival. English made similar changes, including the decline and disappearance of case distinctions and word order differences, as well as of gender-inclusive terms (for example, forms such as 'poetess' and 'editress' have died out in favor of 'poet' and 'editor' for both sexes; and, more recently, 'server' replaced 'waitress/ waiter'), and hence some Germans view such language changes as Americanisms. However, since similar developments occurred long ago in other Germanic languages such as Swedish, Norwegian, Danish, and Dutch, it could more plausibly be argued that they are inherent in the development of Germanic languages. It is nonetheless true that the influence of American English on contemporary German is considerable.

English-Language Influence

The fact that Germany lost two major wars to the Allies including England and the United States surely contributed to pressure on the German language from English. The American prominence in the Allied victory over Germany in World War II is a strong factor in the very noticeable influence of specifically American English in the twentieth and twenty-first centuries. Hollywood films have popularized many American expressions in Germany—actually a case of immigrants "sending" their new language back home, since the American film industry throughout the twentieth century was dominated by German and Austrian refugees. Popular music has provided a second strong cultural influence, beginning in the postwar years with rock 'n' roll and continuing on to the folk and protest music of the 1960s and 1970s, to the rock music of the late twentieth and early twenty-first centuries. In film and music it is difficult to sort out the historical factors from the economic ones. Germany and Austria (the Nazi version of Großdeutschland) were defeated and then occupied by American, British, Russian, and French forces—but the economic and political might of the United States in the postwar world had a pull of its own, and after the fall of the Soviet Union the United States was the sole standing superpower. Even though the practitioners of rock music took a stance as cultural outsiders, their influence abroad could hardly be divorced from their American origins, and so rock music became another aspect of American power.

Lexical borrowing from American English is so widespread that especially the older generation is annoyed by the prevalence of English words in public discourse. However understandable the annoyance, it is temporary, since either the words will disappear quickly or they will be well and truly absorbed by German, at which time every native speaker will understand them. The borrowing of words into a language has historically had a positive, rather than a negative, influence on the borrowing language, enriching vocabulary but not causing language decline.

A different case is presented by long-term extensive public use of a nonnative language as an alternative means of communication. This often results in the decline or death of the native language, even if that process takes a long time. Some people question whether English is having, or will in the future have, this effect upon German.

English as a Lingua Franca

Of considerable concern to many in the German-speaking countries has been a tendency for English to serve as a lingua franca even within German environments, as an inducement to attract foreigners who have not learned German. This phenomenon is increasingly happening at German universities, which are marketing programs to foreign students. Ursula Kimpel of the University of Tübingen, Germany, provides a startling example (quoted in a University of Maryland newsletter): "German universities are offering more courses in English because of the large number of students coming from abroad. German is unfortunately a language in decline. We need and want our professors to be able to teach effectively in English" (University of Maryland 2005, 13). Is this tendency only bowing to the inevitable, or is it also a contribution to the decline of German? German scholars, in the past far more accepting of English influence than, for example, the French, are debating the point. Linguist Peter Eisenberg argues that "the influence of English is still marginal compared to the deep changes of the derivational and inflectional system caused by Latin and French" (2004, 135). Still, the highly visible and audible presence of English in both the popular and the professional spheres of German is causing disquiet among some observers.

Academic writing specifically comes under the microscope of several German linguists. Konrad Ehlich, for example, predicts that "one of the probable globalization victims will be the linguistic diversity of scientific communication" (2004, 174), and calls for strengthening of European multilingualism, arguing that "the philosophical reflection and theoretical foundation of science are unavertibly thrown back to those languages from which the language of science was supposed to differentiate itself" (2004, 177). Ulrich Ammon mentions the need for "continuously modernizing German as a language of science," adding that "it seems at times that German scientists and scholars are not up to the task. They often simply adopt English terms, even in the humanities" (Ammon 2004, 168).

Winfried Thielmann also believes that the widespread use of English for scientific publications has impeded the development of new academic and technical vocabulary in German and other European languages. In addition, he raises the point that German-speaking scholars' writing in English is often misunderstood or unread abroad, in particular when its syntactic and argument structures are too directly translated from German. "The major difficulties of writing English . . . lie in areas still hardly understood, such as text organisation and everyday scientific language," Thielmann writes (2003, 95), calling for more support for German scholars who write in English, either to help them learn the pragmatic demands of English academic writing or for more sophisticated translation services. He laments governmental pressure on German universities "to follow the trend and offer lectures in English to serve the foreign market" (2003, 96).

Although issues of English influence and the future of German as a prestige language of science are matters of discussion among academics, they are far from the daily concerns of ordinary people. In five German-speaking countries (Germany, Austria, Switzerland, Luxembourg, and Liechtenstein) people continue to speak German as they always have and to communicate in their common language across their borders, even though the standard German of these five nations differs somewhat.

Spelling Reforms

English-speaking readers may be unfamiliar with the concept of governmentally induced language reform, but it is a fact of life in Europe. In the United States, for example, publishers of dictionaries and grammar books poll professional writers and other educated people on the acceptability of evolving grammatical (*it is I/it's me*) and spelling (*catalogue/catalog*) conventions. The results guide entries in subsequent editions of the reference works. In German-speaking Europe, by contrast, spelling reform has been driven primarily by government action. However, newspaper and book publishers both in German-speaking and in English-speaking countries commonly set, and alter, their own spelling and grammar standards in-house. Of course, as a practical matter, in democracies it is only in the public schools that spelling regulations can be enforced by government decree, as the reader will see below.

After failed attempts beginning in 1876, the first international spelling reform of German took place in 1901 (Zabel 1995, 6). The reformed spelling was introduced almost immediately thereafter in schools of all the German-speaking nations, making it the only aspect of language benefiting from almost unanimous consensus among German-language nations (Clyne 1995, 30). The reform was a modest one, amounting to validating regularizations already recommended by the *Vollständiges orthographisches Wörterbuch* published in 1880 by the Leipzig firm of Duden (which remains the publisher of language reference works most widely considered authoritative in Germany). The modest changes from earlier practice that were thus ratified by the German government included: (1) elimination of the silent *h* after *t*. Examples are *Tür* for *Thur* 'door', *tun* for *thun* 'do'; (2) replacing *c* in loanwords with *k* or *z*, depending upon the pronunciation. Examples are *zentral* for *central*, *Klasse* for *Classe*, *Medizin* for *Medicin*. (3) Replacement of *aa* with *a*, as in *Wagen* for *Waagen*. At the time, it was recognized that more spelling reform was needed and that these changes were provisional. "Since 1902 virtually every year has seen a (failed) attempt to achieve the reforms," writes Sally Johnson (2000, 109).

The second reform was initiated after a multiyear study by an international committee of the German-speaking nations and ended with their recommendations in 1996. These were adopted by an agreement signed in Vienna by the governments of Germany, Austria, Switzerland, and Liechtenstein. During a specified transition period until August 2005, both the traditional and the new spellings would be acceptable. A list of the changes fills many pages (see a complete accounting in Zabel 1995). The 1996 spelling reform includes, among other changes, new rules for syllabic division, punctuation, and separation of certain compound verbs (for example, *radfahren* 'to ride a bicycle' became *Rad fahren*). Probably the most noticeable for foreigners are the new rules for (but not abolition of) the German character *ß* and the new approval of tripled consonants in compound words. *Daß* 'that' is now *dass*, although *Straße* 'street' remains *Straße*; and *Schiffahrt* 'journey by ship' is now *Schifffahrt*.

The new rules were implemented, as planned, in schools of the signing nations as of the 2004–2005 school year. However, the Rechtschreibereform 'spelling reform' has so far not quite settled into peaceful acceptance. Resistance emerged almost immediately. The German states of Bavaria and North Rhine Westphalia officially rejected the new rules and refused to institute them in public schools. Switzerland accepted the new rules overall but, since it had long ago stopped using the *ß*, continued to replace it in all cases with *ss*, having obtained special dispensation to do so. Luxemburg did not sign the agreement. Hundreds of prominent German authors, including Günter Grass, Siegfried Lenz, Martin Walser, Hans Magnus Enzensberger, and Walter Kempowski, protested against the new rules and took the case to the German Supreme Court, which upheld the legality of the spelling reform.

After a chaotic few years during which major publications refused to accept the new spelling standard, the German *Kultusministerkonferenz* announced in 2006 a revised spelling reform which revoked some of the most controversial spelling changes. This compromise calmed most of the resistance and resulted in a spelling standard to which most German-language publications now adhere (Rat für deutsche Rechtschreibung 2009, n.p.). It is debatable whether all of the controversy concerning the spelling reform is to be taken at face value.

First, the long period between the approval of the new rules (1996) and the directive making them official policy (2005) may, rather than easing the transition, have aggravated it by providing time for opposition to organize. Second, it is possible that resistance to the reforms is actually expression of resistance to other cultural and government institutions (Johnson 2000, 125).

For whatever reasons, currently the publications that may be most confidently relied upon to reflect the new German spelling include government publications, German and Austrian dictionaries, and, ironically, German language textbooks published in non-German-speaking countries such as the United States.

German at Home: Four National Standards

Four of the German-speaking countries—Austria, Germany, Luxem-burg, and Switzerland—have their own national variety of Standard German. In addition, these four have regional dialects, and two have non-German national languages as well: Luxemburg (with French and Lëtzebuergesch) and Switzerland (with French, Italian, and Romansch). A fifth country, Liechtenstein, has several regional dialects but uses the German national standard in school teaching and in official communica-tion. The four national varieties are mutually understandable, even if their pronunciation, spelling (in the case of the Swiss lack of β), and idiomatic phrases differ. Michael Clyne describes German as pluricentric, that is, "a language with several interacting centres, each providing a national variety with at least some of its own (codified) norms" (Clyne 1995, 20).

This pluricentricity, however, does not imply symmetry; rather, the standard language of Germany is clearly dominant, both within the German-speaking world and in the world outside. This means that the German national variety is often seen as the standard against which the other varieties are perceived. Moreover, this view is the most common one not just in Germany but also in the other three German-speaking countries. In German as well as in Austrian and Swiss publications, the Standard German of Germany is sometimes referred to as *Binnendeutsch* ('internal German'), implicitly accepting its primacy (Clyne 1995, 24). However, nationalist sentiments and traditions keep the other national standard varieties of German alive and flourishing in Austria, Luxemburg, and Switzerland as well.

Outside of the German-speaking world, the German national stan-dard is almost always the variety taught in German language classes;

and German, rather than Austrian or Swiss, habits of pronunciation and idiom are the goal for nonnative German language learners abroad. Both learners and teachers assume that the German variety will be understood in all German-speaking countries and often consider Swiss, Austrian, and Luxemburg national varieties to be merely dialects or regional variants. The first assumption—that German Standard German is universally understood—is accurate. The second—that the other national varieties are not standard, but dialects or regional variants—is not. In reality, each of the four German-speaking nations has codified its own standard German language. In each of the four nations, publications, school lessons, and radio and TV broadcasts reflect the national standard. However, the differences in phonology (pronunciation), vocabulary, and syntax (grammar) between the four national varieties are not very great.

In fact, some Swiss and Austrian standard forms overlap with regional dialect forms of Germany. Examples are Austrian *Jänner* for German Standard *Januar* 'January', or the Austrian use of *sein* 'be' as an auxiliary with *stehen* 'stand', *liegen* 'lie', and *sitzen* 'sit', where German Standard calls for *haben* 'have' (Clyne 1995, 25); all of these are present in Bavarian dialects of Germany as well. The greeting *guten Tag* 'good day' common in north and central Germany becomes in both Austria and (South German) Bavaria *grüß Gott* 'God greet you', and in Switzerland *grüezi/grüessdi/grüessech* (variants reflect differing degrees of formality) '[...] greet you'. However, Austrian or Swiss usages such as these, accepted in bordering areas of Germany such as Bavaria, do not meet with general acceptance nationwide in Germany.

The national standard languages of Germany, Austria, Switzerland, and Luxemburg reflect not just regional tradition, but national identity. Especially since the end of the Nazi regime in 1945, the other German-speaking countries seem to have viewed their language difference from Germany as a way of signaling as well their national separation from it.

Germany

The odd-sounding name German Standard German (following Clyne's terminology) repeats "German" in two different senses: the first instance referring to the nation of Germany, the second instance to the language itself. This is the standard variety of the language used for all official purposes and in the national media of Germany. While there is no governmental or other official board of language usage, both language professionals (including teachers of language, writers, and editors) and the educated elite take care to follow, and to enforce others' following, uniform standards of grammatical, syntactic, and lexical correctness in formal writing and speaking. The codification of correct usage is set by publications such as the Duden series of dictionaries (called by Clyne "the most widely used and most authoritative . . . in the German-language countries," 1995, 209). These include the *Duden-Rechtschreibung*, Mannheim edition, containing definitions and pronunciation; the *Duden-Fremdwörterbuch*, containing foreign words and their pronunciation, and several other specialized dictionaries. Also very highly regarded is the extensive *Deutsches Wörterbuch* (first edition, 1968), edited by Gerhard Wahrig. The ultimate model of German Standard German pronunciation guidelines remains Theodor Siebs's 1897 *Deutsche Bühenaussprache* (German stage pronunciation), still largely followed by subsequent dictionaries.

The intellectual elite in Germany is much more inclined to follow "correct" usage and to comment harshly on deviation from it in public writing and speaking, than is the case, for example, in the comparatively free-for-all linguistic arena of American English, where criticism of language incorrectness, though not unknown in upscale publications, is often regarded by even the educated public as petty and its practitioners as scolds.

Of the German-speaking countries, Germany shows by far the greatest dialect diversity, not surprising since it comprises by far the largest geographical area. Further, the standard originated not in the dialect of the dominant or capital city, as was the case for English (London) or French (Paris). For German it was, rather, the result of amalgamation of regional varieties on an east-central German base (see chapter 4). So it was that German Standard German was for centuries after its birth no one's *native* language, but by the end of the nineteenth century it became every educated German's *second* language.

The native languages of Germany were, and to a limited extent still are, the dialects. The four major dialect regions—Saxon, Franconian, Alemannic, and Bavarian—reflect roughly the premedieval or medieval territories of Germanic tribes of those names. As regards these names, however, linguists have cautioned that, because of the migration of tribes, changes in dialects through time, and mixing of tribal identities among Germanic groups, contemporary dialects are not traceable to particular Germanic tribes (Wells 1987, 363–64). In the eastern regions (the former German Democratic Republic) the primary dialects are

Low German and Central German (Low and Middle Saxon); in the western and southern regions, Saxon, Franconian, Alemannic, and Bavarian. Probably fewer than one-third of Germans know a dialect, and those who do are more likely to have receptive or passive competence rather than speaking or writing fluency (Wells 1987, 365). Nonetheless, these dialects are still alive, flourishing in some regions as a home language, in some as a vehicle of popular culture (including the lyrics to locally popular rock music), in others surviving as regional styles of usage rather than as full-fledged dialects, in all cases more likely to be spoken variants than written ones.

Far more commonly spoken in Germany than either dialects or German Standard German (primarily a written standard, in any case a norm for formal rather than everyday use) is the colloquial language called in German *Umgangssprache*. Wells (1987, 365) writes that *Umgangssprache* "might more properly be relabelled 'Normal' or 'Alltagssprache' [i.e., everyday speech]," since "few if any Germans speak the standard language at all outside the formal circumstances of the lecture hall, pulpit, classroom, radio or television interview, or official ceremony." *Umgangssprache* is colored by regional pronunciations and colloquialisms. It is somewhat different in every region, though it is for the most part understandable everywhere (Chambers and Wilkie 1984, 32). While foreigners learn the norms of the written German Standard German in school, *Umgangssprache* is acquired through experience, in reading of popular books and casual periodicals and in listening to and speaking with native speakers. Some characteristics of the *Umgangssprache* are (Keller 1978, 519–522.):

- *Phonological*: coalescence of *b/p, d/t, g/k,* especially in southern and central Germany; coalescence of *ch/sch* in Frankfurt and surrounding regions;
- *Consonant reductions*, such as *nich* or *net* (for *nicht*), *nix* (for *nichts*), *ham* (for *haben*);
- *Shortening of articles*: *e* (for *ein*), *ne* for (*eine*), *ner* for (*einer*), *s* for (*das*);
- *Loss of ending on verb forms*: *ich hab, ich sag, ich hol* (for *ich habe, ich sage, ich hole*);
- *Loss of genitive*: *die Pfeife von meinem Vater* or even *meinem Vater seine Pfeife* (although this variant is considered substandard) for *die Pfeife meines Vaters* 'my father's pipe'; also, use of the dative after "genitive" prepositions: *wegen dem Wetter* (for *wegen des Wetters* 'because of the weather');

- *Loss of distinction between dative and accusative* (in northern Germany); loss of distinction between nominative and accusative (in Rhenish areas);
- *Replacement of personal pronouns by demonstrative pronouns*: <u>der</u> (for *er*) *bleibt nich lang* 'he won't stay long'; <u>die</u> (for *sie*) *lesen das* 'they read that';
- *Word order changes*: Placement of prepositional or adverbial elements outside the "verbal bracket," that is, after the final verb. For example, *Der hat mir n neuen Ball gebracht gestern abend* (for *Er hat mir gestern abend einen neuen Ball gebracht* 'He brought me a new ball yesterday evening').

Today, however, Germans are more mobile than ever, and it is no longer unusual for Germans to make their adult homes and careers in regions other than the ones they grew up in. While many people may have some command of the dialect of the region of birth or childhood, they do not know the dialect of the region they moved to as adults, and their children will likely grow up without knowing any dialect at all. German Standard German, tempered in conversation by its regionally colored relative, *Umgangssprache*, is closer than ever before to becoming the universal mother tongue of native speakers all over Germany.

Austria

Ostarrîchi, the linguistic forerunner of *Österreich* 'Eastern Kingdom', the German name for Austria, appears for the first time in a document issued by Emperor Otto III in 996 AD. While the original inhabitants of the territory that is today Austria were likely Slavs, considerable mixing with Celtic and Germanic tribes had already occurred by medieval times; and after the final Turkish siege of Vienna in 1683 the Emperor sent German-speaking settlers to the depopulated eastern territories as these were reclaimed from the Turks. By 1784 Emperor Joseph II decreed German as the official state language in the "eastern territories" which were to become Austria, although several other languages, primarily Slavic and Hungarian languages and dialects, were spoken by significant portions of the inhabitants.

Austria was created as a nation from the remains of the collapsed Austro-Hungarian Empire at the end of World War I (1918). In 1910 only 23.5 percent of the 48.8 million citizens of the Austro-Hungarian Empire had been native speakers of German, and this ethnic and linguistic mix was to have aftereffects in the new Austrian nation. After

World War I there was tension in Austria between those sympathetic to pan-Germanism and those wishing independence from Germany; as early as 1914 the Austrian writer Arthur Schnitzler recorded that *echt deutsch* "genuinely German" was a term of approval, *echt österreichisch* "genuinely Austrian" of disapproval (Clyne 1995, 31). The principle of national self-determination favored by the Allies after World War I lay behind the creation or re-creation of several European nations (including Austria) and was meant as a balm for the tensions of Central Europe. However, in the event, this principle was inadequate to the geographical, historical, and ethnic issues in the region, which festered and later became contributing factors to World War II. In Austria this meant a revival of the großdeutsch-kleindeutsch question which had been settled only superficially by the creation of the German Reich in 1871 (Keller 1978, 482 ff.). In 1938 Nazi Germany, with the support of the large component of the Austrian population that was pro-German, annexed Austria, but the annexation was annulled by the Allies in 1945, making Austria once again a nation.

This history may explain why many Austrians (often in jest, but just as often seriously) denigrate Austrian Standard German and assume the superiority of German Standard German (Clyne 1995, 33). As is usual in such situations, the reverence is one side of a coin which has as its other side a certain resentment of the (in relative terms) Gargantua to the north, whose population and economy dwarfs that of Austria. Austrian Standard German, however, flourishes in writing and for all formal and official uses, while the local dialects remain primary for home and casual uses.

Most of Austrian dialects are of the Upper German family, closely related to the dialects in neighboring German Bavaria; in Austrian Vorarlberg, the dialect is Alemannic, related to Swiss German dialects.

Popular Austrian attitudes toward their nation's dialects are ambivalent, writes Sylvia Moosmüller. Austrians regard their dialects both as a symbol of low educational and social status, and as a sign of directness and authenticity (Moosmüller 1995, 269). Educated Austrians consider the German spoken in the Austrian media to be artificial, and they prefer as an everyday standard the German spoken in Vienna by the middle and upper-middle classes (Moosmüller 1995, 259–260), even while expecting their fellow citizens to be competent in both the standard language and their local dialect. It is likely that the linguistically flattening effect of the postwar electronic age has not yet been fully digested in Austria and that a few more decades will help to make popular attitudes toward the dialects and the standard language more consistent.

Table 6.1.   Austrian Standard German versus German Standard German

Austrian	German	English
Obers	*Sahne*	cream
Jause	*Zwischenmahlzeit*	snack
Greisler	*Lebensmittelhändler*	grocer
Sessel	*Stuhl*	chair
Fauteuil	*Sessel*	easy chair
Trafik	*Tabakladen*	tobacconist's

After Stedje 2001, 187.

In Table 6.1 Astrid Stedje lists several vocabulary items of Austrian language use (which she calls *Austriazismen*, Austrianisms) and contrasts them to German Standard German.

Switzerland

The nation of Switzerland lies between France, Germany, Italy, and Austria and is bounded by the Rhine, the Alps, and the Jura Mountains. It is named after Schwyz, one of its twenty-two cantons, the local units of the confederation of Switzerland. Its national origins may be traced to a thirteenth-century alliance of three of its cantons, Schwyz, Uri, and Unterwalden. This territory increased through new confederation and military conquest and asserted its independence in 1499 (Keller 1978, 341). The country was first recognized in international law by the Peace of Westphalia in 1648, but it did not encompass the whole of its current territory until the nineteenth century (Bonjour, Offler, and Potter 1952, 3).

Switzerland's official name, the Latin *Confoederatio Helvetia* (abbreviated to *CH*) , pays tribute to its early inhabitants, the Celtic tribe known to the Romans as *Helvetii*. Celts in Roman times built communities of lake dwellings on stilts and sought their fortune away from the overpopulated valleys of their homeland by becoming mercenaries as early as the third century BC. Other early peoples include the non-Celtic, non-Germanic Raetians and Ligurians. Not until the fifth and sixth centuries AD, when Roman rule had collapsed, did Germanic peoples, Alemannians and Burgundians, enter Switzerland.

"Again and again the toponomy of Roman settlements betrays a Celtic origin," writes Bonjour and his co-authors. Examples include *Nyon* (Noviodunum), *Thun* (Dunum), *Yverdon* (Eburodunum), their early names in parentheses indicating with the Celtic suffix –*dunum* a fortified place. *Geneva, Avenches,* and *Lausanne* are Celtic names as well (1952, 32–33).

The mountains and valleys made for inward-looking communities, but outsiders seeking passage across the mountains for trade and settlement brought foreign influences and new languages to Switzerland. Most of the major passes through the mountains which are used today by motor traffic and railways were known to and used by the Romans, as were the long stretches of water routes in the Alps, such as that over Lake Lucerne, Lake Constance, and Lake Zürich and its connected river, the Limmat.

Today's Switzerland is a land of four official languages: German, French, Italian, and Romansh (sometimes called Rhaeto-Romansh). Romansh is a daughter language of the Latin that survived among the locals who fled into isolated mountain areas in the fifth and sixth centuries to escape invading Germanic peoples. Currently, it is spoken by only about one percent of the Swiss. Italian, the mother tongue of about 6 percent of Swiss, is spoken in areas south of the Alps and contiguous to Italy. The linguistic boundary that represents tribal settlement patterns is that between French and German. French is spoken in the southwest of Switzerland, around Lake Geneva, while German is spoken in the northeast. German is the native language of over 70 percent of the population (Bonjour, Offler, and Potter 1952, 17–18).

The Germanic Völkerwanderung, the withdrawal of Roman troops early in the fifth century, and the complete collapse of the western Roman Empire in 476 brought waves of Germanic invasions into fifth-century Switzerland. The seat of the (Germanic) Burgundian king was established in Geneva, and the Burgundians pressed outward from there. Although the Germanic tribesmen exerted political control over this area, they did not dominate linguistically, but assimilated into the Romano-Celtic population and adopted their speech, a variety of Latin that was to evolve into French. Today the territory settled by the Burgundians from the fifth century is the area of French-speaking Switzerland (Bonjour, Offler, and Potter 1952, 38–39).

The Germanic Alemannians, who migrated into and settled north and central Switzerland in the fifth and centuries, were far more numerous than their cousins the Burgundians, and the territory they occupied had been less thoroughly Romanized than the southwest. They dominated not only politically, but eventually also linguistically. The Alemannic territory is more or less the area of today's German-speaking Switzerland.

Today's Swiss German dialects (known as *Schwyzertüütsch*) are used in ordinary conversation and to some extent also in public speaking (Keller 1978, 516). All the dialects but one are of the type Alemannic (Upper German); the exception is the Tyrolian dialect of one village in the Lower Engadine. The dialects are numerous and often unintelligible beyond their small territories, probably due to the isolation of the mountain communities where they developed. This has led to the development of a kind of super-dialect, which is neither the Swiss standard nor any particular dialect, but a kind of dialect lingua franca. It enables the Swiss to understand each other without switching to Swiss Standard German, which is learned in school as a second language and as a result never becomes a comfortable spoken alternative for many Swiss who are not engaged in the intellectual professions.

Swiss Standard German, called in Switzerland *Schriftdeutsch* 'written German', is used in writing, lecturing, teaching, preaching, the stage, and the media (Keller 1978, 516). Certain characteristics in the written language (such as lack of the German letter *β*, which has been replaced by *ss*) differentiate it from the other national standard German languages. The spoken Swiss standard shows specifically Swiss pronunciation, but it is easily understandable by speakers of German also in Germany, Austria, and Luxembourg.

Table 6.2 provides some *Helvetismen* "Swissicisms" in Swiss colloquial German.

"In Switzerland language adheres to territory and not to people," writes Keller (1978, 478), attributing to this cultural view the peaceful (though not entirely tension-free) Swiss acceptance of a four-language nation. The borders of the language areas have changed somewhat in

Table 6.2. Swiss Standard German versus German Standard German

Swiss	German	English
träf	*treffend*	suitable
der Fürsprech	*der Anwalt*	attorney
das Großkind	*der Enkel/die Enkelin*	grandchild
die Tochter [lit. 'daughter']	*weibliche Angestellte*	female employee
welsch	*französisch, italienisch*	French, Italian
hausen	*sparen*	save

After Stedje 2001, 188.

modern times. For example, the formerly German-speaking border town of Biel is now bilingual with French because of the immigration of industrial workers from the French-speaking area to the west; the canton of Grisons, formerly Romansh-speaking, is now bilingual with German. Speakers from the language groups (particularly German and French) stereotype each other in unflattering terms, and there is some resentment at the dominance of German, but this is generally *pro forma* and is overbalanced by the strong sense of Swiss national identity.

Luxemburg

Part of the Netherlands since 1815, the Grand Duchy of Luxemburg in 1867 became an independent state. Its dialects are Franconian, the branch of Germanic that also includes the Netherlandic languages.

Three languages have official status in Luxemburg: Luxemburg Standard German, French, and Lëtzebuergisch. Virtually all Luxemburg citizens are competent to some extent in the first two; Lëtzebuergisch is the home language of the native population. The three languages have different domains: German is used in the early grades at school; French is the school language of the higher grades through high school; Luxemburg's single university uses both French and German. Court cases are held in French, though translators are available for the other two languages on request. Jean-Paul Hoffmann describes French as the long-time prestige language, with the "greatest social glitter" (Hoffmann 1985, 89), while in some circles both German and Lëtzebuergisch (learned by virtually no nonnatives and insufficient for use on the job) are spoken languages only, with writing reserved for French. In addition, the significant numbers of Portuguese "guest workers" find it easier to learn French than German. The prestige of French, its dominance in writing, and its frequent adoption by immigrants result in a sense that the dominant language of public discourse is French, while Lëtzebuergisch is the dominant language of private discourse.

Lëtzebuergisch is a Franconian language, with Germanic syntax but with a vocabulary heavily influenced by French. It is generally not understood by German speakers who have not studied the language or lived in Luxemburg. Though it is not used anywhere but in Luxemburg, it is flourishing, largely because of historical factors leading Luxemburgers to preserve and emphasize their national identity (the national motto is *Mir wëlle bleiwe wat mir sin* 'We want to remain what we are').

Nazi Germany invaded and occupied Luxemburg in 1940, while the Luxemburg royal family went into exile in England. The Germans drafted male Luxemburgers to fight in the war in spite of strong opposition in Luxemburg, leading to a general industrial strike against the occupying Germans—one of only two such anti-German strikes in Europe during the war. Luxemburgish passive resistance included a refusal to speak German. The French language was forbidden by the Nazi occupiers, and in response Luxemburgers resurrected the formerly declining Lëtzebuergisch language, which was not forbidden. The Allies liberated Luxemburg in 1944; Lëtzebuergisch, having been resuscitated during the occupation, began to thrive, and it was one of the winners of the conflict. Today it seems to have a firm place in Luxemburg life.

Luxemburg Standard German is used in official publications and in the media, and it is taught in the schools. It is more like the standard German of Germany, Austria, and Switzerland than like Lëtzebuergisch or its regional dialects, but it maintains some regional distinctions. One example is the use of *méi* as a comparative: *méi lang* (Standard German: *länger*), probably based on the French model *plus long* (Keller 1978, 15).

German as an International Language

Although English appears to be pushing against German in some contexts, German is still to a considerable extent regionally an international language. Visitors to Eastern Europe will notice that German is a second language in many areas of Poland, Romania, Czech Republic, and Russia, sometimes as a result of German invasions during World War II, but just as often as a result of historic ancestral connections.

For example, Russian Empress Catherine the Great invited German workers to Russia during the eighteenth century and guaranteed them the right to maintain their culture and their language. The result was generations of German-speaking "Volga Germans," many of whom migrated back to their ancestors' homeland after the fall of the Soviet Union. In other Eastern European nations, too, entire villages are historically German-speaking, although currently German is more often a second language, one learned in school rather than at home.

Further, because of the economic and industrial prominence of Germany and its borders with Poland, the Czech Republic, and other Eastern European nations, Germany has been a desired destination for young people who wanted to improve their job prospects.

Internationally, in the humanities and the arts, mastery of German is still a desired skill for philosophers, musicians (especially singers) and historians (especially those of twentieth-century Europe). Additionally, anyone who specializes in the history of academic disciplines or of art must be able to read documents in their original versions, which very often, especially for the eighteenth and nineteenth centuries, means German.

German has contributed significant numbers of words to other languages, including English, Turkish, Japanese, Finnish, and French. One reason may be its tendency toward compounds, making one word in German do the work of several words in other languages (example *Schadenfreude* 'taking joy in the sorrows of others'), providing a handy portmanteau to replace the borrowing language's multiword equivalent. Other expressive German compounds that have traveled widely to other languages include the following (from Limbach 2007): *Weltanschauung* (French, Spanish, English), *Leitmotiv* (Spanish, French, English), *Kaffeeklatsch* (English), *Kindergarten* (English), *arbeito* 'work' (Japanese, from *Arbeit*), *Hinterland* 'behind-land' (Italian, English), *szlafmyca* 'lazybones' (Polish, from *Schlafmütze* 'nightcap'). Sometimes the borrowing languages have created their own portmanteaux, compressing German phrases into one word, as with *vigéc* (Hungarian, from *wie geht's* 'how are you' for door-to-door salesman), and *le vasistdas* (French, a small window above the door, from *was ist das* 'what is that?'), which is attested in this meaning in the nineteenth-century writings of Victor Hugo. One final example is provided by the Polish *wihajster* 'thingamajig' from German *wie heißt er* 'what's it called'.

Language Contact and Language Change: The Case of Finnish

Finnish speakers are next-door neighbors to the Germanic homelands in southwestern Scandinavia and northern Germany; their language presents an interesting linguistic case. Like the Germanic homeland, Finland is a geographically large area which was exposed to millennia of Indo-European influence. Later in its history, Finnish survived nine hundred years of mostly subordinate coexistence with an Indo-European daughter language, Swedish, in quasi-familial and often uncomfortable bilingualism. Given this history, the survival of Finnish seems unexpected; yet survive it has, and within Finland (officially bilingual in Finnish and Swedish) it is now the overwhelmingly dominant language.

Finnish belongs to the Finno-Ugric family, along with Estonian, Hungarian, and several languages spoken by small populations in northern areas of Scandinavia and the former Soviet Union. Its constant linguistic companions since earliest times have been the Indo-European languages surrounding Finnish territory. The story of Finnish contributes to our narrative of Germanic by providing a historical as well as present-day example of the process of language change.

The Fenno-Scandinavian peninsula was settled after the last Ice Age, probably around 7500 BC, by the ancestors of today's Sámi (formerly known as Lapps). It is unknown what language the ancient Sámi spoke, but probably it was not any form of Proto-Finno-Ugric, though the modern Sámi languages belong to the Finno-Ugric family. The Sámi homeland today covers the far northern reaches of Norway, Sweden, Finland, and Russia, where, irrespective of national borders, the old ways of reindeer herding are still followed (though now with snowmobiles, cell phones, and laptop computers). Thousands of Sámi people, however, also live the city life in Oslo, Stockholm, and Helsinki as citizens of Norway, Sweden, and Finland respectively.

The ancestors of today's Finns, early speakers of Proto-Finno-Ugric, arrived in Finland and replaced the Sámi people and the indigenous Sámi language in southern and central Finland, but the specifics of the story are still unsettled among linguists, archaeologists, and anthropologists. Scholars believe Proto-Finno-Ugric speakers migrated to Finland between 5000 BC and 3000 BC (Karsten 2004, 68). At that time both Proto-Finno-Ugric and Proto-Indo-European were two among a large number of languages, most now disappeared and untraceable, spoken across Eurasia.

Historical evidence of the arrival of the Proto-Finno-Ugric speakers in Sámi territory is provided by archaeological findings of new types of weaponry and pottery from the east and southeast as well as by genetic '"footprints" of a new population inflow (this might have included speakers of PIE as well, though PIE did not endure in the region; Mallory 1989, 259). It is certain that the indigenous population, the reindeer-herding Sámi, subsequently migrated north to the Polar regions; it is uncertain whether this migration signaled following the reindeer moving north because of a warming climate, or being driven out by the newcomers who wanted the more southerly lands for farming. Either way, the Sámi stopped speaking their old language (of which no trace has been identified) and began speaking a Finno-Ugric one, like the newcomers, who in one widely accepted historical narrative had come from the Russian steppes, in another from farther south.

The Finno-Ugric family, though typologically different from Indo-European, nevertheless shows a strong connection to it. For example, striking similarities between grammatical verb and noun endings in Proto-Indo-European and Proto- Finno-Ugric suggest to linguists that the two coexisted at an early time in the forest-steppes or steppes of the Volga-Ural region (Mallory 1989, 149–151). Further, there is evidence of Pre-Germanic borrowing in Finno-Ugric, including Sámi, dating as far back as 2000 BC (Karsten 2004, 208–209).

During early Indo-European settlement of Northern Europe and continuing into Germanic times, trade among various tribes of the North flourished, with furs, amber, and metals bought and sold throughout the Baltic lands, the trade in these typically northern goods reaching as far away as the Mediterranean. At this time a considerable number of words were borrowed by Proto-Finnic from its Germanic neighboring language, Gothic (Koivulehto 1988). Finnish borrowed even its word for 'mother' from Gothic (Finnish *äiti*, cf. Gothic *áithei*), surely an indication of a close relationship between Finnic and Gothic speakers. Some scholars (see Salmons 1992, 13) consider early Proto-Finnic and Proto-Germanic a *Sprachbund*, that is, two geographically neighboring languages that share many features with neither one entering the language family of the other. However, while Proto-Finno-Ugric borrowed many features from PIE and later from Gothic, this borrowing does not seem to be mutual (see also the discussion in chapter 1 on possible Finno-Ugric influence on the Germanic Sound Shift). An example of the few Finno-Ugric loanwords into Indo-European languages is 'tundra,' from Sámi *tundar* 'high-topped hill' (*American Heritage Dictionary* 2000).

Through the centuries, Finnish survived as a language exception in the increasingly Indo-European Baltic and North Sea areas, where PIE had given rise to Slavic, Baltic (i.e., Latvian and Lithuanian), and Germanic languages. Finnish continued to borrow vocabulary from its neighbors, particularly German and Swedish, the languages of its largest trading partners, but it so changed these borrowings according to its own sound rules that they are not easily recognizable today by speakers of German or Swedish (example: Ger. *schön*, Swe. *skön*, and Finnish *kaunis*, all three meaning 'beautiful'). Finnish and the other Finno-Ugric languages remain structurally distinct from Indo-European languages, despite the many lexical borrowings.

Probably the most striking characteristic of Finnish and other Finno-Ugric languages is that they are *agglutinative*. This means that the grammatical and pragmatic information often indicated in English by word order, prepositions, or intonation is expressed by word suffixes, which may be appended in theoretically unlimited number. An example is *Taloissanikinko* "[Do you mean] in my houses, too?" This rather typical one-word question can be analyzed as follows:

talo /   i /   ssa / ni / kin / ko
'house'/ plural/'in' / 'my'/ 'also'/ question-marker

Other specifically Finno-Ugric characteristics include a lack of tonality in spoken utterances (e.g. questions, surprise, or emphasis are not expressed by rising or falling tone, but with particles), and a conjugated verb meaning "[does/do] not," rather than a negative adverb such as English "not" or German *nicht*.

The Finno-Ugric essence remains, although many Finnish words are of Germanic origin. "Lexical borrowing, even on a massive scale, is highly unlikely to lead to a change in the genetic affiliation of a given language," as Hock explains (1991, 423).

Finland currently maintains both Finnish and Swedish as official languages, with Finnish strongly dominant. It was not always so. Centuries of Swedish administration of Finland, beginning in the twelfth century AD when Finland became part of the Kingdom of Sweden, resulted in the dominance of Swedish, the sole language of administration and education. Finnish, though the native language of the majority, remained in the background as a collection of dialects for rural and home use, lacking a national standard. Sweden lost control of Finland to Russia in the early eighteenth century, making Finland an autonomous Grand Duchy of the Russian Empire, while Swedish laws and language remained in force (Reuter 1979, 171). Swedish remained the language of government and had become the home language among many in the educated class, even those who were ethnically Finnish, since knowledge of Swedish was necessary for professional and mercantile success. However the Finnish language received a boost in 1863 when the Duchy, which had the Czar's guarantee of linguistic autonomy, raised Finnish to the status of an official language alongside Swedish. By midcentury the rise of Finnish National Romanticism (part of a pan-European movement, both artistic and political) served to revive and give artistic expression to Finnish folk culture and the Finnish language. Finnish-language literature blossomed. Elias Lönnrot's 1835 book-length poem *The Kalevala* transformed folk legends into a national epic of archaicized and stately Finnish verse, brought Finland its first international literary recognition, and inspired Henry Wadsworth Longfellow's American epic *The Song of Hiawatha* (1855), which Longfellow wrote in the

Kalevala's unrhymed trochaic tetrameter after having studied Finnish, Danish, Swedish, and German languages and literatures in Europe.

In 1917 Finland won independence from Russia and, after a long and bitter debate on the language question, retained both Finnish and Swedish as official languages. Finnish citizens have a constitutionally protected right to use either Finnish or Swedish in administrative dealings with the government or in cases at law. Accordingly, civil servants must pass a language examination in both Finnish and Swedish, although in practice many government employees lack competence in spoken Swedish (Reuter 1979, 175). Finnish is now clearly dominant. Finns from Swedish-speaking families outside of the intensively Swedish areas of Finland's west coast and western islands currently use Swedish only at home and possibly in school (though only if they are in a Swedish school), while Finnish is the language of the workplace and public discourse (Reuter 1979, 176). The situation seems to suggest further weakening in the position of Swedish in Finland. In 2003, 5.6 percent of the Finnish population listed Swedish as its mother language, a percentage that has fallen steadily as Finnish has gained in prestige. In 1610 the percentage of Swedish speakers stood at 17.5 percent—a minority, but a high-status one at the time, comprising most of the nation's civil servants, teachers, writers, and Lutheran Church hierarchy down to the parish priests.

In prehistoric times, Finnish was not unseated by PIE in spite of the evident linguistic influence of PIE and, later, Germanic. In the seventeenth and eighteenth centuries Swedish seemed poised to supplant Finnish but did not succeed. After independence, the fact of Swedish language dominance in government, education, and all public speaking did not prevent Finnish from surviving and even thriving in the new democracy. The survival of Finnish against all expectations is a reminder that social, economic, and power relations make language change and survival difficult to predict.

Early Germanic Language in a Deep Freeze: The Case of Icelandic

In the year 870 Norwegian Viking adventurers in longships arrived in Iceland, bringing their Germanic language, Old Norse, to this unoccupied island of glaciers and volcanoes. During the next sixty years the adventurers were joined by as many as twenty thousand additional settlers, Celtic as well as Norse. They came from Norway, but also from coastal Scotland, Ireland, northern England, the Shetland Islands, the Orkneys, Hebrides, and the Isle of Man, where earlier Norse adventurers had invaded and settled. Many of the settlers of Iceland were these same Norsemen and their Celtic wives; other Celtic people came along as slaves or servants. All mixed as the centuries passed, to become the Icelandic population. In subsequent centuries the settlers slowly tamed their wild, beautiful, and partially forested land into farmsteads and a town or two.

By the twenty-first century Iceland had morphed into an industrial democracy, its modern cities and technology-equipped sheep stations and pony ranches heated by hot springs, powered by waterfalls, and set amidst the still beautiful fire and ice of its now almost treeless landscapes. Iceland's glaciers, mountains, and volcanoes had resisted the effects of civilization. Not so its once-abundant trees, which fell victim to clear-cutting by the early settlers. Wide-ranging and voraciously grazing sheep, a cooling climate (from the fourteenth to the nineteenth centuries), volcanic ash, and soil erosion impeded tree regrowth. Today's Iceland has only one forest (*Hallormstadaskógur* in eastern Iceland), although a massive tree-planting project is under way.

The language of Iceland, nearly as resistant to change as its glaciers, remained deep-frozen among the mountains, geysers, ranches and cities: today's Icelandic is in many respects unchanged from the language of its ninth-century pioneers (Halldórsson 1979, 76).

The modern population consists almost entirely of the descendants of those original settlers, their Norse-Celtic admixture still traceable. A twenty-first century DNA project (suspended in 2004 because of governmental concerns about citizens' privacy; Abbot 2004, 429) documented that a majority of females in the Icelandic founding population had Celtic ancestry, while the majority of males had Scandinavian ancestry (Helgason 2000, 697). The language of the founding settlers was, however, Old Norse; only a few Celtic borrowings entered Icelandic.

Iceland's *kristnitaka* 'Christianization' in the year 1000 occasioned borrowings from other Scandinavian languages for church-related words such as *biskup* 'bishop' and *kirkja* 'church.' Otherwise, the isolation of Iceland tended to preserve the old language, and the vocabulary and grammar of Modern Icelandic is still to a large extent Norse. In thirteenth-century Norway, by contrast, significant changes occurred in the Norse language, as the heavy inflection in verbs, nouns, and adjectives wore away. But in Iceland, except for those church-related words and some shifts in pronunciation, the Norse language stayed as it had been (Halldórsson 1979, 85).

In 1523, plague-weakened Norway and with it Iceland fell under the control of the Danish crown, but Danish did not replace the Icelandic language. The 1540 Lutheran Reformation in Iceland and the subsequent 1584 translation of the Bible into Icelandic brought into common use many new words from German, Danish, and Swedish without changing the basic structure of Icelandic. However, Icelanders soon recognized that their language was different from the Old Norse of the settlers, and gave it the name *íslenzka* 'Icelandic.' In Norway, the Danish language was so dominant that even church preaching was in Danish; as a result Norwegian was substantially and permanently changed by Danish, to which Norwegian was already very similar. However, Icelandic's significant grammatical differences prevented Danish from gaining a foothold as the everyday language on the island. Pastors preached in Icelandic, not Danish; the ordinary people of the congregations didn't know Danish, though Danish prestige as the language of learning and sophistication meant that the elites of Iceland were bilingual in Icelandic and Danish.

The 1780 statutes of the Icelandic Society for the Learned Arts (*Eens íslenzka Lærdoms-lista Félags Skraa*) called for protection and preservation of Icelandic from foreign words. This movement for linguistic purism (*nýyrðastefna*), which even today enjoys wide popular support (Halldórsson 1979, 78), has helped to insure the continuation in Icelandic of Old Norse structure, though with a vocabulary fully adequate to a technological society. By general agreement, and through a language commission, Icelandic words for new and foreign inventions are coined from Old Norse roots. An example is *veðurfræði* 'meteorology,' a compound of *veður* 'weather' and *fræði* 'studies.' Though there are regional pronunciation differences, genuine dialects have never developed in Iceland, and people from all parts of the small country understand each other without difficulty (Halldórsson 1979, 85).

Overall, written Icelandic has changed little since the eleventh century Icelandic sagas, or historical epics; only the addition of significant numbers of vocabulary items in modern times makes it likely that a saga author would have difficulty understanding the news in today's *Morgunblaðið*, the daily newspaper of Rejkavik, Iceland's capital city. *Morgunblaðið* readers, on the other hand, can read Old Icelandic relatively easily, though they may prefer to use a glossary to get the fine points. Notable Old Icelandic writings include historiography such as the *Landnámabók* ('Book of settlements'), the

Íslendingabók ('Book of the Icelanders,') of Ari Þorgilsson (1067–1148) and the *Heimskringla* ('The circle of the world') and *Prose Edda* of Snorri Sturlusson (1179–1241), as well as the skaldic, or court, poetry of Snorri and other poets, and the mythological and heroic poetry of the *Poetic (Elder) Edda*, the principal source of modern knowledge of Norse pagan mythology.

The nineteenth-century National Romantic movement in Iceland and in Europe caused renewed interest in the sagas and other Old Icelandic writings, in the process giving cultural validation to the retention of Modern Icelandic's traditional grammatical forms. These cultural and historical gems are still read not only in Icelandic schools, but world wide in university programs in Scandinavian studies and Germanic historical linguistics, though they are considerably more difficult for those foreign students and scholars than for Icelandic schoolchildren.

Danish rule continued in Iceland until the twentieth century. Modern Icelandic independence is the result of a 1944 plebiscite in Iceland, taken during the Nazi occupation of Denmark but later accepted by the postwar Danish government, though Iceland retains close political and cultural ties to Denmark.

Conclusion

We have followed the fortunes of German and its linguistic ancestors at their turning points, beginning in the bogs of what is today Denmark in the fifth millennium BC, to its unexpected victory in a bruising contact with the overwhelming power of the Roman Empire, through the splintered history of its home territories in medieval and early modern Europe, its emergence as a language of biblical and worldly authority, the solidification of its pluricentric written and spoken standards, and its twentieth-century human and military disasters.

In the twenty-first century, German is the second most widely spoken language in Europe (after English); it is an official language in seven European nations: Germany, Austria, Switzerland, Liechtenstein, Luxemburg, Belgium, and Italy. Worldwide, twenty million people are learning German; and Germany has the strongest economy in the European Union.

Though there has been much influence on German from American English lexicon and idiom, there has never been much doubt that German would remain the home language of Germans and Austrians. Even increased future dominance of English as a worldwide lingua franca is unlikely to change this, for "a lingua franca, which by definition serves a restricted range of communication only, will never be able to threaten the national role of languages nor to exclude them totally from international life," writes Hans Joachim Meyer (2004, 73).

However, English has seriously challenged German dominance as a second language in Central Europe in the postwar years and into the twenty-first century. Whether German will be able to maintain its current position as a lingua franca throughout Central and Eastern Europe is not certain, but it will unquestionably remain a principal language of five European nations.

Timeline: From the End of World War I to the Present

Year	In German-speaking Europe	In the Rest of the World
1918	End of World War I: Allied victory, France, England, U.S., and Germany sign armistice (Nov. 11); German republic at Weimar proclaimed; Austria becomes a republic; eight-hour workday introduced in Germany	War statistics: 8.5 million killed, 21 million wounded, 7.5 million prisoners and missing; ex-Czar Nicholas and his family executed in Russia; women over 30 get the vote in Britain; Czechoslovakia declared independent republic
1920	Adolf Hitler announces his 25-point program at the Hofbräuhaus, Munich; Swiss psychiatrist Herman Rorschach devises the "inkblot" test	In U.S., Eighteenth Amendment (Prohibition) passed; American novelist Edith Wharton, *The Age of Innocence*; Danzig (Poland) declared a free city
1921	Hitler's Storm Troops (SA) begin to terrorize political opponents; rapid fall of German mark, start of hyperinflation (a glass of beer could cost as much as four billion marks); German population 60 million	Radio station KDKA in Pittsburgh transmits the first regular programs in U.S.; U.S. population 107 million, Japan 78 million, Great Britain 42.5 million

continued

Year	In German-speaking Europe	In the Rest of the World
1925	Hitler reorganizes Nazi Party with 27,000 members and publishes Vol. I of *Mein Kampf*; German architect Walter Gropius moves the Bauhaus school of architecture and design to Dessau from Weimar	Scottish inventor John Logie Baird transmits images via television; Tennessee schoolteacher John T. Scopes tried for teaching evolution
1933	Adolf Hitler becomes Chancellor of Germany; Hermann Göring named Prussian Prime Minister; 92% of German electorate vote for the Nazis; first concentration camps built in Germany; approximately 60,000 authors, actors, painters, and musicians emigrate from Germany	Japan withdraws from the League of Nations; starvation in U.S.S.R. reaches disastrous proportions; Twenty-first amendment repeals Prohibition in U.S.; popular films in U.S: *Little Women*, starring Katharine Hepburn; *She Done Him Wrong*, starring Mae West
1939	World War II begins: Germany invades Poland	Britain and France declare war on Germany Sept. 3; U.S. President Franklin D. Roosevelt declares U.S. neutral
1940	Germany invades Norway, Denmark, Holland, Belgium, Luxemburg, France.	Germany begins all-night bombing of London ('Blitz'); Italy declares war on France and Britain; Lascaux caves with prehistoric paintings discovered in France
1941	Germany invades Russia; Germany and Italy declare war on U.S.	Japanese bomb Pearl Harbor, Hawaii, Dec. 7; U.S. and Britain declare war on Japan Dec. 8; U.S. declares war on Germany and Italy; German playwright Bertolt Brecht, in exile in Sweden, *Mother Courage and Her Children*

Timeline (continued)

Year	In German-speaking Europe	In the Rest of the World
1945	Hitler commits suicide; Germany capitulates May 7; Allied Control Commission divides Germany into four zones; Hermann Hesse, *Das Glasperlenspiel*	U.S. drops atomic bombs on Hiroshima and Nagasaki; Japan surrenders; end of World War II; Nuremberg trials of Nazi war criminals begin; black markets for food, clothing, and cigarettes develop throughout Europe; women win right to vote in France
1949	Three Allied zones of Germany (British, French, U.S.) unite to become German Federal Republic; Russian zone becomes German Democratic Republic; U.S.S.R. blockade of Berlin (begun 1948) lifted, U.S. airlift operation to bring supplies to West Berlin ends after 277, 264 flights	Clothes rationing ends in Britain; Rodgers and Hammerstein musical *South Pacific*; American physician Philip Hench discovers cortisone
1957	The Saarland, part of France since 1945, joins the Federal Republic of Germany	U.S.S.R. launches Sputnik I and II, first earth satellites; Cold War between U.S. and the Soviet Union; seventy-one world cities exist with over one million inhabitants, compared to sixteen in 1914
1965	Six former Auschwitz prison officials sentenced to life imprisonment; Shakespeare is the most performed playwright in German theaters, followed by Schiller and Shaw	Race riots in Watts district of Los Angeles; Martin Luther King heads procession of 4,000 civil rights demonstrators in Alabama

continued

Year	In German-speaking Europe	In the Rest of the World
1971	Women win the right to vote in Switzerland; summer Olympics held in Munich, and Arab terrorists kill two Israeli athletes, nine other hostages; German novelist Heinrich Böll wins Nobel Prize for Literature	Apollo 16 astronauts John Watts and Charles Duke spend 71 hours on the moon; Apollo 17 crew, Eugene Cernan and Dr. Harrison Schmitt, stay 74 hours, 59 minutes; Soviet spacecraft Venus 8 lands on Venus
1989	The fall of the Berlin Wall, and GDR President Erich Honeker and later the Communist government resign and a reform government takes power; West Germans Boris Becker and Steffi Graff win Winbledon tennis singles championships	Iranian Ayatollah Khomeini announces a *fatwa* (death sentence) on author Salman Rushdie; thousands of Chinese students die in Tiananmen Square, Peking, in an anti-government demonstration; archaeologists uncover the remains of the Elizabethan Globe Theater in London
1995	Schengen Treaty goes into effect, eliminating border controls between Germany, France, Belgium, the Netherlands, Luxemburg, Portugal, and Spain; World Bank ranks Switzerland first in per capita income ($36,410), followed by Luxemburg	Iranian government says it will no longer issue death threats to author Salman Rushdie; Egypt demands return of Egyptian art treasures from Berlin museums, including a bust of Queen Nefertiti
2000	German President Johannes Rau begs forgiveness in the Israeli Parliament (Knesset) "for what the German people have done"; the oldest excerpt from St. Paul, the Apostle's Book of Hebrews, discovered in the Austrian National Library	U.S. companies that had factories in Germany during World War II to establish a fund for paying restitution to slave laborers; skeletal remains of the longest dinosaur, which must have been about 164 feet long and weighed fifteen tons, found in Patagonia

Timeline (continued)

Year	In German-speaking Europe	In the Rest of the World
2005	Germany elects its first female chancellor, Angela Merkel	
2008	U.S.A. elects its first black president, Barack Obama	Worldwide economic crises

Bibliography

Abbot, Alison. 2004. "Icelandic Database Shelved as Court Judges Privacy in Peril." *Nature* 429: 118.

Aikio, Ante. 2000. "On German-Saami Contacts and Saami Prehistory." *Journal de la Société Finno-Ougrienne* 91: 9–55.

Aikio, Ante, and Aslak Aikio. 2002, September. "Suomalaisten fantastinen menneisyys." *Kaltio. Pohjoinen Kultuurilehti.* www.kaltio.fi/index.php?362 (accessed Aug. 29, 2009).

American Heritage Dictionary of the English Language, 4th ed. 2000. Boston: Houghton Mifflin.

Ammon, Ulrich. 2004. "German as an International Language of the Sciences—Recent Past and Present." In *Globalization and the Future of German*, ed. Andreas Gardt and Bernd Hüppauf, 157–172. Berlin: Mouton de Gruyter

Anglo-Saxon Chronicle. 850–1150/1912. Trans. James Ingram and J. A. Giles. Reprint, London: Everyman Press. Online Medieval and Classical Library, Release #17. http://omacl.org/Anglo/ (accessed Aug. 31, 2009).

Anthony, David W. 2007. *The Horse, the Wheel, and Language. How Bronze-Age Riders from the Eurasian Steppes Shaped the Modern World.* Princeton, N.J.: Princeton University Press.

Antonsen, Elmer. 2002. *Runes and Germanic Linguistics.* Berlin and New York: de Gruyter.

Arndt, Erwin. 1962. *Luthers deutsches Sprachschaffen. Ein Kapitel aus der Vorgeschichte der deutschen Nationalsprache und ihrer Ausdrucksform.* Berlin: Akademie-Verlag.

Barbour, Stephen, and Patrick Stevenson. 1990. *Variation in German: A Critical Approach to German Sociolinguistics.* Cambridge: Cambridge University Press.

Barraclough, G. 1963. *The Origins of Modern Germany*, 4th ed. New York: Capricorn.

Baumstark, Reinhold, and Frank Büttner. 2003. *Großer Auftritt: Piloty und die Historienmalerei.* München: Pinakothek-Dumont.

Bayer, Oswald. 2003. "Luther as an Interpreter of Holy Scripture." In *The Cambridge Companion to Martin Luther*, ed. Donald K. McKim, trans. Mark Mattes, 73–85. Cambridge: Cambridge University Press.

Beja-Pereira, Albano, et al. 2006. "The Origin of European Cattle: Evidence from Modern and Ancient DNA." *Proceedings of the National Academy of Sciences of the USA*. 103 (21), May 23, 8113–8118. www.pubmedcentral.nih.gov/articlerender. fcgi?artid=1472438 (accessed Aug. 29, 2009).

Berigsen, Ulf. 2003. "Using DNA to Help Solve the Riddle of Ancient Germanic Migration." *Mankind Quarterly* 44, 1 (Fall): 91–99.

Billinger, Robert D., Jr. 2004. "The Revolutions of 1848, 1848–49: Interpretive Essay." In *Events that Changed Germany*, ed. Frank W. Thackeray, 7–18. Westport, Conn.: Greenwood.

Birnbaum, Norman. 2006. "The Strange Silence of Günter Grass. *The Nation* (August 18, 2006). www.thenation.com/doc/20060828/birnbaum (accessed Aug. 29, 2009).

Blair, John. 2000. *The Anglo-Saxon Age: A Very Short Introduction*. Oxford: Oxford University Press.

Bonjour, E., H. S. Offler, and G. R. Potter. 1952. *A Short History of Switzerland*. Oxford: Clarendon.

Brüggemeier, Franz-Joseph, and Gerhard Hoffmann, eds. 1999. *Menschen im Jahr 1000*. Freiburg im Breisgau: Herder.

Bury, Ernst. 2005. *Deutsche Sprachgeschichte kennen lernen*. Lichtenau: AOL-Verlag.

Busbecq, Ogier Ghiselin de. 1595. *A. G. Busbequii D. legationis Turcicae epistolae quattor* (Four Turkish Letters). Paris: Ex officina plantiniana.

Caesar, Julius. 58–47 BC. *The Gallic Wars*. Trans. W. A. Devitte and W. S. Bohn. New York: Harper. http://classics.mit.edu/Caesar/gallic.html (accessed Aug. 29, 2009).

Campbell, Joseph. 1969. *The Flight of the Wild Gander: Explorations in the Mythological Dimension*. New York: Viking.

Cassius Dio Cocceianus. 200–222(?)/1914–1917. *History of Rome*. Trans. Earnest Cary. Reprint, Cambridge, Mass.: Harvard University Press..

Cavalli-Sforza, Luigi. 2000. *Genes, Peoples, and Languages*. Trans. Mark Seielstad. New York: Farrar, Straus and Giroux.

Chambers, W. Walker, and John R. Wilkie. 1984. *A Short History of the German Language*. New York: Methuen.

Chirita, Diana. 2003. "Did Latin Influence German Word Order? Aspects of German-Latin Bilingualism in the Late Middle Ages." In *Aspects of Multilingualism in European Language History*, ed. Kurt Braunmüller and Gisella Ferraresi, 173–100. Amsterdam: John Benjamins.

Christensen, Arne Søby. 2002. *Cassiodorus, Jordanes, and the History of the Goths: Studies in a Migration Myth*. Copenhagen: Museum Tusculanum Press.

Clair, Colin. 1976. *A History of European Printing*. London: Academic Press.

Clunn, Tony. 2005. *The Quest for the Lost Roman Legions: Discovering the Varus Battlefield*. New York: Savas Beatie.

Clyne, Michael G. 1995. *The German Language in a Changing Europe.* Cambridge: Cambridge University Press.

Collinder, Björn. 1966. "Distant Linguistic Affinity. In *Ancient Indo-European Dialects: Proceedings of the Conference on Indo-European Linguistics Held at the University of California, Los Angeles, April 25–27, 1963,* ed. Henrik Birnbaum and Jaan Puhvel, 199–200. Berkeley: University of California Press.

Comrie, Bernard. 2002. "Genes and Language, with Special Reference to Europe and the Caucasus." In *Global Perspectives on Human Language: Scientific Studies in Honor of Professor Joseph Greenberg,* ed. Bernard Comrie. http://greenberg-conference.stanford.edu/Comrie_Abstract.htm (accessed Aug. 31, 2009).

Coulmas, Florian. 1995. "Germanness: Language and Nation." In *The German Language and the Real World: Sociolinguistic, Cultural, and Pragmatic Perspectives in Contemporary German,* ed. Patrick Stevenson, 55–68. Oxford: Clarendon Press.

Country Reports. 1997–2007. Germany. www.countryreports.org/history/historyDetail.aspx?countryid=91&hd=ra47e.aspx&de0066 (accessed Aug. 29, 2009).

Crompton, Samuel Willard. 1997. *One Hundred Battles that Shaped World History.* San Mateo, Calif.: Bluewood.

Crowley, Terry. 1992. *An Introduction to Historical Linguistics.* Auckland: Oxford University Press.

Crystal, David. 1997. *The Cambridge Encyclopedia of Language.* 2nd ed. Cambridge: Cambridge University Press.

Detwiler, Donald S. 1999. *Germany: A Short History.* 3rd ed. rev. Carbondale: Southern Illinois University Press.

Diamond, Jared. 2001. "Deaths of Languages." *Natural History* 110 (April): 3.

Doyle, Christine. 2003. "Singing Mignon's Song: German Literature and Culture in the March Trilogy." *Children's Literature* 31: 50–70.

Duden Jiddisches Wörterbuch. 1992. Ronald Lötsch, ed. Mannheim: Duden.

Durant, Will. 1957. *The Reformation. A History of European Civilization from Wyclif to Calvin: 1300–1564.* The Story of Civilization, Part VI. New York: Simon and Schuster.

Durschmied, Erik. 2000. *The Weather Factor. How Nature Has Changed History.* London: Hadden and Stoughten.

Eggers, Hans. 1963. *Deutsche Sprachgeschichte I. Das Althochdeutsche.* Reinbeck bei Hamburg: Rowohlt.

Ehlich, Konrad. 2004. "The Future of German and Other Non-English Languages for Academic Communication." In *Globalization and the Future of German,* ed. Andreas Gardt and Bernd Hüppauf, 173–184. Berlin: Mouton de Gruyter.

Eisenberg, Peter. 2004. German as an Endangered Language? In *Globalization and the Future of German,* ed. Andreas Gardt and Bernd Hüppauf, 121–137. Berlin: Mouton de Gruyter.

Eller, Cynthia. 2000. *The Myth of Matriarchal Prehistory. Why an Invented Past Won't Give Women a Future.* Boston: Beacon.

Elliott, John, and Tom Robbins. 2001. "Genetic Survey Reveals Hidden Celts of England." *Sunday Times of London,* December 2.

Ernst, Peter. 2005. *Deutsche Sprachgeschichte: Eine Einführung in die diachrone Sprachwissenschaft des Deutschen.* Wien: UTB Basics, WUV.

Evangelical Lutheran Church in America. 1994. "Declaration of the Evangelical Lutheran Church in America to the Jewish Community." www.elca.org/ ecumenical/interreligious/jewish/declaration.html (accessed Aug. 29, 2009).

Evangelical Lutheran Church of America. 2001. MOSAIC Television: "The Morning Star of Wittenberg." Transcript. http://archive.elca.org/mosaic/Luther/ katiescript.html (accessed Aug. 29, 2009).

Evangelische Kirche Deutschlands. 2007. Glauben. Bibelausgaben. 1. Lutherbibel. www.ekd.de/bibel/bibel.html (accessed Aug. 29, 2009).

Evangelisch-Lutherische Kirche in Bayern. 1998. "Erklärung zum Thema 'Christen und Juden.'" Internationaler Rat der Christen und Juden. Heppelsheim, Germany. http://jcrelations.net/de/?item=2861 (accessed Aug. 29, 2009).

Fagan, Brian. 2000. *The Little Ice Age: How Climate Made History* 1300–1850. New York: Basic Books.

Ferris, I. M. 2000. *Enemies of Rome: Barbarians through Roman Eyes.* Phoenix Mill, UK: Sutton.

Flood, John L. 1998. "The Book in Reformation Germany." In *The Reformation and the Book*, ed. Jean-François Gilmont, trans. Karin Maag, 21–103. Aldershot, UK: Ashgate.

Frost, Peter. 2006. "European Hair and Eye Color: A Case of Frequency-Dependent Sexual Selection?" *Evolution and Human Behavior* 27, 2 (March 2006): 85–103.

Fulbrook, Mary. 2004. *A Concise History of Germany.* 2nd ed. Cambridge: Cambridge University Press.

Furman, Nelly, David Goldberg, and Natalia Lusin. 2007 (Nov. 13) "Enrollments in Languages Other Than English in United States Institutions of Higher Education." Modern Language Association Enrollment Study. Web publication. www.mla.org/2006_flenrollmentsurvey (accessed Aug. 29, 2009).

Füssel, Stephan. 2003. "The Book of Books: The Luther Bible; A Cultural-Historical Introduction," trans. Christiane Roth. Supplement to the Luther Bible of 1534. Köln: Taschen

Gardt, Andreas, and Bernd Hüppauf, eds. 2004. *Globalization and the Future of German.* Berlin. Mouton de Gruyter.

Geary, Patrick. 1988. *Before France and Germany: The Creation and Transformation of the Merovingian World.* New York: Oxford University Press.

Gerhard, Gesine. 2004. "The Unification of Germany, 1871: Interpretive Essay." In *Events that Changed Germany*, ed. Frank W. Thackeray, 29–41.Westport, Conn.: Greenwood.

"German Influence Dying in America." 1918. *New York Times*, June 23.

Gilmont, Jean-Francois, ed. 1998. *The Reformation and the Book*, trans. Karin Maag. Aldershot, UK: Ashgate.

Gimbutas, Marija. 1991. "Deities and Symbols of Old Europe and Their Survival in the Indo-European Era: A Synopsis." In *Sprung from Some Common Source:*

Investigations into the Prehistory of Languages, ed. Sydney M. Lamb and E. Douglas Mitchell. Stanford, Calif.: Stanford University Press.

———. 1999. *The Living Goddesses*. Ed. and supplemented by Miriam Robbins Dexter. Berkeley: University of California Press.

Glück, Helmu, and Wolfgang Werner Sauer. 1995. "Directions of Change in Contemporary German." In *The German Language and the Real World: Sociolinguistic, Cultural, and Pragmatic Perspectives in Contemporary German*, ed. Patrick Stevenson, 95–116. Oxford: Clarendon Press.

Goertz, Hans-Jürgen. 2004. *Deutschland 1500–1648: Eine zertrennte Welt*. Paderborn, Germany: Schöningh.

Goffart, Walter. 2006. *The Migration Age and the Later Roman Empire*. Philadelphia: University of Pennsylvania Press.

Green, Dennis. 1999. "Linguistic Evidence for the Early Migrations of the Goths." In *The Visigoths from the Migration Period to the Seventh Century: An Ethnographic Perspective*, ed. Peter Heather, 11–32. Woodbridge, UK: Boydell.

Green, Dennis H. 1998. *Language and History in the Early Germanic World*. Cambridge: Cambridge University Press.

Grietsch, Eric W. 2003. "Luther as Bible Translator." In *The Cambridge Companion to Martin Luther*, ed. Donald K. McKim, 62–72. Cambridge: Cambridge University Press.

Grimmelshausen, Hans Jacob Christoffel. 1993. *The Adventures of Simplicius Simplicissimus*. Trans. and introduction by George Schulz-Behrend. 2nd ed. Columbia, S.C.: Camden House.

Grun, Bernard. 2005. *The Timetables of History: A Horizontal Linkage of People and Events*, 4th ed. New York: Simon and Schuster.

Halldórsson, Halldór. 1979. "Icelandic Purism and Its History." *Word* 30, 1–2: 76–86.

Heather, Peter. 1996. *The Goths*. Oxford: Blackwell.

Helgason, Agnar, et al. 2000. "Estimating Scandinavian and Gaelic Ancestry in the Male Settlers of Iceland." *American Journal of Human Genetics* 67: 97–717.

Herf, Jeffrey. 1984. *Reactionary Modernism: Technology, Culture and Politics in Weimar and the Third Reich*. Cambridge: Cambridge University Press.

Hillerbrand, Hans J. 2003. "The Legacy of Martin Luther." In *The Cambridge Companion to Martin Luther*, ed. Donald K. McKim, 227–239. Cambridge: Cambridge University Press.

Hobsbawm, Eric. 2008. "Diary. Review of Eric Weitz." *Weimar Germany: Promise and Tragedy*. *London Review of Books*, v. 30, 2 (Jan. 24, 2008). www.lrb.co.uk/v30/n02/hobs01_.html (accessed Aug. 29, 2009).

Hock, Hans Henrich. 1991. *Principles of Historical Linguistics*. 2nd ed. Berlin: deGruyter.

Hoffmann, Jean-Paul. 1985. *Standard und Dialekt in der saarländisch-lothringisch-luxemburgischen Dreiländerecke*. Luxemburg: Sankt-Paulus-Druckerei.

Horrocks, Geoffrey. 1997. *Greek: A History of the Language and Its Speakers*. London: Longman.

Ing, Janet. 1988. *Johann Gutenberg and His Bible: A Historical Study*. New York: The Typophiles.

Jeep, John. 1995. *Alliterating Word-Pairs in Old High German*. Studien zur Phraseologie und Parömiologie 3. Bochum: Universitätsverlag.

Johnson, Sally. 2000. "The Cultural Politics of the 1998 Reform of German Orthography." *German Life and Letters* 53 (1): 106–125.

Jordanis. 551/1913. *Gotengeschichte. Nebst Auszügen aus seiner Römischen Geschichte* Trans. and ed. Wilhelm Martens. Reprint. Essen: Alexander Heine.

Julku, Kyösti, ed. 1992. *Suomen varhaishistoria. Tornion konressi* 14–16.6. 1991 (Finnish Ancient History Congress at Tornio, June 14-16, 1991). Rovaniemi: Pohjois-Suomen Historiallinen Ydhistys.

Kallio, Petri, Jorma Koivulehto, and Asko Parpola. 1997. "Kantagermaanin suomalais-ugrilainen substraatti: perusteeton hypoteesi." *Tieteessatapahtuu* 8. www.tieteessatapahtuu.fi/arkisto.htm (accessed Oct. 1, 2008).

Karsten, T. E. 2004. *Die Germanen: Eine Einführung in die Geschichte ihrer Sprache und Kultur*. Wiesbaden: Marixverlag.

Kaufmann, Thomas. 2006. *Martin Luther*. München: Beck.

Keller, R. E. 1978. *The German Language*. London: Faber and Faber.

Klindt-Jensen, Ole. 1957. *Denmark before the Vikings*. Trans. Eva and David Hudson. London: Thames and Hudson.

Koivulehto, Jorma. 1988. "Alte Indogermanische Lehnwörter im Finnisch-ugrischen." *Ural-Altaische Jahrbücher* NF 8, 1–7.

Kolbenhoff, Walter. 2008. *Schellingstraße 48: Erfahrungen mit Deutschland*. Reprint. München: Süddeutsche Zeitung GmbH.

König, Werner. 1994. *DTV-Atlas deutsche Sprache*. Reprint. München: Deutscher Taschenbuch Verlag.

Krause, Arnulf. 2005. *Die Geschichte der Germanen*. Frankfurt: Campus Verlag.

Labov, William. 1993. "The Social Motivation of a Sound Change." *Word* 19: 273–309.

Lankheit, Klaus. 1984. *Karl von Piloty: Thusnelda im Triumphzug des Germanicus*. München: Hirmer Verlag

Lehmann, Winifried P. 1961. "A Definition of Proto-Germanic." *Language* 37: 67–74.

———, ed. 1967. *A Reader in Nineteenth Century Historical Indo-European Linguistics*. Bloomington: Indiana University Press. www.utexas.edu/cola/centers/lrc/books/readT.html (accessed Oct. 1, 2008).

Limbach, Jutta, ed. 2007. *Ausgewanderte Wörter*. Reinbek bei Hamburg: Rowohlt.

Lockwood, W. B. 1976. *An Informal History of the German Language*. Reprint. London: Andre Deutsch.

———. 1972. *A Panorama of Indo-European Languages*. London: Hutchinson.

Lowenthal, David. 2005. "Why Sanctions Seldom Work: Reflections on Cultural Property Internationalism." *International Journal of Cultural Property* 12, 3: 393–423.

Lucy, Sam. 2000. *The Anglo-Saxon Way of Death. Burial Rites in Early England*. Phoenix Mill, UK: Sutton.

Lull, Timothy F. 2003. "Luther's Writings." In *The Cambridge Companion to Martin Luther*, ed. Donald K. McKim, 39–61. Cambridge: Cambridge University Press.

Lutheran Church-Missouri Synod. 1983. "Luther's Anti-Semitism." www.lcms.org/pages/internal.asp?NavID=2166 (accessed Aug. 29, 2009).

Magee, Bryan. 1999. "Sense and Nonsense." In *Philosophy: Basic Readings*, 2nd ed., ed. Nigel Warburton, 29–38. London: Routledge.

Mallory, J. P. 1989. *In Search of the Indo-Europeans. Language, Archaeology and Myth*. London: Thames and Hudson.

Mallory, J. P., and D. Q. Adams. 1997. *Encyclopedia of Indo-European Culture*. London: Fitzroy Dearborn.

Markey, T. L., and John A. C. Greppin, eds. 1990. *When Worlds Collide: The Indo-Europeans and the Pre-Indo-Europeans*. Ann Arbor, Mich.: Karoma.

Marty, Martin. 2004. *Martin Luther*. New York: Viking.

Mason, Patricia. 1979. "Social Implications of Borrowing: The Visigothic Element in Hispano-Romance." *Word* 30, 3: 257–272.

Meiklejohn, John Miller Dow. 1907. *The English Language: Its Grammar, History and Literature*. Boston: Heath.

Meyer, Hans Joachim. 2004. "Global English: A New Lingua Franca or a New Imperial Culture?" In *Globalization and the Future of German*, ed. Andreas Gardt and Bernd Hüppauf, 65–84. Berlin. Mouton de Gruyter

Milisauskas, Sarunas. 1978. *European Prehistory*. New York: Academic Press.

Montgomery, James E. 2000. "Ibn Fadlan and the Rusiyyah." *Journal of Arabic and Islamic Studies* 3: 1–25.

Moosmüller, Sylvia. 1995. "Evaluation of Language Use in Public Discourse: Language Attitudes in Austria." In *The German Language and the Real World: Sociolinguistic, Cultural, and Pragmatic Perspectives in Contemporary German*, ed. Patrick Stevenson, 257–278. Oxford: Clarendon Press.

Musset, Lucien. 1975. *The Germanic Invasions: The Making of Europe A.D. 40–60*. Trans. Edward and Columba Jones. London: Paul Elek.

Nestingen, James A. 2003a. "Approaching Luther." In *The Cambridge Companion to Martin Luther*, ed. Donald K. McKim, 240–256. Cambridge: Cambridge University Press.

———. 2003b. *Martin Luther: A Life*. Minneapolis: Augsburg Books.

Nettle, Daniel. 1999. *Linguistic Diversity*. Oxford: Oxford University Press.

Neue Pinatothek. 2003. *Katalog der Gemälde und Skulpturen*. München: Pinakothek-Dumont.

Oberman, Heiko A. 1992. *Luther: Man between God and the Devil*. Trans. Eileen Walliser-Schwarzbart. New York: Doubleday.

Ozment, Steven. 2004. *A Mighty Fortress: A New History of the German People*. New York: HarperCollins.

———. 1992. *Protestants: The Birth of a Revolution*. New York: Doubleday.

Phillips, Patricia. 1980. *The Prehistory of Europe*. London: Penguin.

Polomé, Edgar C. 1992. "Germanic, Northwest Indo-European and Pre-Indo-European Substrates." In *Recent Developments in Germanic Linguistics*, ed. Rosina Lippi-Green, 47–55. Amsterdam/Philadelphia: John Benjamins.

————. 1997. "The Impact of Marija Gimbutas on Indo-European Studies." In *From the Realm of the Ancestors: An Anthology in Honor of Marija Gimbutas*, ed. Joan Marler, 102–107. Manchester, Conn.: Knowledge, Ideas, and Trends.

Price, T. Douglas. 2000. *Europe's First Farmers*. Cambridge: Cambridge University Press.

Prince, Morton. 1918. *The Creed of Deutschtum: And Other War Essays, Including The Psychology of the Kaiser*. Boston: Richard D. Badger, The Gorham Press.

Prinz, Friedrich. 2005. *Kelten, Römer und Germanen: Deutschlands Frühgeschichte*. München: Piper.

Rat für deutsche Rechtschreibung. 2009. Zusammenfassung der Änderungen. http://rechtschreibrat.ids-mannheim.de/rechtschreibung/aenderungen.html (accessed Dec. 8, 2009).

Reallexikon der germanischen Altertumskunde. 1998. Berlin: de Gruyter.

Reinbothe, Roswitha. 2006. *Deutsch als internationale Wissenschaftssprache und der Boykott nach dem Ersten Weltkrieg*. Duisburger arbeiten zur Sprach-und Kulturwissenschaft, 67. Frankfurt: Lang.

Renfrew, Colin. 1987. *Archaeology and Language: The Puzzle of Indo-European Origins*. Cambridge: Cambridge University Press.

————. 1990. "Archaeology and Linguistics: Some Preliminary Issues." In *When Worlds Collide*, ed. T. L. Markey and John A. C. Greppin, 15–24. Ann Arbor, Mich.: Karoma.

————. 2000. "At the Edge of Knowability: Towards a Prehistory of Languages." *Cambridge Archaeological Journal* 10, 1: 7–34.

————. 1991. "The Origins of Indo-European Languages." In *The Emergence of Language: Development and Evolution. Readings from Scientific American Magazine*, ed. William S-Y Wang. (Reprint from *Scientific American*, 1989.) New York: W. H. Freeman.

Reuter, Mikael. 1979. "Swedish in Finland: Minority Language and Regional Variety." *Word* 30, 1–2: 171–185.

Richards, Julian D. 2005. *The Vikings: A Very Short Introduction*. Oxford: Oxford University Press.

Robinson, Orrin W. 2004. "Luther's Bible and the Emergence of Standard German." In *A New History of German Literature*, ed. Hans Ulrich Gumbrecht, Anton Kaes, Joseph Leo Koerner, and Dorothea E. von Mücke, 231–236. Cambridge, Mass.: Harvard University Press.

————. 1992. *Old English and Its Closest Relatives: A Survey of the Earliest Germanic Languages*. Stanford, Calif.: Stanford University Press

Roelcke, Thorsten. 1997. *Sprachtypologie des Deutschen*. Sammlung Göschen. Berlin: de Gruyter.

Royal Society of Edinburgh. 2007. *The Vikings of Scotland: Impact and Influence*. Report of a Conference organized by the Royal Society of Edinburgh, 20–22. September 2006.

Salmons, Joe. 1992. *Accentual Change and Language Contact: Comparative Survey and a Case Study of Early Northern Europe*. Stanford, Calif.: Stanford University Press.

Sampson, Geoffrey. 2006. "What Was the Earliest Ancestor of English Like?" www. grsampson.net/Q_PIE.html (accessed Aug. 29, 2009).

Schmidt, Georg. 2003. *Der dreißigjährige Krieg.* München: Beck.

Schmidt, Wilhelm. 1993. *Geschichte der deutschen Sprache.* 6. Auflage. Stuttgart: S. Huzel.

Schulze, Hagen. 1998. *Germany: A New History.* Trans. Deborah Lucas Schneider. Cambridge, Mass.: Harvard University Press.

Seidel, Eugen, and Ingeborg Seidel-Slotty. 1961. *Sprachwandel im Dritten Reich. Eine kritische Untersuchung faschistischer Einflüsse.* Halle (Salle): VEB Verlag Sprache und Literatur.

Sheerin, Daniel. 1996. "Christian and Biblical Latin." In *Medieval Latin: An Introduction and Bibliographical Guide,* ed. F. A. C. Mantello and A G. Rigg. Washington, D.C: The Catholic University Press.

Smyser, H. M. 1965. "Ibn Fadlan's Account of the Rus with Some Commentary and Some Allusions to *Beowulf.*" In *Franciplegius: Medieval and Linguistic Studies in Honor of Francis Peabody Magoun, Jr.,* ed. Jess B. Bessinger, Jr., and Robert P. Creed, 92–119. New York: New York University Press.

Stedje, Astrid. 2001. *Deutsche Sprache gestern und heute.* 5. Auflage. München: Fink.

Strabo. 1917–1932. *Geography* (8 vols.). Trans. H. L. Jones. Loeb Classical Library. Cambridge, Mass.: Harvard University Press. http://penelope.uchicago.edu/ Thayer/E/Roman/Texts/Strabo/home.html (accessed Aug. 29, 2009).

Swadesh, Morris. 1952. "Lexicostatistic Dating of Prehistoric Ethnic Contacts." *Proceedings of the American Philosophical Society* 96, 4: 452–463.

Tacitus, P. Cornelius. 109. *Annals.* Trans. Alfred John Church and William Jackson Brodribb. Internet Classics Archive, MIT. http://classics.mit.edu/Tacitus/ histories.html (accessed Aug. 29, 2009).

Thackeray, Frank W., ed. *Events that Changed Germany.* Westport, Conn.: Greenwood.

Thielmann, Winfried. 2007. "Luther als Übersetzer—ein Pragmatiker am Werk?" In *Texte und Diskurs: Festschrift für Konrad Ehlich zum 65. Geburtstag,* ed. Angelika Redder. Tübingen: Stauffenburg.

———. 2003. "The Problem of English as the Lingua Franca of Scholarly Writing from a German Perspective." In *Proceedings of the Conference: A Celebration of the European Year of Languages at ANU: Language Policies and Issues,* ed. T. Liddicoat and K. Muller, 95–108. Melbourne: Language Australia.

Thorpe, I. J. 1996. *The Origins of Agriculture in Europe.* London: Routledge.

Tilley, Christopher. 2003 (repr. 1996). *An Ethnography of the Neolithic: Early Prehistoric Societies in Southern Scandinavia.* Cambridge: Cambridge University Press.

University of Maryland. International Programs. 2005. "German Professors Visit Maryland English Institute to Refine Their English for the Classroom." *Maryland International Newsletter* 11 (Fall): 13.

Vasold, Manfred. 2003. *Die Pest: Ende eines Mythos.* Stuttgart: Theiss.

Vennemann, Theo. 2003. *Europa Vasconia—Europa Semitica.* Trends in Linguistics, Studies and Monographs 138. Ed. Patrizia Noel Aziz Hanna. Berlin: Mouton de Gruyter.

Wade, Nicholas. 2006. *Before the Dawn: Recovering the Lost History of Our Ancestors.* New York: Penguin.

Waterman, John T. 1966. *A History of the German Language.* Seattle: University of Washington Press.

Watkins, Calvert. 2000. *The American Heritage Dictionary of Indo-European Roots.* Rev. 2nd ed. Boston: Houghton Mifflin.

Weinreich, Max. 2008. *History of the Yiddish Language.* V. 1–2. Ed. Paul Glasser. Trans. Shlomo Noble with the assistance of Joshua A. Fishman. Reprint. New Haven, Conn.: Yale University Press.

Wells, C. J. 1987. *German: A Linguistic History to* 1945. Oxford: Clarendon Press.

Wells, Peter S. 2008. *Barbarians to Angels. The Dark Ages Reconsidered.* New York: Norton.

———. 1999 *The Barbarians Speak: How the Conquered Peoples Shaped Roman Europe.* Princeton, N.J.: Princeton University Press.

———. 2003. *The Battle that Stopped Rome: Emperor Augustus, Arminius, and the Slaughter of the Legions in the Teutoburger Forest.* New York: Norton.

West, M. L. 2007. *Indo-European Poetry and Myth.* Oxford: Oxford University Press.

Wiik, Kalevi. 1999. "Europe's Oldest Language?" *Books from Finland* 3/1999. www.lib.helsinki.fi/bff/399/wiik.html (accessed Sept. 8, 2008).

———. 2003. "Finnic-Type Pronunciation in the Germanic Languages." *Mankind Quarterly* 44, 1 (Fall): 43–90.

Wolfram, Herwig. 2005. *Die Germanen* 8. Überarbeitete Auflage. München: Beck.

———. 2001. *Die Goten und ihre Geschichte.* München: Beck.

Zabel, Hermann. 1995. *Die neue deutsche Rechtschreibung.* Gesellschaft für deutsche Sprache. Niedernhausen: Falken/Ts.

Index

Note: Page numbers in *italics* refer to charts.

architecture, 25
Arianism, 67, 69, 71, 81
aristocracy, 96, 159, 165–66
Ari Þorgilsson, 210
Arius of Alexandria, 67
Armenian language, 13
Arminius, 44–45, 47–48, *52, 53, 55, 88*
Arndt, Erwin, 146, 147
Arthur, King, 61, *111*
articles, 32, 195
Ashkenaz, 102
Asia Minor, 58, 65, 67, 68, 79, *112*
astrology, 104
attested languages, 11
Attila the Hun, 69, *90*, 92
Augustus, Emperor of Rome, 43, 44, 46–47, 104
Aurelian, *89*
Aurogallus, Matthäus, 140
Australia, 180
Austria: and Austrian Standard German, 197, *198*; bureaucratic language of, 165; dialects in, 197; and emigration to America, 188; and Frankfurt National Assembly, 160; and German Standard German, 197, *198*; language spoken in, 190, 192, 193, 196–98; national origins of, 196–97; and Nazis, 182; official language of, 210; pronunciation in, 164; and Revolution of 1848, 160; and the Rugians, *55*; and spelling reforms, 191
Austro-Hungarian Empire, 160, 196
Avestan language, 17

Balkans, 58, 65, 69
Baltic regions and languages, 13, 34, 51, *55, 56,* 64
Barcelona, 70
Barraclough, Geoffrey, 129, 135, 162
Basic Rights Law, 160
Basque language, 13, 49
Battle of Aquae Sextiae, *56*
Battle of Camlan, *111*
Battle of Hastings, 62–63, 76, *113*
Battle of Kalkriese, 43–49, *53,* 79, 80, *88, 89*
Battle of the Teutoburg Forest, 44
Battle of the Weser River, 47
Bavaria and Bavarian languages: and Altbairisch 'Old Bavarian', 94; and dialects, 159, 193–95, 197; and eighth century Germanic languages, 98; and German Bibles, 144; and German confederation, 159, 160; and Germanen tribes, *56,* 79, 82, 84; and Lutheranism, 130; and Old High German, 99–100; and the Peace of Augsburg, *153*; and Roman limes, 80; and sound shift, 94;

and spelling reforms, 191; and the *Völkerwanderung*, 79
Beethoven, Ludwig van, 176, 180
Belgium, 49, 60, 126, 210
Bengali language, 13
Benrath Line, 92–93, 98–99
Beowulf, *52*, 61, *113*
Berber language, 35
Berlin, 157, 171
Berliner Gesellschaft für deutsche Sprache (Berlin Society for German Language), 166
Bible, 117–51; Bible German, 145–46, 150–51; bootlegged versions, 142, 143; Celts mentioned in, 58; *Codex Argenteus* (Silver Bible), 65; first printed versions, *115*; gospels of, 65, 72; and Gothic language, 65, *66,* 69, *89*; Hebrew Bible, 120; and High German, 157; and the Inquisition, *114*; King James Bible, 148–49, *149, 153*; and language selection, 137–42; and Latin, 150–51; and Luther's background, 123–25; Mazarin Bible, 119–20; Mentelin Bible, 144; New Testament, 58, *89*, 120, 140, 150, *152*; and Old English, 62; Old Testament, 140, 146, *152*; and printing of Europe, 118–21; proverbs, *148*; readership of, 121–22; and the Reformation, 128; and the *Septembertestament*, 117–18; and ties to Rome, 143–44; and translation, 145–50; Vulgate Bible, 117, 124, 139, 144, 148, 149
bilingualism, 13, 37–38, 201, 203, 209
Billinger, Robert D., Jr., 159, 160–61
Birnbaum, Norman, 184
Bismarck, Otto von, 157, 162, 170, 171, *172*
Black Death, 63, 102, *115*
Black Sea, 12, 65, 68, 69, 72
Blair, John, 61
"block book" printing, 119
Blubo (for *Blut und Boden*), 181, 186
Blut ('blood'), 181
Bøgebakken archaeological site, 9–10, *40*
Bohemia, 60, 131
Böll, Heinrich, 183
Bonjour, E., 198
book fairs, 120, 141
Bopp, Franz, 11
Bora, Katharina von, 124
borrowed words: effects of, 39, 188; and English, 188; and Finnish, 206; and German, 203, 210; and the Germanic homeland, 34; and Germanic Sound Shift, 29, 31; and Icelandic, 208, 209;

borrowed words (*continued*)
and language prestige, 35–39; and
linguistic purity, 166; from non-Indo-
European languages, 35–36; and PIE
language, 33, 34, 36–37, 38–39
Brandenburg-Prussia, 161
Brecht, Bertolt, 6, 179, *212*
Bretagne, 49
Breton, 59
Britain: and Anglo-Saxons, 60–63; and
Battle of Kalkriese, 49; and the Celts, 58,
59–60; and the Frisians, *54*; and German
immigrants, 180, 181; and German Jews,
178; and the Jutes, *54*; and the Saxons,
55; and the Vikings, 73; and the
Völkerwanderung, 78, 79
Bromme, Denmark, *39*
Bructeri, 45
Brythonic languages, 59
Bugenhagen, Johannes, 140
Bulgarian language, 13
Burgundians, *52, 110*; founding of
Burgundian Kingdom at Worms, *90*;
and Hun invasions, 63, 65; in
Switzerland, 198, 199; and the
Völkerwanderung, 78, 79
burial practices: and the Battle of
Kalkriese, 47; and the Celts, 58; and the
Goths, 71; and pictorial representations,
41; and prehistoric cultures, 4, 9–10, 13,
20–23, 25; and the Vikings, 74
Busbecq, Ogier Ghislain de, 72
Byzantine Empire (Eastern Roman
Empire), 68, 78, 111

Caesar, Julius, 58, 86
Campbell, Joseph, 9
camp followers, 45, 46
Canary Islands, 68
The Canterbury Tales (Chaucer), 63
case system, 28, 77
Cassel Glosses, 100–101
Cassiodorus, 68
Cassius Deo, 45
Catalan language, 13
Catherine II, Empress of Russia, 202
Catholic Church : and anti-Jewish doctrine,
102; and Arianism, 67, 71; and Bible
translations, 117; and book printing, 122;
and family structure, 96–97; and
Kulturkampf, 169–70; and Latin, 151; and
Luther, *116*, 122–24, 136, 143–44; and
the Luther Bible, 140; and the Peace of
Augsburg, *153*; and the Reformation, 79,
127–28, 142–43; and sixteenth-century
life, 126; and *theodiscus*, 93; and the Thirty
Years' War, 132; and Vatican II, 151

celestial bodies, 18
Celtic people and language, 58–60; in
Austria, 196; Continental Celtic, 12; and
English, 38; and gender ratios, 23; and
Germanic tribes, 51, 59, 196; Icelandic, 207–8; and Latin, 49;
perceptions of, 58, 85; and Roman
Empire, 49, 58–59, 60; and the substrate
hypothesis, 109–10; surviving languages
of, 59; in Switzerland, 198–99
Central German dialect, 195
Chaldaean astrology, 104
Chamberlain, Houston Stewart, 169
Chambers, W. Walker, 167
chancery German, 127, 138, 145, 147
Charlemagne, Emperor, 70, 99, 100, *112*
Charles V, Holy Roman Emperor, 124,
144, *152*
Chatti, 45, *52, 53*
Chaucer, Geoffrey, 63
Cheruscans (Cherusci), 45, *53, 88*
Cherusker, 48
Christensen, Arne Søby, 68
Christianity, *110*; and Arab invaders, 70;
and the Celts, 61; and conversion of
Germanic tribes, 81; and decline of
paganism, 126; and the Goths, 65, 67,
69, 72; and Iceland, 208; and influence
of Latin, 107; and Old High German,
99–100; and the Vikings, 73, 76; and
weekday names, 105. See also Catholic
Church
Cimbri, *53, 56*
cities of Germany, 170, 171. See also *specific
cities*
clans, 50, 81
classes. See social structure
Claudius, Emperor of Rome, 59, 80
climate changes, 21
Cloister of Werden, 65
Clovis, King of the Franks, 79, *110*
Clunn, Tony, 44
Clyne, Michael, 163, 192, 194
Cochlaeus, Johannes, 122
Codex Argenteus (Silver Bible), 65, *66*, 72
colloquial language (*Umgangssprache*),
195–96
Cologne, 101, 145
common people, 165–66
Communist movement, 168–69
comparative method, 11, 14
compounding, 185–86, 203
confoederatio, 65
conjugations, 31
consonants: and Indo-European mother
language, 5, 26, 33; and sound shifts,
27–29, 30, 32, 82, 93, 94–95, 99, 106–10;

Indo-European, *40*; and the Franks, *53*, 82; and the Goths, 69; and Hun invasions, 64; and Roman Empire, 43; and the Suebi, *56*; and the Visigoths, 68; and the *Völkerwanderung*, 65, 79
Gdansk, Poland, 67
Geary, Patrick, 87
Gemeindeutsch, 127
Gemeinsprachetendenzen, 147
gender in language, 28, 186–87
genetic studies, 4, 18, 23, 59–60, 61, 63, 204, 208
Geneva, 199
genitive case, 186, 195
Geography (Strabo), 85–86
Gepids, 63
German Confederation (*Deutscher Bund*), 158, 159–61, 163, 167
German Democratic Republic, 184–85, 194
Germanen: ancestors of, 18; and Britain, 60–63; and the Celts, 58; and destruction of Roman fortifications, 81–82; early Latin influence, 106–7; life and society of, 86–87; and Proto-Indo-European language (PIE), 13; religion of, 81; and Roman rule, 80–81; Roman views of, 84–86; in Rome, 46–47; term, 19
Germania (Tacitus), 50–51, *88*
Germanic Franks, 49
Germanic homeland, 19–25
Germanic languages: adjectives in, 32; borrowed words in, 29; and the eighth century, 98–99; and Germanic homeland, 19; and Germanic populations, ca. 800 AD, 82–84; and Germanic Sound Shift, 39; Indo-European roots of, 13, 22; and the Negau helmet, 26, 27; Proto-Germanic roots of, 27; and Roman influences, 49; speakers of, 3, 19; syllabic stress in, 28; vocabulary of, 33, 35
Germanic Sound Shift. *See* under sound shifts
German language: adjectives in, 31; alliteration in, 31; and book printing, 121; dialects of, 159; and Finnish, 205, 207; German Standard German (GSG), 163–64, 193–96, 197, *198*, *200*; and Icelandic, 209; Indo-European roots of, 13; influence of English on, 187–90; as an international language, 202–3; and linguistic nationalism, 166–67; as a literary language, 167–68; and Luxemburg Standard German, 201, 202; name of, 93; as national language of Prussia, 157; national standards in,

192–202; and Nazis, 6, 180–82; noun cases of, 32; pluricentricity of, 192; prestige of, 182, 183, 190; Proto-Germanic roots of, 27; and Second Sound Shift, 93; as a state language, 158; status of, 163, 176–80, 182–83, 189; study of, as foreign language, 181–82, 192–93; and *Umgangssprache* (colloquial language), 195–96; verb forms in, 32; vocabulary of, 33; and the *Völkerwanderung*, 78; and weekday names, 104–6, *105*; and West Germanic, 76. *See also* Germany; *variants, including* Modern German language
German Reich, 169, 170, 177, 197
German Stage Pronunciation (Siebs), 164, 194
Germany: and appearance of agriculture, 24; and the Catholic Church, 126; cities of, 170, 171; and German Standard German, 163, 192, 193–96, 197, *198*, *200*; German unification, 130, 135, 162, *172*; and High German, 157; languages spoken in, 190, 193–96, 210; and Latin influence, 49; and the Reformation, 128; and spelling reforms, 191; and the Thirty Years' War, 131–34; and the *Völkerwanderung*, 79. *See also* German language
Gestapo, 186
Getica, sive de origine actibusque Gothorum (Jordanes), 67, 68
Gimbutas, Maria, 17
Glück, Helmu, 186
Goethe, Johann Wolfgang von, 98, 167, 176, 179–80
Goidelic languages, 59
Gønghusvej settlement, 19
gospels, 65, 72
Götaland, 67
Gothiscandza, 67
Goths and Gothic language, 65–72; about, 5–6, *54*; alphabet, *66*; and Christianity, 65, 67, 69–70, 81, *89*; Crimean Goths, 69, 71–72; and East Germanic, 76; extinction of, 5–6, 67, 68–69, 70–71; and Finnish, 205; and Germanic Sound Shift, 29, *30*, 31; and Hun invasions, 63, 64–65; Jordanes's account of, 67–68; migration of, 68–69; and Roman Empire, *88*, *89*; sample of, 72; and Spanish language, 70–71; surnames, 70; and the *Völkerwanderung*, 79; as written language, 65–66, *66*, 83
Gotland, 67
grammar, 14, 28, 150, 157, 186
Grass, Günter, 183–84